iPad® in Education

FOR DUMMIES®

A Wiley Brand

2nd Edition

by Sam Gliksman

FOR DUMMIES®
A Wiley Brand

iPad® in Education For Dummies,® 2nd Edition

Published by: **John Wiley & Sons, Inc.,** 111 River Street, Hoboken, NJ 07030-5774, www.wiley.com

Copyright © 2015 by John Wiley & Sons, Inc., Hoboken, New Jersey

Published simultaneously in Canada

For general information on our other products and services, please contact our Customer Care Department within the U.S. at 877-762-2974, outside the U.S. at 317-572-3993, or fax 317-572-4002. For technical support, please visit www.wiley.com/techsupport.

Wiley publishes in a variety of print and electronic formats and by print-on-demand. Some material included with standard print versions of this book may not be included in e-books or in print-on-demand. If this book refers to media such as a CD or DVD that is not included in the version you purchased, you may download this material at http://booksupport.wiley.com. For more information about Wiley products, visit www.wiley.com.

Library of Congress Control Number: 2014941050

ISBN 978-1-118-94698-5

ISBN 978-1-118-94699-2 (ebk); ISBN 978-1-118-94700-5 (ebk)

Manufactured in the United States of America

10 9 8 7 6 5 4 3 2 1

Table of Contents

Introduction

. . . .

*B*ack in 2010, the first iPad was sold at the Apple flagship store in New York City. Its release was heralded with heady anticipation and excitement. Apple had done it again! Although it was not the first tablet computer to hit the market, it quickly became the one to define it. Within a couple of short years, iPad sales into schools have soared above MacBook sales by a margin of 2:1. That demand comes partly from the overall popularity of iPads, but it also stems from the recognition that technology has the potential to revitalize our educational systems.

The iPad and its Mini counterpart are light and easy to carry, intuitive to use, and (best of all) relatively inexpensive. However, be careful about putting the iPad cart before the horse. If we expect the iPad to be an agent of change, it's important that technology use serves our greater educational vision and doesn't become an objective in itself. The only time *computer* should come before *education* is in the dictionary.

Mobile technology can be used to re-envision education. That's the goal of this book. There will be loads of "how to" information in these pages, but along the way, I'll try and address the question of "why" we use technology in class as well. Instead of using iPads to deliver and drill content, we should strive to empower students to create, investigate, and innovate. In doing so, we encourage students to develop the skills they'll require to become lifelong learners who can thrive in our exponentially changing world.

Feeling a little overwhelmed? Don't be. You've already made the first important step by buying this informative and easy-to-read book. Just stick with me, and I will guide you through the wonderful and exhilarating world of iPad use in education.

About This Book

You've seen what kids look like when they handle an iPad. With little hesitation, they jump right in, and, within minutes, they start drawing, reading, or finding some other activity that motivates and engages them. It's their canvas, and given the freedom to explore and express themselves, students can be wonderfully creative and imaginative with technology.

Albert Einstein once wrote, "It is a miracle that curiosity survives formal education. If we are to develop our students' sense of curiosity, we must be mindful to carve out time to allow our students to inquire and explore."

This book examines ways we can use utilize iPads to unlock some of those possibilities in educational settings.

Here are some of the things you can do with this book:

✔ Learn how to use iPads to address 21st-century skills and literacies

✔ Discover techniques to manage a classroom of iPads

✔ Learn how to find and purchase apps for yourself or in volume

✔ Learn how to use the built-in multimedia tools for digital storytelling and creative expression

✔ Discover how to create and blend various media into eBooks

✔ Explore ways the iPad can be used to explore, investigate, create, and collaborate

✔ Learn how technology can be used to empower and engage students

✔ Discover ways other teachers are using iPads innovatively in their classrooms

This book uses a few specific conventions in this text for ease of comprehension. When I tell you to type something (in a box or a field, for example), I put it in **bold.** When I refer to text that you see onscreen, I put it in a typeface that `looks like this`. Terms in *italic* are defined as they relate to using the iPad in the classroom. And when I provide a URL, it looks like this:

`www.dummies.com/extras/ipadineducation`

Foolish Assumptions

You know what happens when you assume . . . but as an author, I have to make certain assumptions about you — my readers — in order to target the book at your needs.

✔ You either own or are considering buying an iPad. The principles discussed in the book apply whether you have the original iPad 1 through to the latest iPad and iPad Mini. You will, however, need an iPad 2 or higher to take advantage of the advice and directions regarding multimedia use.

✔ You are not a "techie." This is a book about education written for teachers, administrators, parents, and anyone else that has an interest in education.

✔ You have access to a wireless Internet connection.

✔ You know technology can be used effectively as an educational tool, but you're just not sure how . . . and the thought of a classroom full of children with iPads scares you just a teensy bit.

✔ You're looking for new and exciting ways to engage and motivate your students.

Icons Used in This Book

What's a Dummies book without icons pointing you in the direction of really great information that's sure to help you along your way? In this section, I briefly describe each icon I use in this book.

The Tip icon points out helpful information that is likely to make your job easier.

This icon marks a general interesting and useful fact — something that you might want to remember for later use.

The Warning icon highlights lurking danger. With this icon, I'm telling you to pay attention and proceed with caution.

When you see this icon, you know that there's techie stuff nearby. If you're not feeling very techie, you can skip this info.

Beyond the Book

Technology use in education is a huge and rapidly growing field, and it's difficult to encompass everything within the confines of any single book. With that in mind, I've added a few juicy bits for you online. Feel free to browse, use, and share the following content.

✔ **Cheat Sheet:**

www.dummies.com/cheatsheet/ipadineducation

The Cheat Sheet for the book contains a list of ideas for digital storytelling projects as well as ten wonderful educational games for learning as you have fun playing.

✔ **Online articles covering additional topics:**

www.dummies.com/extras/ipadineducation

Learn about additional topics by reading the additional articles included on the Extras page:

- Learn how to create and access educational content on any topic using Apple's iTunes U.

- Read about popular tools and apps that can be used for collaborative learning with iPads.

- Browse a list of some of the more important iPad accessories you'll want to consider purchasing for educational use.

✔ **Updates:** Each *For Dummies* technical book explains where readers can find updates in case the book changes substantially. (For example, the book includes an entire chapter or part on the importance of Facebook Fan pages and then Facebook does away with Fan pages.) Updates will be posted to the Downloads tab on the book's product page. On the book's Extras landing page (www.dummies.com/extras/ipadineducation), an article will either describe the update or provide a link to take readers to the Downloads tab for access to updated content. For programming books, this is where errata will appear.

Where to Go from Here

This book can be read in any order you choose. Each chapter stands on its own and can help you tackle specific tasks. For example, if you have just started thinking about using the iPad in your classroom but don't know where to begin, head to Part I. Your first stop might be to read the table of contents and find the sections of this book that you need at any time.

Part I

Getting Started with the Educational iPad

getting started with

the
Educational iPad

In this part . . .

✔ Examine the evolving educational needs of students in the 21st century

✔ Learn the basics about navigating and using an iPad

✔ Explore options for deployment and management of iPads in schools

✔ Find out how to make volume purchases of apps and eBooks

Chapter 1

Education in the 21st Century

In This Chapter

▶ Re-evaluating educational objectives for a world of constant change

▶ Examining how iPads meet the needs of a 21st-century education

▶ Reviewing what this book is — and is not

*I*t's nine and a half inches long and less than one third of an inch thick. At less than a pound and a half, it can go anywhere with you. It boasts a crystal-clear display, has a microphone and two cameras, and is a great little device for taking photos and video. Whether you prefer to prop it up on a table or lay it in your lap, just tap a button and you'll instantly connect with people and information anywhere on the planet. Yes, the iPad is the face of modern technology . . . and given the opportunity, technology such as iPads has the potential to revitalize our educational systems.

Investigating New Educational Models

We've come a long way in such a short time. Many of us grew up in an age of relative stability. Personal computing was still in its infancy, and we'd never heard of anything called the Internet. If you wanted to communicate with your cousin in another country, you'd pull out a pen and paper, write a letter, slap on a stamp, and walk to the nearest mailbox. Imagine that! Welcome to the 21st century, where we find ourselves launched into the beginnings of a new era characterized by extreme, exponential change. The fuel that's feeding that change is technology. Computers have evolved from massive machines that weighed several tons and required several people to operate them to sleek, super-powerful, tiny devices that perform incredibly complex tasks and move information between remote locations at lightning speed. Fifty years ago, people were amazed at being able to deliver a heavily abbre-viated message overseas with a telegram that might arrive at its destination a day later. Nowadays, kids complain that email takes too long! The mobile devices we carry around in our pockets today are thousands of times more powerful than those enormous computers were just a few decades ago.

Of course, change isn't a new concept, but it's the amazing speed at which society is changing that takes your breath away. Inventions such as the telephone and radio took generations to become common household items, yet after just a few short years, iPods, iPhones, and iPads have sold several hundred million units. A service such as Facebook didn't even exist ten years ago; now it has a user base exceeding 1 billion. We just reached 7 billion people on planet Earth, and there are more than 5 billion cellphone subscriptions.

Re-evaluating educational objectives in a changing world

Technology has changed almost every facet of our daily life — at work, home, and leisure. Given the right opportunity, it can also transform our educational systems; however, our school systems have largely struggled to keep pace. Take a stroll around many schools today, and they look largely the same as they did when you went to school. The problem is twofold:

- ✔ **Lacking technology:** Students lead technology-filled lives outside of school, yet many of them have only minimal access to personal technology for learning within school itself.

- ✔ **Using technology for a 20th-century education:** Simply adding a dose of technology to the standard educational mix may not be enough if that technology is patched over outdated objectives and pedagogies.

The incredibly rapid changes occurring all around us are having a significant impact on the skills students need when they graduate school. Old models of content delivery and frontal teaching — lecturing from the front of the class — aren't addressing the evolving needs of a society where information is available freely and instantly, and constantly changing. The technology revolution that encompasses us has changed all our educational paradigms. We need to consider iPad use within the framework of educational objectives that address the needs of our rapidly changing society:

- ✔ **Replacing rote memorization with real skills:** Skills such as critical thinking, communication, and creativity have increasingly greater value than the rote memorization of content. After all, the vast majority of content can be easily accessed within seconds on most mobile devices. We've even created a verb to describe it. What do you do when you want to know something? You "google" it!

✔ **Navigating the information jungle:** Historically, an important function of education was to provide students with access to textbook content and teacher expertise. Today, content and expertise are abundantly available online. There's so much information available that new educational priorities are needed to help students navigate the vast volumes of content. Information literacy skills help students access, organize, filter, evaluate, and use the enormous amount of information available online. The core question is morphing from "What do you know?" to "What can you do with what you know?"

✔ **Working in groups (because there's no *I* in *teamwork*):** We live in an emerging global society, and the development of collaborative skills — the ability to work effectively in teams — outweighs traditional demands that students sit still, listen, and work only on their own.

✔ **Incorporating multimedia literacy:** Text remains an important medium for conveying information, but multimedia is becoming the language of new generations, and its use should be encouraged in schools. Further, we need to discuss and develop standards that assist students in creating media that communicate the intended message effectively.

✔ **Saying goodbye to the 30-pound backpack:** At higher grade levels, most courses are still delivered and structured around the use of a single textbook — often one that was printed several years ago. That's a stark contrast to a world where news and information are always up to date and available from a wide variety of sources and perspectives.

✔ **Reaching beyond the school walls:** School is still the central hub for learning, but technology now enables us to be constantly connected. The old model of learning within the physical confines of a classroom or school campus is being completely redefined. In the age of the Internet, learning can occur anywhere and is available on demand.

✔ **Staying flexible is key:** Instruction and curriculum need to constantly adapt to new information, technologies, and interests.

✔ **Differentiated instruction and assessment:** Some students are great auditory processors. Explain something once to them and they get it. Others need to sit and read. Many students lean to more visual modes of learning. Technology offers options for differentiated instruction and alternative forms of assessment, which free us from a "one size fits all" teaching model. (And in reality, that model never worked anyway!)

✔ **Limiting frontal teaching:** New technologies placed in the hands of students empower them to research, explore, and create. Use of technology can and should move us from frontal, content-delivery models of education to more student-centered, discovery-based, and interactive learning practices.

✔ **Knowing that learning never ends:** We're all students who must continually learn and adapt to constant change. School is only part of our educational journey. Instead of focusing on preparation for assessments and certificates, we need to rediscover the joy that's inherent in the process of learning itself. Our objective should be to develop students who are independent, lifelong learners who can continue to thrive in a society of continual and rapid change.

Implementing iPads for 21st-century learning

As Ringo Starr reminded us, "It Don't Come Easy." Adding expensive technology to school environments requires significant budgeting, planning, and infrastructure development and training. With all the investment of money, time, and effort, it's even more important to focus the use of technology on critical 21st-century learning goals. The iPad is well equipped to meet those educational challenges.

✔ **Learning on the go:** An iPad weighs less than a pound and a half and is well suited to the goal of "anytime, anywhere" education. You can take it with you wherever you go. Store it easily in a bag or backpack, or just carry it on your person. Plus, the iPad's battery has up to ten hours of life, so you won't have to deal with cords and electrical outlets. Charge your iPad overnight, and it will be ready and available all day long.

✔ **Kicking back and relaxing:** Use your iPad any way that feels comfortable. There aren't any annoying upright screens forming a barrier between teachers and students. It's easily passed around when used in a group setting. Turn it on easily while sitting, standing, or even when lying down (although don't say I didn't warn you that keeping your iPad next to your bed will make it extremely difficult to get up on time in the mornings)!

✔ **Turning on, tuning in:** The iPad turns on with the simple tap of a button. You don't wait long for it to start, and you don't have to log in to use it. It's instantly accessible and can be integrated effortlessly into any activity inside the classroom or outside. Access any website, look up any information, jot down notes and appointments — all within seconds.

✔ **Touching and swiping is as easy as A-B-C:** Have you ever seen a small child using an iPad? It's quite incredible how easily children take to the multitouch interface. After all, we grow up manipulating the world around us by directly touching objects: We pick them up, move them, open, and use them. A computer that uses direct touching of its interface is a natural extension of that process.

✔ **Accessing the library at your fingertips:** You can purchase, download, and read digital books (see Figure 1-1) right from within iBooks and other book-reading apps on your iPad. Change the display to meet your taste or reading preference. Highlight or underline text, make notes, look up a word definition, and search for anything in the book . . . even use the VoiceOver feature to have the book read to you. The Apple iBooks Store now also includes digital textbooks with interactive and constantly updated content from major publishers.

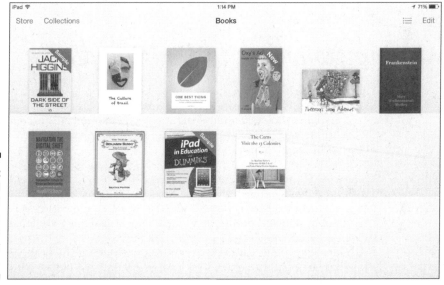

Figure 1-1: Download and read books using the iBooks app on your iPad.

✔ **Empowering students:** Put it all together, and iPads have the potential to empower students. It enables them to research and analyze information, connect to people, develop and collaborate on solutions to problems, express knowledge in a variety of media . . . in short, technology empowers students to develop independent learning skills that are essential for success in today's society.

✔ **Including everyone through assistive technologies:** With features such as VoiceOver reading, and the capability to change interface colors, fonts, and size of text, the iPad offers a custom and differentiated learning environment that can bend to the needs of individual learning styles. In addition, several apps are specifically designed for people with special learning needs, such as those with limited vision or motor skills.

✔ **Focusing on student-centered learning to garner out-of-the-box results:** It's important for educators to understand the potential power of technology use, but you don't need to become an expert. There's a good chance you already have 20 of those tech-savvy students sitting in your classroom. Way too much of our traditional educational models is standardized, scripted, and controlled. The power of using iPads in education is revealed when they're put in the hands of students and we loosen the educational reins. Technology is the language of their daily life, and the magic of using technology in education is when students are given opportunities to use it innovatively to produce creative results that we never predicted.

Moving from Text to Multimedia

You more than likely grew up using reading and writing for most of your learning in school. The invention of the printing press and the mass production of paper completely altered the way we communicate and learn. In fact, the printing press is thought of as one of the most revolutionary inventions of the second millennium!

Do anything long enough and it becomes difficult to imagine that there are other ways to accomplish the same objectives. If you look at schooling at any time during the 20th century, you'll notice that education was built on the consumption and production of text. You learned by reading and you expressed your knowledge by writing about it. Remember those big, heavy textbooks you were expected to read? Many students still have them and drag that 30-pound backpack to school every day just like we did. And most of the work submitted in school is still written the way it was in our day, old-timer.

However, if you stop and take a long look outside the gates of school, you'll see a brand-new world of communication and learning . . . and it doesn't look anything at all like the one in which we grew up.

The world of the 21st century is now awash in colorful, vibrant, and interactive media. Important messages are most often expressed in videos and images. When many of us want to learn something, we often look for video tutorials on sites such as YouTube.

Multimedia has quickly become the language of modern communication. Your iPad has a sparkling display with built-in audio and video tools (iPad 2 or higher; see Figure 1-2) for the creation and use of all forms of multimedia. Use it to take and edit video or photos, record podcasts and class lectures, and create animated presentations, multimedia stories, and more. With embedded cameras, microphone, and wide range of multimedia apps and tools, the iPad is a little multimedia powerhouse that will become as indispensable to our students as our pens and notebooks used to be back in the day.

Apps

Front camera

Rear camera

Figure 1-2:
The iPad 2 or higher has an integrated microphone and camera.

Touchscreen   Home button

Asking Why You Want iPads

In his book *Start with Why,* author Simon Sinek claims that we all know *what* we do. You often define yourself by what you do: "I'm a teacher," for example. You usually also know how you should do whatever you do. People usually develop a routine to make their tasks easier. Very few people or organizations constantly discuss and debate *why* they do something. Only by reflecting on the question of why are we able to develop and articulate a meaningful vision for what we should be doing . . . and that certainly applies to education. Let me explain.

We all have a vision for the ideal education, and it's highly likely that we'll disagree on many of its components. There is, however, one common thread that most of us would agree upon. As strange as it may sound, we aren't teaching children to become good students in school. Yes, you read that correctly. After all, school is simply a transitional stage of their lives. Our objective is to educate and prepare them for life *outside* school. Ideally, we'd like to give them the necessary skills to become happy, productive adults and solid citizens.

When you live in an era of change, asking why helps evaluate whether you are preparing your students appropriately for their lives outside school. It's a natural tendency for humans to fall into routines, to focus on what we do and how we do it without regard for whether it's still relevant. Many people continue following the same educational routines and processes without asking whether they are really preparing our children for their lives in an ever-changing society full of technology.

Simply purchasing and using technology to address questions of how we teach won't advance education. If we buy technology as a means of reinforcing the same old educational processes, then we may be totally missing the point. Here are some examples:

- ✔ Continuing to use lecturing as a primary pedagogical process but using technology to project the documents and presentations rather than delivering material orally or in printed formats.

- ✔ Continuing content-based educational practices by having students read a chapter and answer the questions at the end but allowing them to use technology to submit typed responses.

- ✔ Continuing to stress memorization of facts but using tools such as flashcard apps to help drill the information.

Asking why and looking outside the school walls may lead us to different visions and new directions. Why only focus on text for exchanging information when the world now communicates with a variety of multimedia, and fluency in media literacy is a valuable skill in the workplace? Why continue using the same old textbooks when we can access updated information on any topic within seconds using the Internet or digital books? Why focus on a static, content-delivery and memorization approach to learning when that pool of content is increasing at unprecedented speed, and it's more important for students to be skilled in finding, analyzing, and using information as they need it? Are we preparing students for tests or are we preparing them for life? We have to ask ourselves "Why?"

Using technology effectively in education requires much more than just having technical skills. Instead, through the use of technology we have the ability to sculpt new educational visions that address the real needs of children entering a new world. It's a fundamental reason for why I am writing this book.

Sharing iPads in Schools

iPads are designed as inherently personal devices. There are no user logins or custom desktops for different users as there might be on a laptop or desktop. Can you start to sense the problem here? Many schools share iPads between classes and students in much the same way they share laptop carts. Laptops can accommodate different user logins and therefore protect individual student data. iPads aren't laptops and can't be used the same way.

Most iPad apps cache your login information. In other words, after you've logged in, they automatically remember your login information and open your data when the app is opened again. The little love letter or risqué rap lyrics that Joey wrote will pop right up on the screen for the next user who opens the app.

A 1:1 environment is where every student gets his own dedicated iPad — and it's unquestionably the preferred model for school use. You'll have to overcome quite a few obstacles if you expect to share iPads between students. iPads just aren't built to be shared. Having said that, there are some considerations that make it a little easier and safer to share them:

  ✔ **Little kids, little problems. Big kids, big problems.** Sharing iPads at lower grade levels is far easier. There's less data produced and the data tends to be less sensitive. In the upper grades, students may be writing papers and keeping notes that need to be kept private.

  ✔ **Stay faithful to your iPad.** Number your iPads, and keep a list or spreadsheet to make sure students use the same iPad every time. At least that way, students' data should be available, and they're only sharing that particular iPad with a small handful of other students. Also, anything that goes wrong will be easier to track. You can always sticker the outside of the iPad with a number, but another approach is to create a large visible graphic with the respective number and make it the wallpaper for each device's home page.

✔ **You *don't* got mail.** Forget setting up incoming email in the iPad Mail app unless you're prepared to let students see each other's email. Changing email accounts in Mail requires going to Settings; that can get messy and time-consuming (although some schools do it that way).

✔ **Access email through the web browser.** Many email services such as Google and Microsoft Exchange have a web interface that you can access through Safari. Just make sure to log out when you're done.

✔ **Log out, log out, log out.** Few apps prompt you to log out when you close them, but many have an option to log out on their Settings menus. Encourage students to always log out (as shown in Figure 1-3) before closing an app or website that requires a login.

✔ **Appreciate the silver lining to your cloud account.** Consider saving data to a cloud-based service such as Google Drive or Dropbox. There are simple ways to move content from the iPad to a cloud storage account. For example, many apps have a Share option that enables you to move content from one app to another. Moving content to the Google Drive app on your iPad makes that content available on any other device or computer that can also access your Google Drive account. You'll still have to delete the files from the iPad, however, if you want to keep the information private.

Encourage students to use logout options.

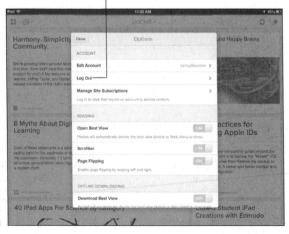

Figure 1-3:
Many iPad
apps such
as Pocket
have options
to sign in
and out.

What This Book Is and Is Not

The objective of this book is to help you successfully integrate the use of iPads into an educational setting.

✔ Although my main objective isn't to teach you mad iPad skills that turn you into the go-to technology expert, you'll pick up a lot of helpful knowledge about iPad use along the way.

✔ It isn't a technical book for the school's "tech guy." He has enough headaches already.

✔ It isn't a directory of app recommendations. There are several hundred thousand apps on the market (and a few more probably came out as you were reading this sentence!). Learning new apps is fun, but the book's focus is firmly on educational objectives. I demonstrate a variety of apps and web tools to help move you in that direction.

✔ The book will be helpful for teachers, school administrators, parents, and anyone else concerned with education.

✔ You will learn how to use iPads effectively as educational tools that engage students and energize learning across age levels and academic disciplines.

✔ At its core, this actually isn't a book about "using iPads in education." Instead, it's a book about "educating using iPads." That isn't just a small semantic difference. It's an important distinction in priorities that stresses the fact that using technology is never the goal.

Technology is a tool that serves the greater objective of preparing students for their lives outside school.

✔ Last, if you've ever spent two minutes with an iPad, you know that this is a book about having fun!

Chapter 2

Getting Acquainted with iPad Technology

*T*he initial days of the very first personal computers were only about 35 years ago. The first *commercially available* "portable" computer, such as the IBM 5100, sold for a whopping $10,000 to $20,000 and contained around 16K to 64K of memory. To put that in perspective, the average personal computer today contains several hundred thousand times the memory and sells for around 5 percent of the cost! Phenomena such as the Internet are revolutionizing how we connect and communicate. Mobile technologies have advanced to the point where portable devices are now smaller and more powerful than we could have imagined back in the early days of computing. Now we're witnessing the emergence of widespread mobile tablet computing with its unique touch interface. Tablets have skyrocketed into prominence over the last couple of years and are changing the face of popular computing. The clear leader in that field is an amazing and powerful little device that is taking the world by storm — the iPad.

Mobile, tablet computers are substantially different from the desktop and laptop computers you've been using for many years. In this chapter, I explain what sets the iPad's physical hardware apart from traditional computers, and

I also demonstrate the different ways you use its software. I walk you through many of the core functions and look at how to find and purchase software "apps." Of course, throughout the process, I make sure to keep my educationally tinted glasses focused on the incredible opportunities that exist for using the iPad as an educational device.

Touring the iPad's Physical Layout

Let's take a quick walk-through of the physical exterior of the iPad. Apple has done a wonderful job designing everything into a small and sleek footprint, and you don't have very many controls to learn.

Along the edges

Let's start at the very top of the iPad, where you find the headphone jack, microphone, and Sleep/Wake button (see Figure 2-1):

- **Headphone jack:** Plug your headphones or earbuds into the 3.5mm headphone jack.

- **Microphone:** Pay attention to the location of the microphone and position it correctly when recording.

- **Sleep/Wake button:** Your iPad can be in any one of three states: powered on, powered off, and sleep mode. Press this button once, and it puts your iPad to sleep. Press it again, and your iPad wakes instantly. (Wouldn't it be great if you could wake your kids up that easily?) Turn it off by pressing and holding the button down for a few seconds and then sliding the onscreen slider to confirm that you want to shut it down. Pressing and holding will also start your iPad.

Putting your iPad into sleep mode rather than turning it off completely uses up a touch more of the battery but keeps it available for immediate use whenever you need it. If you're using a SmartCover or an alternative, the iPad automatically goes into sleep mode when you close the cover and magically wakes up when you open it. You can also set your iPad to go to sleep after a period of inactivity in Settings, under the General menu and Auto-Lock.

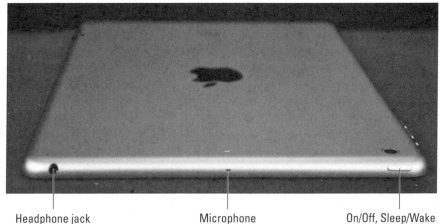

Figure 2-1:
The top side
of an iPad.

Headphone jack　　　　　　Microphone　　　　On/Off, Sleep/Wake

With the iPad screen facing you, look along the right edge to find the Volume
Control and the Mute Switch/Rotate Lock (see Figure 2-2):

✔ **Volume control:** The volume is a single button. Press the upper part to
turn the volume up, and press the lower part to turn the volume down.
As an aside, the same button can also be used as a camera shutter
button on the iPad 2 or later.

✔ **Mute switch:** Slide the Mute switch to the down position, and it turns off
any unexpected sounds such as notification noises from apps. Note that
this doesn't affect the sound coming from sources such as music and
video. You have the option of using this button as a Screen Orientation
Lock instead of a Mute switch. When the Screen Orientation Lock option
is off, the iPad switches orientation when you move it from portrait
to landscape and back. To change the button's function, tap Settings
and go to the General section in the margin. Scan down to see the two
options for using the side switch.

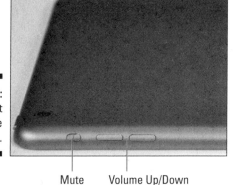

Figure 2-2:
The right
side of the
iPad.

Mute　　Volume Up/Down

Take a look at the bottom of your iPad to see the built-in speaker and the dock connector port (see Figure 2-3):

- ✔ **Speaker:** It's the little speaker that could. It's not overly powerful and mono not stereo, but it's still fine for personal listening.

- ✔ **Dock connector (or lightning connector):** This port is used most often to charge your iPad. It does have other important functions as well, such as connecting your iPad to a computer for synchronizing content, connecting to a Camera Connection Kit to transfer images, and connecting to AV connectors for screen projection.

Built-in speaker   Lightning connector

Figure 2-3:
The bottom
of the
second-
and third-
generation
iPad (below)
and fourth-
generation
and later
(above).

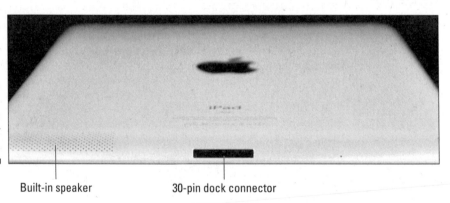

Built-in speaker   30-pin dock connector

Looking at the front and back

Moving on, let's take a closer look at that dazzling display:

- ✔ **Screen:** It starts with the beautifully clear display — amazingly crisp if you have a third-generation iPad. This is where it all happens and where you find icons for all your apps.

- ✔ **Home button:** Directly below the screen you find the indispensable Home button. Think of it like Hansel and Gretel's breadcrumb trail. Wherever you are, just press the Home button to take you back.

- ✔ **Front and rear cameras:** If you have an iPad 2 or later, you have one camera in the front and another in the back. Just toggle between them as needed. Take it from me, though; there's nothing quite so startling as preparing to take a picture only to have your face suddenly fill the screen because you're using the wrong camera!

It's Not Your Father's Computer

For many years, people who were going to make a presentation at a different location had only one option: pack up the desktop computer and lug it along with them. Today, you can just drop your iPad into your bag, and off you go. With its sparkling display, built-in media tools, and Internet connectivity, it has most everything you need. Let's see what makes it tick.

How iPads differ from laptops

Don't waste your time looking for the keyboard and mouse. The most fundamental difference between an iPad and a traditional computer is that the iPad uses the same input device you've been using to manipulate objects since the day you were born. The iPad's "touch" interface is based upon manipulating objects on the screen with your fingers. Drag them, drop them, size them (the objects, not your fingers!) . . . everything is based on gestures you make with your fingers. The touch interface is what makes iPads such a natural fit for children. We grow up learning about the physical world around us by touching objects. The iPad interface is a simple extension of that process.

You've probably developed certain work habits on computers that will need to change a little when you start using your iPad. Some of the most fundamental changes include the following:

- **See me, feel me . . . touch me:** The iPad has a very simple and intuitive touch interface. There's no physical keyboard or mouse. Everything you need to move or type is right there onscreen — under your fingertips. Using an app is as simple as tapping the icon onscreen with your finger. When you need to type anything, the iPad automatically slides a virtual keyboard up on your screen.

- **Don't look for folders:** iPads don't use the folder and file storage structure that computers use. Files are associated with apps and accessed through them.

- **No drives, no ports:** iPads don't have a USB port or a CD or DVD drive. The most common ways to transfer content on and off your iPad are cabling it to a computer and synchronizing your content wirelessly. Add a dose of cloud storage to the mix, and your content is available on any device in any location. Magic. Universal access to all your information. You get a closer look at those options in Chapter 3.

- **Stay focused!** iPads only keep one open app on the screen at a time. You can, however, keep several apps open and then switch between them as needed; refer to the handy Tip later in this chapter.

- **Network cables? Phooey.** IP4, IP6, TCPIP, DHCP . . . all those technical acronyms are enough to give anyone a headache. The iPad doesn't have an Ethernet port, which is really just a fancy way of saying you can't plug in a network or Internet cable. Set up a simple connection to your wireless network, and the iPad connects to the Internet automatically and effortlessly. The only acronym you need is SBAR — Sit Back and Relax!

- **What you see is what you get:** The iPad doesn't have an open architecture. You can't open it and mess with components. The bad news is that you can't add more hard drive space or additional memory. The good news? You can't mess it up by trying.

- **Save the trees:** You can't cable your iPad to a printer. Chapter 19 provides some options for printing, but there are also many possibilities for paperless, digital communications.

- **It just plain works!** In the two decades that I've worked with computers, one of the biggest differences between an iPad and a traditional computer that I've noticed is probably also the most important: Turn the iPad on and it just works. It's intuitive to use, and you just don't run into many technical issues. You can spend your time being productive and having fun instead of connecting cables and calling for technical support.

Apps versus software

You may be accustomed to purchasing and installing computer software yourself. You know what I mean: Purchase a CD or download it from the publisher's website and then run through some installation procedure that often requires you to configure options, file locations, and more. Not so on the iPad. Software programs for any iOS device such as your iPad are called *apps* — short for *applications.* Apps need to be approved by Apple, and then they are listed for purchase and downloading directly through the App Store (see Figure 2-4). Tap the button to buy an app, and within seconds, the icon appears on your screen. No setup screens, no file locations, and very few ways to mess it up. For most of us, that's got to be a great thing.

You need an iTunes account to purchase apps . . . don't go away. I discuss that in the next few pages.

Figure 2-4: Tap the price button to purchase an app in the App Store.

Where's the keyboard?

Your iPad has a virtual keyboard (see Figure 2-5) that appears onscreen when needed. It intelligently detects when you tap in an editing field and just automatically slides up, ready and waiting for you to type.

One of the advantages of the virtual keyboard is that you actually get access to several keyboards that change according to the context in which they're being used. For example, when typing an email address, the keyboard automatically adds an @ key.

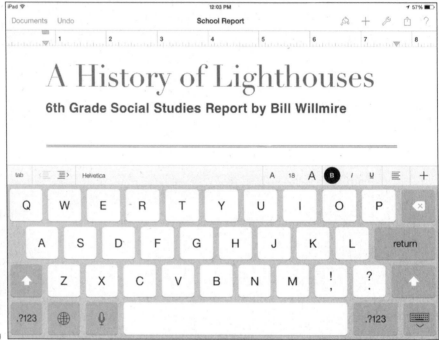

Figure 2-5:
The iPad has a virtual keyboard that displays onscreen as needed.

Storing and moving files

You have many options to create content on iPads. You'll be creating and editing documents, photos, presentations, video, and more. However, there's no way to directly access and move files and folders on an iPad in the same way you can on a laptop or desktop. Although there are some wireless utilities to work around it, there's no USB port to plug a flash drive into your iPad.

You'll want to move content off your iPad for synchronization with other computers and devices and also for backup purposes. This issue of "workflow" — moving content on and off iPads — is even more critical in a classroom setting where teachers have to deliver content, and students need to share and collaborate on content that gets returned to the teacher.

Don't run off to get your headache medication just yet. What happens on the iPad doesn't have to stay on the iPad. You have lots of options for moving files — so many, in fact, that I devote all of Chapter 20 to workflow options.

Adding an international keyboard

One of the advantages of using a virtual keyboard is that you can switch keyboards with a couple of taps. Adding a foreign language keyboard is a fairly simple process:

1. Tap the Settings icon on your iPad Home screen.

2. Select and tap the General option, then scroll down and tap the Keyboard option.

3. Tap Keyboards.

4. On the next screen, tap Add New Keyboard.

5. Select your language of choice.

Your international keyboard is now installed, and you can display it as needed. Whenever you want to switch languages for typing, simply tap the Globe icon in the bottom left of your keyboard, select your language, and start typing.

Planning for the Essential Extras

The iPad is an amazing device that will open up rich opportunities for you to create and use media, read books, listen to music, connect through the Internet, and much more. You do, however, need to create the right environment to get the most out of your iPad. Two of the more important factors are the strength of your wireless Internet connection and being able to find and purchase apps — especially in a school environment.

Connecting wirelessly

One of the major strengths of the iPad lies in its capability to connect you to information, people, events, media, books, and more. Having an iPad that can't get a connection out to the Internet is almost like having a car without any gas. Unless you have an iPad that supports a connection with a data plan through your cell network, you'll be connecting using Wi-Fi. Of course, not all connections are created equal. There are two considerations when planning the setup of your Wi-Fi network:

✔ **The speed of your incoming connection:** Internet connectivity is becoming faster and cheaper. Depending on the area in which you live, you may or may not have many options for fast Internet service. The amount of bandwidth you need depends on the following:

   • *The number of people using the wireless connection — especially concurrent users.*

   • *The type of activity occurring wirelessly.* For example, emailing and texting won't require much bandwidth, but watching high-resolution streaming video will gobble it up quickly.

✔ **The distribution of the wireless signal:** You've signed a tremendous deal to get oodles of fast Internet connectivity for your home, school, or office. Don't get too smug yet. You're only halfway done. Your Internet Service Provider (ISP) will bring its connection into a central, wired point on your property. If you expect to get a wireless signal, you need to distribute that Internet signal throughout the required areas. If you're setting up a home Wi-Fi network, then a fairly inexpensive router (less than $100) will probably do the trick. The larger the area, the more important it becomes to invest in a solid wireless infrastructure with robust access points for managing and distributing the wireless signal. This is extremely important when considering the strength of your wireless system across the school campus.

No other factor will more quickly kill enthusiasm for the budding use of technology on campus than the inability to get it working when needed. There will be areas to save on your technology budgets. This is most definitely not one of them.

Tuning your iTunes account

There are many methods for handling the purchasing and downloading of apps, books, music, and other content for your iPad. Let's start with the easy way. In order to get personal access to content in the iTunes or App Store, you must have your own Apple ID. If you don't already have one, you have two easy ways to open an account: the first from your computer and the second from your iPad:

On a computer:

1. **Go to www.apple.com/itunes/download to download and install iTunes on your computer.**

2. **Open iTunes on your computer.**

   From the Store menu, choose Create Account and follow the prompts. You'll need to provide personal details along with a valid method of payment, such as a credit card. The billing information will be used if and when you purchase apps and content.

3. **When asked, verify your email address and log in.**

   You're set to go.

On an iPad:

1. **Tap the Settings icon on your Home screen.**

2. **Tap the iTunes & App Store menu item in the left column.**

3. **Tap Create New Apple ID and follow the prompts (see Figure 2-6).**

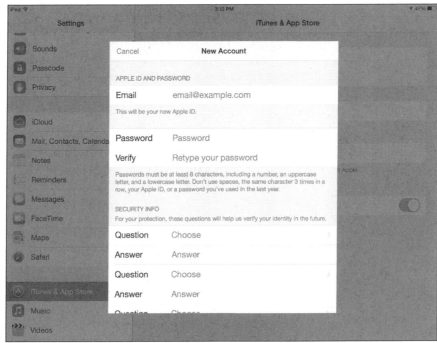

Figure 2-6:
You need to create an Apple ID to download apps.

4. When asked, verify your email address and log in.

After you've created and verified your Apple ID and billing information, you'll be able to start using it to acquire apps, music, books, and more.

Some schools create Apple IDs that are used across devices and aren't accessible to students. A preferable method might be for all students to have their own Apple IDs so that content and services can be stored, synchronized, and accessed through their accounts on any device. That was a problem until recently, as there's a minimum age of 13 when signing up for an Apple ID. However, the new Apple ID for Students program allows institutions to upload a list of student IDs being requested, and an email asking for consent is sent to the parent or guardian. The Apple ID is issued to the student after the consent has been given. You can find more information on Apple's website at www.apple.com/education/it/appleid.

As long as you're using a modest number of iPads, the tools provided by Apple should be sufficient to manage your iPads. Several companies offer Mobile Device Management (MDM) software solutions for the larger-scale deployment of iPads in schools and organizations. MDM products provide a central administration point where devices can be configured wirelessly. If you're managing hundreds or thousands of iPads, then researching and purchasing an MDM solution will be well worth the investment of time and money. Chapter 3 covers management alternatives.

Using Apple's Volume Purchase Program

Apple's Volume Purchase Program (VPP) is what most schools use to purchase larger quantities of apps and books at a discount. Once purchased centrally, they can then be distributed to school employees and students. Chapter 3 explains how to set up and manage an institutional account for the Volume Purchase Program.

One additional option that is worth considering is purchasing iTunes Gift Cards in set, smaller amounts and giving them to teachers to buy and try individual apps for their classes. If an app looks promising, the teacher can recommend that the school use its VPP to purchase that app in larger quantities.

Email

When the first iPad was released, many argued that it was just a fancy device for the consumption of media. Along came the release of the iPad 2 with its built-in cameras and apps, and all of a sudden the iPad was a more-than-capable device for production and creative expression. One characteristic was largely overlooked in the debate over whether the iPad was capable of both consumption and production: The iPad is a wonderful device for connecting and communicating with others in a wide variety of methods. One of the most prominent communication features is the iPad's superlative Mail app (see Figure 2-7).

I'm not going to run through all the options for setting up and managing your email. Most are fairly straightforward. If you work at a school, you may be lucky enough to have a tech person set up email on your iPad for you.

If you have to set up your email account, the simplest option is to have your email accounts, calendars, and contacts placed on your iPad as part of the overall iTunes synchronization process. If you have Mac Mail, Microsoft Outlook, Gmail, or Yahoo! Mail set up on your computer, you can synchronize them directly with your iPad. The other option is simply to set it manually. You can do that by going to Settings and tapping the Mail, Contact, Calendars menu option in the left column.

Email is not only a great communication medium, but it's also an enormously useful tool in the iPad classroom. Most apps that enable you to create content also contain an option to email that content directly to a recipient. That makes email one of your options for moving content, whether it's emailing a file to yourself so that you can continue working on it, delivering something to a student, or as a way for students to submit work to a teacher. Chapter 4 delves more deeply into email.

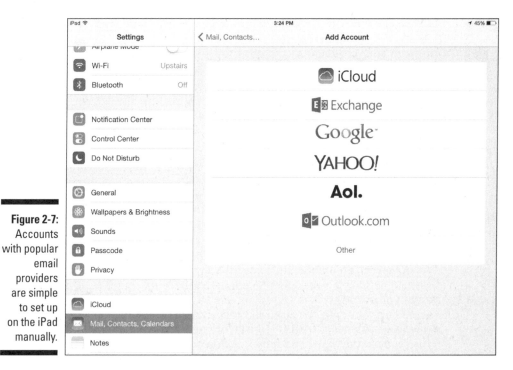

Figure 2-7:
Accounts
with popular
email
providers
are simple
to set up
on the iPad
manually.

Operating an iPad

Tablet computers such as the iPad have taken a refreshing new look at how people and machines should interact. The emphasis has been placed on keeping everything compact and mobile and using the sense of touch to directly manipulate objects and operate the iPad. There are no external components such as a mouse, keyboard, USB, or CD drive. Just pick up your iPad and take it anywhere. That's all you need — and I know you're going to love using it. My only word of caution is that you keep close tabs on it. Your family and workmates will constantly find reasons to borrow it, or as my youngest son would say, "just to look something up for a second." Uh-huh . . .

The iPad actually uses a common operating system with the iPhone and iPod touch. It's called, naturally, iOS. If you can use an iPhone, then you're well on the way to using an iPad; they use similar iOS features. If you've never used an iOS device before, then just settle back, grab a cup of tea or coffee or other beverage of choice, and browse through the following pages. I assure you the iPad will be the easiest and least technical device you've ever had to learn. Now let's get started.

You can connect to the Internet through a wireless network or, if you purchased the model that supports Wi-Fi and 3G or 4G, you can connect directly through your cellular service provider by subscribing to a monthly data plan. For the purposes of this book, I assume you're using a Wi-Fi–only model. That's because this is the predominant model being used in education.

Turning on

You've set up an Apple ID, your wireless network is up and running, and you're all set to go . . . except for one simple thing. Where's the On button? Press the Sleep/Wake button on the upper-right corner of the iPad. Hold it down for a few seconds, and your iPad will power up. Turn it off the same way; hold the Sleep/Wake button down for a few seconds until a large slide control appears at the top of your screen. Slide the red arrow across to turn off the iPad.

If you've used an iPhone, then you also know that you can lock your iPad without actually powering it off completely. Locking your iPad is a convenient way of protecting it. You can even create a passcode to prevent anyone from accessing your data. It's also ready and can be turned back on very quickly whenever you need it. The iPad will lock automatically after a few seconds (you can set the time in Settings), or you can just tap the Sleep/Wake button quickly. Tap the Sleep/Wake button or the Home button to turn it back on.

Staying in charge

Your iPad comes with a USB power adapter. Plug in the adapter to charge your iPad. Charging it from empty to 100 percent can take a few hours. This is the fastest method for charging, but you also may be able to charge your iPad by plugging it into the USB port of your computer. You should note, however, that it requires a high-power USB port.

Pumping up the volume

You can adjust the volume on your iPad in several ways. The most accessible way is to use the volume control on the right side of the physical frame, pressing the upper portion to increase volume and lower part to decrease it. Many apps also have sound controls built into them, and you can change the volume from there as well. Lastly, system sounds such as calendar alerts and new emails can be controlled by using the iPad's native Settings app. Look for Sounds under the General category in the left menu.

Using the built-in cameras

The camera functionality on the iPad varies from model to model. If you have an original iPad, you were a trailblazer . . . but not in a photographic sense. Unfortunately, that iPad doesn't have a camera. If you have an iPad 2 or later, you have both a front- and rear-facing camera (see Figure 2-8). The difference in image quality is substantial, however, with the iPad 3 boasting a 5-mega-pixel (rear-facing) iSight camera with autofocus and HD video recording.

Accessibility to a built-in camera has allowed for the simple integration of media into a variety of educational activities. Chapter 4 more fully explains how to take photos with the Camera app.

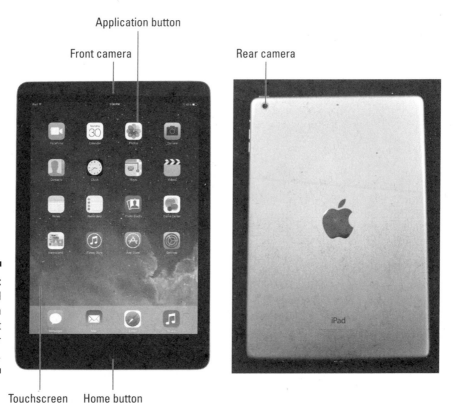

Figure 2-8:
The iPad has both front and rear cameras.

Getting Comfortable

You won't need years of computer science training to master the iPad, but you will need a basic familiarity with some of the core functions. Ironically, the younger you are, the less training you'll need.

The following sections take you on a quick tour of some of the basic functions. I suggest taking a look at the general *iPads For Dummies* series of books for a more detailed discussion of the core iPad features and apps.

Navigating the Home screen

Tap the large round Home button at the bottom of your iPad, and it will take you to the Home screen (see Figure 2-9). Each icon on the Home screen represents a different app, and your iPad comes stocked with around 17 to 20 apps, depending on your version. Apps included with your iPad include Settings, App Store, Mail, Calendar, Contacts, iTunes, Maps, Photos, and more.

Figure 2-9: Each icon on your Home screen represents an app.

Swipe the home page to the left with your finger, and it takes you to another screen of apps. As you start to purchase and download more apps, you'll notice they are automatically arranged into more screens.

The Dock is the row of apps at the bottom of the screen that can hold up to six icons. When you swipe from one screen to the next, the Dock remains. It's a good idea to keep your most commonly used apps in the Dock so that you can tap and start them from any screen.

Putting your apps in order

You can move app icons to any screen and location. Simply press any icon and hold your finger on it until you notice the icons begin to jiggle. Now you can press and drag any icon to move it. If you want to move it to another screen, then press and swipe it out to the very edge of the screen; the next screen will appear. You can also move apps down into the Dock area at the bottom of the screen. Move your popular apps down into the Dock so that they'll be available on all screens.

You can even organize your icons into folders. Try it:

- ✔ Press and hold your finger on an icon until all the icons start jiggling.

- ✔ Press an icon and drag it over the top of another icon that you want grouped with it in a folder.

- ✔ A new folder is automatically created with a folder name that's based on the nature of the apps in the folder. You can rename the folder and continue dragging other icons into it.

- ✔ Removing apps from a folder is done in a similar manner. Press and hold any folder until it jiggles, and then drag any icon out of it. Now, if only organizing my desk was that simple!

You can also arrange and delete icons and also Home screens when you're cabled to a computer with iTunes. If you have a lot of housecleaning to do, then it's probably a more efficient method.

Pressing and holding icons isn't just for moving them. When they start to jiggle, you'll notice that a little X appears in the top-right corner of most app icons (with the exception of the native iPad apps that cannot be deleted). Tap the X to remove that app from your iPad. Don't worry — it's just removed from your iPad. You can restore it next time you sync your devices or by going to the App Store and downloading it again.

Learning multitouch gestures

Computers have largely been using external input devices such as keyboards and mice since the popularization of the first personal computers. In retrospect, it seems so much more natural to directly touch and manipulate objects with your fingers than to use an external device . . . and although the iPad isn't the first computer to use a touch interface, it probably is the simplest and most advanced.

Some of the gestures vary between iPads and operating systems. The basic gestures, however, are common to all and include:

- ✔ **Tap** basically selects something. Tap with your finger to open and activate items such as apps and menu selections.

- ✔ **Flick** is a quick and easy way to scroll up and down pages and lists. Stop the scrolling by tapping on the page or list. You can also flick left or right on an item in a list to delete it.

- ✔ **Two-finger stretching** zooms into a page or image. If you've never done this before, it's sure to elicit a "wow" the first time you try it. Just pick any two fingers, place them on the screen, and move them apart. Pinch them closer together and the screen zooms back out. You'll never have to search for one of those little magnifying glass icons again. By the way, double-tapping with your finger often has the same effect.

- ✔ **Drag** is when you tap and hold your finger on the screen and then move it in any direction. You'll often drag to move an object or to move around in a web or other page.

 Apple introduced some cool new gestures back when it released the iOS 5 operating system. You'll have to make sure Multitasking Gestures are enabled in the General category within the Settings app. If you want to impress your friends and work colleagues, try some of the following and bask in the glow of admiration!

- ✔ Swipe up with four or five fingers to reveal a list of windows showing all currently open apps.

- ✔ If you're in an app, swipe to the left or right with four or five fingers to switch to the next/previous open app.

- ✔ Pinch with four or five fingers inside any app to return to the Home screen.

Creating and editing text

I don't mean to freak you out, but your iPad is pretty smart and often can sense what you need. Don't you wish you had more people in your life who could do that? Let's say you want to send an email. The second you open a new email message and tap in a field that requires text, your virtual keyboard automatically pops up on the screen, ready for you to type.

One of the features that helps many users type more fluently on the iPad is Auto-Correct. Yes, there's no doubt that it does lead to the occasional hysterical error, but overall, it helps correct many common errors that occur when you accidentally tap the wrong keys. Turn Auto-Correct on or off with the following steps:

1. **Tap the Settings icon on your Home screen.**

2. **Tap General.**

3. **Scroll down and tap Keyboard.**

4. **On the Keyboard screen, turn Auto-Correction on or off.**

Here are some other tips that will enhance your iPad keyboarding skills:

- **Special characters:** Hold down many of the keys for a list of alternative characters. For example, hold down the dollar key and you'll get a pop-up list of characters for other currencies. If you hold down keys such as I or N, you'll get a list of foreign language equivalents of those characters.

- **Adding periods:** Double-tap the spacebar at the end of a sentence and it automatically adds a period at the end of the sentence.

- **Quick keys:** You can tap, hold, and slide up on some keys for easy insertion of other characters. For example, tap and hold the comma key, and then slide your finger up and it adds an apostrophe. Swipe the period key and you get double quotation marks.

- **Split keyboard:** Have you ever noticed that your kids are masters at typing text messages with their thumbs? If that's your thing, then you'll love this tip. First, make sure that you've turned on the Split Keyboard option using Settings⇨General⇨Keyboard. Now return to any app that uses the keyboard. If you have iOS 5 or later, press and hold the keyboard key in the bottom right of your keyboard. It gives you the option to Undock your keyboard and move it anywhere onscreen. A second option splits the keyboard into two parts, as shown in Figure 2-10. In portrait mode, splitting the keyboard makes it easy to type with your thumbs, but I don't recommend it for those of us over the age of 30!

✔ **Typing in all-caps**: Double tap the Shift key to type something in ALL CAPS (if enabled in Settings➪General➪Keyboard➪Enable Caps Lock).

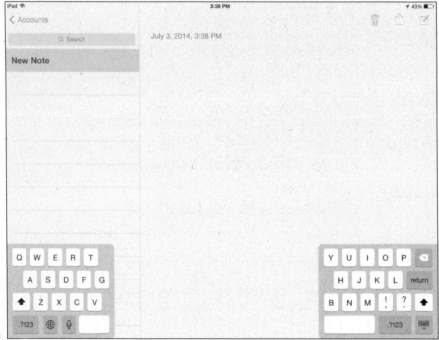

Figure 2-10: iOS 5 and later allows you to move and split the virtual keyboard.

Using copy and paste can be a valuable timesaver when you're typing a lot of text. Tap and hold any text in an email, document, or web page. A magnifying bubble appears, enabling you to move to text that you want to copy. Lift your finger and a little pop-up menu offers you options to Copy or Select All. The highlighted text has handles in two corners, as shown in Figure 2-11, that you can drag outward to expand your selection. Tap Copy when you're done.

The copied text is now in the iPad's clipboard and can be pasted into any app that has a text field. Simply tap wherever you want and select Paste from the pop-up menu. And if you feel a little more ambitious, here are a couple of cool shortcuts:

✔ Double-tap on any word to automatically select it.

✔ Tap four times quickly on text to select the entire paragraph.

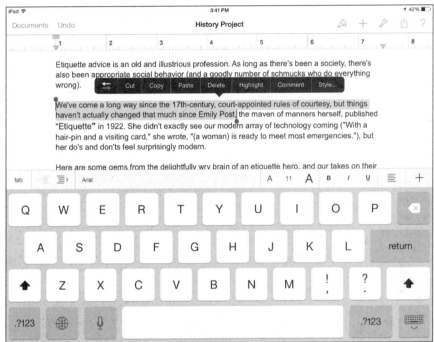

Figure 2-11:
Tap, hold,
and drag the
handles to
select text.

Switching between apps

Although you can't have more than one app open on your screen at the same time, the iPad does allow you to keep several apps open and then switch between them as needed.

Here's how you can quickly switch between open apps:

✔ Double-tap the Home button on the bottom of your iPad to reveal a row of windows showing the list of currently open apps, as shown in Figure 2-12. If you're using iOS 6 or below, you'll get a list of icons along the bottom of your iPad.

✔ Swipe to the left or right with your finger if the app you're looking for isn't there. There are usually more open apps than the windows can display at any one time.

✔ Tap any window to switch to it or tap the icon of the app if you're using iOS 6 or earlier. The app will open full screen, usually at whatever state you left it.

Remember: You can also swipe left or right with four or five fingers from within any app to slide between open apps. (Refer to the earlier section "Learning multitouch gestures.")

Figure 2-12:
Double-tap
the Home
button to
switch
between
open apps.

Using iPhone apps

When you search the App Store, you'll find that apps can be designed for use on the iPhone/iPod touch or iPad. In many cases, the app developer will have a version for both, and in other cases there are hybrid apps that adapt their display to the device being used. The main distinction between them is the size they occupy onscreen. iPhone apps are designed for the smaller iPhone screen, but most will work equally well on your iPad (unless they require iPhone-specific features such as dialing a number).

When using an iPhone app on the iPad, it defaults to running in its original size. You'll see a little 2x button in the lower-right corner of your screen. Tap it and the app will expand to fill the entire screen. You'll notice immediately that the image isn't as crisp, but I find it especially useful when the app has a keyboard and I need larger keys for typing.

Some apps are hybrids and work across iOS devices. They automatically detect the device and adjust their screen display accordingly. You'll find them listed in the App Store with a small + sign in the corner of the icon.

Putting Auto-Correct to work for you

Auto-Correct can be a great way of creating shortcuts for words and phrases that you often need to type. Let's say that you work for the New Horizons for Global Economic Change. The facility has a great cafeteria, and you're always asking people to meet you there for lunch. Their vegetable lasagna has this amazing tomato . . . sorry, I digress. You send several people an email and have to type **New Horizons for Global Economic Change** every time. That's quite a challenge. One slipup and Auto-Correct will have them searching the New Horizons for Glorious Economical Cheese. Here's a slick and easy little solution. Use Auto-Correct to create typing shortcuts. Here's how:

1. **Tap to open the Settings app.**

2. **Tap General in the left menu, and then tap Keyboard from the menu of options in the main window.**

At the bottom of the main window, you see the section for Shortcuts.

3. **Tap to Add New Shortcut.**

You have two choices:

✔ **Phrase:** Type the long-hand version of the text you want to appear. That's **New Horizons for Global Economic Change.**

✔ **Shortcut:** Type a short series of letters that the iPad will then expand and auto-correct for you. For example, you might type NHGEC. Now every time you type **NHGEC,** Auto-Correct will jump in and presto — it automatically expands the text into New Horizons for Global Economic Change. Now don't forget to try the lasagna.

Searching your iPad

If you go to your Home screen and swipe to the left, you'll find yourself on the Spotlight Search page, as shown in Figure 2-13. This is your one-stop-shop for finding anything in your iPad. Things you can search for include

✔ **Apps:** As you get more and more apps that fill multiple screens, this often becomes the easiest way to find an app quickly.

✔ **Mail messages:** Searches the From, To, CC, BCC, and Subject fields**.**

✔ **Media:** This includes music, podcasts, videos, and more.

✔ **And more:** Including contacts, events, reminders, messages, and notes.

Type your search term in the field at the top of the page. You can type any part of the item that you're searching, and the results will narrow down as you continue typing the term. The results are categorized by type. Tap the item you want, and it opens in the appropriate app.

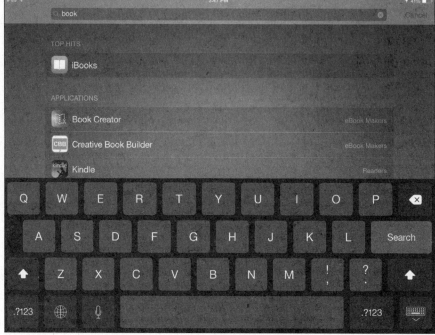

Figure 2-13:
Spotlight
Search
categorizes
your search
results by
type.

Accessorizing Your iPad

I've yet to meet anyone who hasn't loved using an iPad. Having said that, a number of accessories can make it even more functional and keep it physically safe and secure. Purchasing accessories is really a matter of taste, but here's a list of some that you may want to consider:

✔ **Physical keyboard:** Everyone has his own favorite type of keyboard. With a little time and practice, most people become quite fluent typing on the iPad's virtual keyboard, but it may take time to become comfortable using it. You do have options. A number of external, physical keyboards can be used with your iPad.

- *Wireless keyboard:* Apple offers its own wireless keyboard that uses Bluetooth and just needs to be placed somewhere near the iPad. The company also offers a separate stand that can prop up your iPad for easier viewing while you type. Similar options are also available from several other companies.

- *Combination case with keyboard:* Some companies, such as Logitech, Belkin, and Zagg, offer iPad covers and cases with built-in keyboards. The case generally opens and props the iPad up on a stand in front of an attached keyboard.

✔ **Screen cleaners:** It won't take very long at all for your screen to be covered with annoying smudges that you want to clean. All-purpose cleaner may do a great job on windows and tabletops, but don't even think of using it on your iPad! Stay away from using any cleaning fluids, abrasive cloths, towels, and paper towels, too. They may damage the screen. Apple recommends using only a soft, lint-free cloth.

✔ **Cases:** The iPad is actually pretty sturdy, but it still makes sense to protect it with a case. There are hundreds to choose from, and I've seen everything from bulky options that look and weigh like military flak jackets to flimsy little covers that would barely protect against the wind. When selecting a case, keep the following in mind:

- *Protect but don't smother.* Make sure your case still gives you access to the buttons and ports. It's very annoying when you have to peel back or take off a case to do something as simple as accessing the volume control.

- *Standing room.* Consider a case that has options for propping up the iPad when opened. Some even have separate stands for vertical and horizontal use. It's often very convenient when you want to stand your iPad up on a table or desk.

- *Corner protection.* Dropping an iPad on its corner will often cause the worst damage to the screen. Select a case that protects the corner edges.

✔ **Earbuds:** When you're blasting that AC/DC music, you'll be doing everyone a favor if you pull out and use a set of earbuds. Generally, any earbuds that work with an iPhone or iPod will work with your iPad as well. Rather than sharing, especially if you're using iPads in a classroom, you may want to consider having children bring their own for sanitary reasons. Their parents likely will prefer that, too. Also, some earbuds include a built-in mic as well, which can come in very handy.

✔ **Belkin Rockstar:** In class, you may often need to have several students listen to audio on an iPad at the same time. The Belkin Rockstar will be your savior. It connects to your iPad and offers five adapters for students to plug in their own earbuds. Be warned, though: It's a "splitter," which means that the volume is shared among the different earbuds and will therefore have lower volume for each.

✔ **Stylus:** I'll leave it to you to decide the value of using a stylus with your iPad. However, if you do want to use a stylus, I recommend trying out a specific model before buying as they vary significantly in comfort and efficacy. Consider higher quality options for writing, such as Wacom's Bamboo stylus or Adonit's Jot. Also, some models are designed for precision handwriting, whereas others excel when used for sketching. Ensure you get the stylus that best meets your specific needs.

✔ **Screen protector:** An invisible screen protector can be an inexpensive way of preventing scratches and keeping the screen clean.

✔ **Adapters:** Your iPad is very compact and mobile. As a result, it doesn't have ports for attaching peripheral devices. However, wherever there's demand there's a product, and you'll find adapters for most of the uses you'll encounter, such as connecting cameras and external displays.

Chapter 3

Managing the iPad Classroom

*I*f you're lucky, you have an IT professional who has been trained in device management and takes care of it for you. If so, you can happily skip to the next chapter knowing that, at least in this instance, ignorance is bliss. Unfortunately, it's more likely that you're at a school that's dealing with a patchwork of misunderstood solutions — some of which work, some that don't, and others that are so confusing nobody understands what to do. If that's the case, then welcome! This chapter is for you.

This chapter provides an overview of the issues that affect iPad rollout and management.

Planning the Deployment

There are several basic stages of an iPad deployment:

▸ **Preparing your infrastructure:** Ensure that your school and IT systems are ready for widespread iPad use.

▸ **Configuring and managing iPads:** Configure the iPads for distribution to staff and students. Administer iPad settings, accounts, restrictions, and profiles.

▸ **Deploying apps and content:** Purchase, distribute, and update apps and content.

Models of device setup and management vary according to the number of iPads being distributed and managed. I'd like to promise you that it will be simple and headache-free. It isn't, but hopefully, with a little guidance, it won't end up being quite as painful as you may fear.

Preparing Your Infrastucture

You've read about all the wonderful things other schools are doing with iPads, and you're eager to dive in and get started. Wait. Even the most well-designed building will topple if it isn't built on a solid foundation. Review your infrastructure and make sure you're ready. Here's a short list of some of the things to consider before purchasing all those devices:

- ✔ **Wi-Fi:** Do you have a Wi-Fi network that is sufficiently robust to handle the number of devices you plan on purchasing? You need a healthy amount of bandwidth from your Internet provider along with a solid wireless infrastructure on campus. Your Wi-Fi network needs to supply a consistent and reliable signal that's strong enough to handle multiple devices connecting at any and all locations around campus. The quickest way to torpedo any technology initiative is to have teachers work hard to prepare wonderful projects for students that are unable to connect when they power up the devices.

- ✔ **Core data systems:** Ensure that your central data systems — such as email, calendars, and databases — are set up to work smoothly with iPads. As one example, an email system that requires its own app as opposed to being configured to use the native iPad Mail app may cause problems down the road. Check that your essential data systems can be managed as needed on iPads.

- ✔ **Management system:** However you plan on configuring and managing the iPads, ensure that you have the configuration in place and well defined. Smaller deployments may need only personal management. Larger installations might require the use of a mobile device management (MDM) solution.

- ✔ **Content storage:** Ensure that you have a system in place for students to store and exchange content created on iPads.

You'll see me frequently refer to MDM solutions. MDM software gives IT departments the capability to enroll devices in a centrally managed environment, wirelessly configure and update their settings, and even to remotely wipe or lock managed devices. Several third-party MDM solutions are available for managing iOS devices. If you Google *MDM management of iOS devices,*

you'll get a comprehensive list of options that you can evaluate. Research the various options and select the one that best matches your budget and requirements.

Configuring and Managing iPads

The truck rolls up and drops several large boxes of iPads at your door. You need to get them ready for class use, but you don't have any training or experience setting up mobile devices. Take a deep breath; I'm going to map out some options. Hopefully, you've already defined the size of your deployment and an appropriate management strategy, as discussed in the previous section.

There are three basic deployment models:

- ✔ **Personally owned and managed:** Staff and/or students own and manage their own devices. This personal deployment is the model being used by millions of iPad users around the world. Users activate the iPad using the Setup Assistant that prompts them when the iPad is first powered up and use their own Apple IDs during setup and management of the device. The same model would also apply in a "BYOD" (bring your own device) environment.

- ✔ **Personally distributed but school managed:** This is a common scenario in 1:1 deployments where each student gets exclusive use of an iPad, but the devices are centrally configured and managed. Devices are usually configured before distribution to users, and an MDM solution is often used to manage the devices and settings. A hybrid alternative would enroll the device using an MDM, which would control settings and organizational apps while allowing users the freedom to separately install their own apps and content.

- ✔ **Shared devices:** iPads that will be shared are typically configured and managed centrally and usually have restrictions set to prevent users from installing apps or changing settings. Apple Configurator is a program that's often used to set up and supervise device settings and profiles.

Of course, you may also have a mixture of any of these scenarios. It's possible that you may allow teachers to manage the devices they are given but student iPads are administered by the IT (information technology) department using an MDM.

Getting Apple IDs for students

A significant part of the iPad management hassles in elementary schools stemmed from the fact that U.S. regulations prohibited institutions from creating web-based accounts such as Apple IDs for students under the age of 13. This has been addressed by Apple in the new Apple ID for Students program. Schools can upload a spreadsheet of student names and IDs to Apple. Emails are sent out to parents requesting their consent to create the Apple ID. Upon receipt of parental consent, Apple creates the ID for their student. With their own ID in hand, students can get individualized access to school materials, iCloud, content, textbooks, and more.

Apple has a Device Enrollment Program that enables institutions to enroll iPads into mobile device management to ensure that all of devices are configured right out of the box. Institutionally owned devices can be automatically enrolled in MDM during activation without ever touching the device. You can set custom settings for your institution, and streamline the entire setup process so users get an abbreviated version of the Setup Assistant and can quickly get up and running when they first start up the iPad. Find out more at `https://www.apple.com/education/it/dep`.

Managing devices

iOS devices are unmanaged by default. They're primarily designed as personal devices, allowing individual users to change settings, accounts, and content as needed. Many institutions decide to adopt a management strategy when purchasing large numbers of devices, and they usually implement it with an MDM solution. iPads are enrolled in the MDM, which has comprehensive controls for configuring and administering the device.

Distributing configuration profiles

Setting up an iPad requires information about email servers, Wi-Fi settings, possible restrictions on use, and more. That information can be encoded in a configuration profile. If you're setting up large numbers of iPads, you can automate the setup by distributing the configuration profile to the devices. That's typically done using Apple Configurator on smaller deployments or wirelessly via an MDM when dealing with larger numbers.

Supervising devices

iPads are also not supervised by default. Configuration settings can be changed by any user. Supervision allows an organization to monitor and change settings on devices that have already been rolled out to users. Supervision is usually enabled as part of the device setup through Apple Configurator or an MDM solution and will lock the configuration profile and prevent individual users from changing it. Changes and new profiles can be distributed with Apple Configurator or the MDM.

Deploying Apps and Content

After you've configured and issued your iPads, you'll want a simple way to purchase and distribute apps and content. Apple's Volume Purchase Program (VPP) allows institutions to purchase apps and books in volume and distribute them to the devices in their organization. Use the following steps to deploy apps and content:

1. **Enroll your school as an educational institution and specify the program manager.**

2. **Set up and manage the administrators who will purchase and distribute content.**

3. **Go to the Apple VPP store online (`https://volume.itunes.apple.com/us/store` for schools in the USA), and find your desired content, and then set the quantity you want to purchase.**

   App developers that have offered educational pricing will offer their apps at a 50-percent discount for purchases of 20 or more units.

4. **Distribute redeemable codes to individual users, or assign the content to larger amounts of user devices with your MDM solution.**

   If the device is supervised, you can install the apps wirelessly. You can also apply redemption codes through Apple Configurator when dealing with smaller deployments.

Management Tips

Managing iOS devices is still a work in progress, and it's likely to undergo several important revisions in the near future. In the meantime, maybe a couple of tips from the field will help make the task a little easier for you.

Using restrictions on student iPads

Whether you manage devices and profiles centrally or by individual device, you'll want to put some thought into how to set the restrictions on iPad use. Of course, the restrictions will vary depending on the users and what they should be doing with the iPads. If you're assigning restrictions directly on the iPad itself, go to the Settings menu, and tap General on the left. Tap Restrictions to see the pane shown in Figure 3-1. You're required to set a passcode that can be used later to change or delete restrictions. Restrictions can also be set as part of a configuration profile that is distributed to devices by Apple Configurator or an MDM.

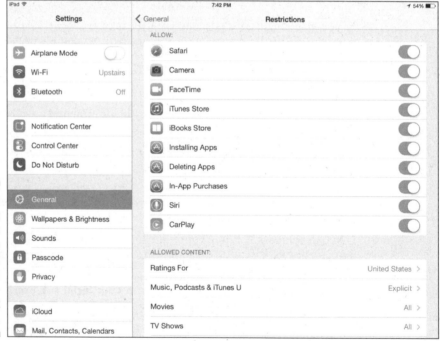

Figure 3-1: Set Restrictions on iPad use on the iPad itself or in a profile management tool.

Here's a quick look at some of the more important restrictions:

✔ Disallow apps such as Safari (in case you want to use a different, filtered browser), FaceTime, and the iTunes Store.

✔ Disable the camera and FaceTime.

✔ Install and/or delete apps.

✔ Disable in-app purchases.

You can choose to prevent changes to the following settings/accounts:

- ✔ Location Services (a good idea if students are posting any data to the web that contains geolocation data, such as photos)
- ✔ Mail, Contacts, Calendars, iCloud, and/or Twitter accounts

In addition, you can choose to prevent access to specific content types for music and podcasts, movies, TV shows, and more.

Tracking devices with Find My iPad

Activating Find My iPad can be a valuable tool in tracking down lost iPads on campus or off. You need an iCloud account to use it, and then you can log into iCloud on any browser to see the location of your iPad on a map if it's powered on.

Go to Settings on your iPad, tap iCloud, and enable Find My iPad. Then if you misplace it, sign in to www.icloud.com from any web browser on a Mac or PC, or use the Find My iPhone app to display the approximate location of your iPad on a map. Find My iPad allows you to play a beep, display a message, lock your iPad remotely, or even wipe your data off it.

Identifying iPads

Each iPad has a specific name. If you open Settings and tap General and then About, it's the first item that appears in the pane on the right. However, when you need to quickly identify an iPad to hand out to a student, that takes too many steps. Sure, you can sticker them (the iPads, not the kids!) on the outside, but stickers fall off.

Some schools identify iPads by creating an image with a number on it and setting it as the wallpaper. That way, as soon as you turn the iPad on, the number shows up on the screen. A nice idea. Why not take this idea a step further, and use a little introductory lesson that is also educational? Why not use the opportunity to have the students tell you something about themselves or their interests? Have them find an image that represents something meaningful to them, which is a task that may be really fun to send home to be done with a parent or relative.

Self-management of iPads

Managing tens and hundreds of iPads can be a difficult process with any tool. Some schools have decided to let older students manage the devices themselves. They are responsible for such things as downloading and updating apps, backing up their content to iCloud accounts, and updating operating systems. Theoretically, you could still set them up with some limited restrictions if needed, and then just hand them over to the students. Granted, it's a leap for many administrators, but it relieves schools of the headache of centralized management while also nurturing student independence and responsibility. Ensure that students have their own iTunes accounts, train them in basic device administration, and meet on a regular basis. Some schools also have an IT office where students can come for help. You could even have it staffed by students themselves! Self-management of devices is definitely worthy of discussion.

Use an app such as Skitch (a free art app) to combine the image with text containing a fact or some identifiable information about the image. It might be something about their favorite car, hero, or maybe their pet (as shown in Figure 3-2). Set it as the iPad wallpaper or Lock screen. The students will be extremely motivated and identify more with their particular iPads.

Figure 3-2:
Have students set the wallpaper for their iPads to help identify them.

Part II
Finding and Using Apps

In this part . . .

- ✔ Use email and browse the Internet
- ✔ Learn how to best utilize your iPad camera
- ✔ Explore the apps that came with your iPad
- ✔ Find and buy apps in the App Store

Chapter 4

Tap Dancing with Your iPad's Apps

. . . .

In This Chapter

▶ Communicating with email on your iPad

▶ Surfing the web

▶ Using the built-in camera to take photos and video

▶ Getting and reading digital books

▶ Organizing your contacts and calendar

▶ Browsing through the apps that came with your iPad

. . . .

You've just brought home that shiny, sleek new iPad from the store. It's crammed full of apps that let you start surfing the Internet, take photos and video, email, video-chat, watch movies, read books, and more. It's there waiting for you . . . as soon as you master a few basics about using your iPad's apps. It's all really very easy. It's just that we start at such a huge disadvantage. After all, we're "adults."

Children pull the device out of the box, power it up, and start using it instantly. They're so tech-savvy; it's almost as if they were using technology in utero. Adults? In the best-case scenario, you look for a user manual. Worst case, you close the box and go find a book to distract you from the need to learn another electronic device. No problem. Just make sure it's this book, and you'll be an expert app user in no time!

The iPad is a tool with almost limitless possibilities after you master some of its core apps. This chapter walks you through using most of the apps that came with your iPad and shows you some of the amazing things you can do with them. It discusses how to use email, access the Internet, use the camera, read digital books, and more. Put on your seat belt and let's get going.

Making Mail a Communication Tool

One of the least heralded characteristics of iPads is that they really are terrific communication devices. The wonderful Mail app is a perfect example.

Many of us have more than one email account. You may have one for work, one for home, and possibly another account for the cousin who constantly sends you jokes you don't want to read. One of the many convenient features of your iPad's Mail app is its capability to collect and display messages from different email accounts in one simple location. Instead of needing to log into different websites to check your personal, work, and school emails, all your messages are organized in one easy-to-access location. You'll never have to worry about which email you've forgotten to check, and you don't have to waste time reentering your username and password again and again. The iPad's Mail app will keep you connected to your email and make it simple for you to track and reply to all your digital correspondence . . . even with your annoying cousin.

Opening Mail accounts

The first step to using the Mail app is to sign in to your email account(s).

1. **Tap the Mail icon on your iPad Home screen.**

   The Mail icon often can be found on the application Dock at the bottom of your Home screen.

2. **Choose your email provider.**

   Mail works with popular email providers, including Google Gmail, Microsoft Exchange, Yahoo! Mail, Outlook, and AOL. They are listed as default options for mail setup. If your email belongs to one of those services, then tap and select it. If you don't see your email provider listed here, tap Other, then Add Mail Account, and enter specific details about your mail provider (see Figure 4-1).

3. **Follow the prompts on your iPad.**

   The Mail app will ask for information such as a username and password during the initial setup.

If you ever need to change details about an existing account, go to your Home screen, tap Settings, and then Mail, Contacts, Calendars. Select the account you want to edit, and modify the information.

The best part about Mail is the capability to have all your emails in one place! You can only do that if you add all your email accounts. To add another account, head back to your Home screen. Tap Settings, tap Mail, Contacts, Calendars, tap Add Account, and follow the onscreen instructions. You'll never miss an email about a staff meeting, an e-vite to your niece's birthday party, or an electronic half-off coupon again!

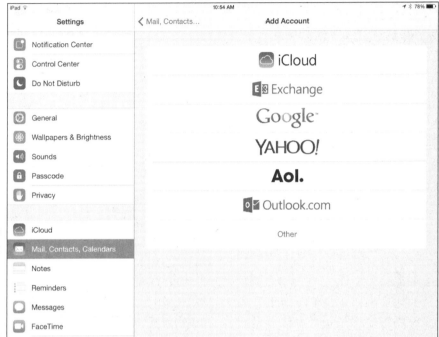

Figure 4-1:
Follow the
prompts
to set up
your email
accounts.

Your iPad Settings give you control over quite a few of the Mail defaults, such as how many messages to show and how to display them. The options are listed under the Mail, Contacts, Calendar menu category in Settings. You'll notice that there's also a choice entitled Fetch New Data. That enables you to set the method and frequency your iPad uses when getting your email. The more often you fetch your email, the more battery you'll use. If you want to prolong your battery life, fetch your email less frequently.

Browsing mail

After you have set up your mail accounts, simply tap the Mail icon on your iPad Home screen to open the Mail app and check your email. If you're holding your iPad in landscape orientation, you'll see the following:

✔ Your accounts are listed on the left (see Figure 4-2). The Mail app has one section for Inboxes and another for all the folders you have in your account. Tap any option in the left pane to start browsing mail.

Compose icon

Reply/Forward/Print icon

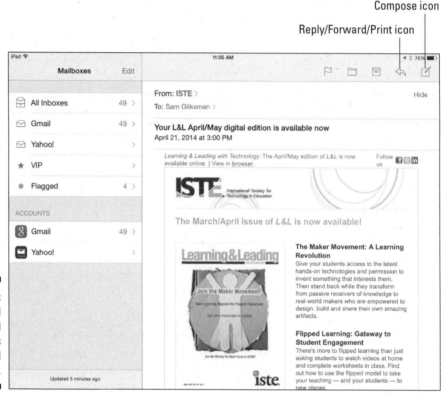

Figure 4-2:
Track all
your email
accounts
in the iPad
Mail app.

✔ When you tap the option, it opens the appropriate folder and lists the mail in it. Scroll through the list and tap any mail to browse it in the pane on the right. Messages may be grouped in threads (that option can be changed in Settings) so that the original email and its replies are kept together in a list.

✔ If an email contains images, the images will appear in the body of the message. Tap and hold any image, and you can save it to your Camera Roll. You can also tap any document attachments such as PDF, iWork, or Word files to open and view them.

✔ If you have iOS 6 or later, you'll notice a separate folder for VIP mail. Add any sender to your VIP list by tapping the sender's name or email address in the email message header, and then scrolling down the pop-up menu and selecting Add to VIP. Mail adds a folder for each VIP, so it's easy to get to their messages.

✔ If you added more than one email account, you'll have the option of tapping the All Inboxes choice on the menus, where you can browse all the messages from all your accounts in one integrated list.

If you hold your iPad vertically, the navigation pane automatically disappears so that you have more space to read your email. Tap the button with the account or folder name in the top-left corner of the screen, and the navigation pane will slide back in.

Creating and sending an email

Creating and sending email is a piece of cake. The top-right corner of your screen includes the Compose icon (refer to Figure 4-2). Tap it to start a new email. The virtual keyboard will slide up when you tap in any text field. Enter the recipient in the To field and fill in the Subject. Tap anywhere in the body to start typing your message. When you're done, tap Send in the top-right corner and your message is on its way!

Everyone asks the same question about email at some point. The answer is, "No, you can't get your message back once you've sent it." The moral is simple: Read your email carefully before tapping that Send button.

Using contacts

Digital address books have been around for quite a few years, and they make tracking and using your contact information simple. Your iPad has a Contacts app as well, and it integrates directly with Mail. You can add contacts in several ways:

- Tap the Contacts icon on your iPad, and then press the + icon to enter data about a new contact directly into the app.

- Tap the name of any person who sent you an email in the From field of the email. A pop-up window will display the sender's details and options to Create New Contact or Add to Existing Contact. Tap either option to add the sender's email address to your Contacts list.

- Synchronize your Contacts list with an existing list as part of your iPad synchronization. Refer to Chapter 3 for more information.

When you compose a new email, you'll notice a + sign on the right of the To field. Tap it to bring up your Contacts list and select a recipient.

You may also notice that your iPad Mail app has an excellent memory. It keeps a history of people whom you have emailed and will pop up a list of suggested names from the history list when you start typing in the recipient field. Now if it could only remember where you put your keys . . .

Deleting email

Swipe from right to left across any email in your mail list, and Mail prompts you to delete it. You can also tap the Trash Can icon on the toolbar above any open email to delete it. Of course, there's always that time you delete an email and then realize you could use that coupon for another power drill after all. Luckily the email isn't permanently deleted right away, so you can still retrieve it.

Mail generally moves deleted email to a trash or archive folder. Tap your account in the menu on the left and look for the folder with your deleted messages. Don't fret — your email is just as you last saw it, and can be accessed there. Your only problem might be explaining that sixth power drill to your wife.

Taking an Educational Internet Safari

What if you're standing in front of the class teaching History and you can't remember the wedding date of Henry VIII's fifth marriage? Talk about egg on your face! Seriously, having quick and easy access to the Internet is an invaluable learning tool. With Safari, iPad's web browser, the Internet is always just a simple tap away.

Browsing and tabs

Safari was given a major upgrade when Apple released iOS 5, and one of the most prominent new features was the capability to keep multiple pages open in tabs within the browser.

- **Opening a new tab:** You see each page displayed in a row of tabs along the top of your browser window (see Figure 4-3), and you can open a new tab at any time by tapping the + icon at the right of the top menu bar.
- **Switching tabs:** Tap any tab to switch focus to that page.
- **Closing tabs:** Tap the little x on the tab to close it.

You can keep multiple pages open in tabs. Safari remembers your open tabs and reopens them when you next browse the Internet.

Tabs

Figure 4-3:
Safari uses
tabbed
browsing
for keeping
multiple
pages open.

Safari was given a major face-lift with the release of iOS 6 in 2012 and iOS 7 in 2013. Features such as browser tabs for multiple pages, Reader, Reading List, smart search field, and more are all significant upgrades to the prior version. We focus on the iOS 7 version of Safari in these discussions, and I strongly recommend that you upgrade to it if you haven't already.

Googling

I have to confess that I'm a sentimentalist at heart. I still treasure the smell and feel of those old encyclopedias I had as a kid, and it's hard to believe that brands such as *Britannica* are no longer published. On the other hand, I absolutely love the fact that I can type a few words in a web browser and access information anywhere in the world instantly — and the most popular key to searching that vast knowledge base is Google.

It has become so popular that the word "Google" is now used as a verb, and we refer to searching as "googling." Jump-start your Google searches by using one of these two shortcuts:

- ✔ **Safari's smart search bar:** This is a great tool to use if, while you are using Safari, you realize there is information you want to look up. Tap the address bar at the top of your Safari screen where you'd normally type the URL of the website you want. Instead of typing a web address such as www.yahoo.com, simply type your search term instead. Try it! Type **Bob's fishing supplies** and tap the large Go key on your keyboard. Your wish is Google's command! The Google search page displays with the results for *Bob's fishing supplies.* It's as simple as that . . . and frankly, Bob could do with the extra business. (Note that you can also use Settings to change the default search engine used by Safari to either Yahoo! or Bing).

- ✔ **iPad's built-in search engine:** Swipe down on any Home screen to reveal the Spotlight Search function. Type your query into the box at the top of the screen, and then tap Search Web. This opens a new tab in Safari with your Google search results.

You can set your default web search provider on the iPad. In order to make sure that Google is your default search engine, go to your Home screen and tap Settings. Then tap Safari in the left navigation pane. The first option allows you to select which search engine to use.

Getting rid of clutter with Reader

It seems like websites are getting more and more cluttered — between the advertisements, stock tickers, and pop-ups, it's hard to identify the actual content you're trying to read. If you're using iOS 5 or later, Safari has added a solution with its Reader function.

When you browse through most websites, a Reader icon that looks like a series of horizontal lines appears in the left side of the address bar as shown in Figure 4-4. Just tap the Reader icon and Safari will display only the article. All the clutter is gone! If only I could do that to my desk . . .

Reader icon

across the Pine Island Glacier, a major ice stream that drains the West Antarctic Ice Sheet.

City-sized iceberg drifts into ocean

(CNN) -- A massive iceberg with an area almost twice the size of Atlanta is moving into the ocean off Antarctica and could threaten shipping during the Antarctic winter, scientists say.

The ice island, known as iceberg B31, covers 255 square miles and could be almost a third of a mile thick, scientists say in a report from NASA's Earth Observatory.

The iceberg calved from Antarctica's Pine Island Glacier last November, according to NASA. The crack that produced it was first spotted in 2011.

Since November, B31 has drifted out of Pine Island Bay and into the Amundsen Sea off the western side of the continent.

"The iceberg is now well out of Pine Island Bay and will soon join the more general flow in the Southern Ocean, which could be east or west in this region," iceberg researcher Grant Bigg from the University of Sheffield in England said in the NASA statement.

Once that happens, the researchers worry it will be difficult track the iceberg during the long weeks of darkness that comprise the Antarctic winter.

And don't expect it to melt. An iceberg of that size could hang around for a year or more, Robert Marsh, a scientist at the University of Southampton in England, said last year.

Figure 4-4:
Safari's Reader function removes clutter and makes it easier to read articles.

Bookmarking

Bookmarking is a must with Safari. Save websites you frequently visit to avoid having to remember and type their addresses manually.

- ✔ **Add a bookmark.** When you are visiting a page you want to bookmark, tap the Share icon on the left of Safari's address bar (see Figure 4-5). It's the icon that looks like a rectangle with an arrow coming out the top of it. This will bring up a menu of options. Tap Bookmark, edit the name if you like, and tap Save. Your bookmark has been added!

- ✔ **View your bookmarks.** Tapping the Bookmark icon at the right of Safari's address bar (see Figure 4-5) displays your list of saved websites. Select any site in the list by tapping it, and it opens in your Safari browser.

- ✔ **Edit your bookmarks.** You can add, delete, and organize your saved websites. Tap the Bookmark icon, and then tap Edit in the bottom-right corner to delete bookmarks, move items in the list, create folders, and more.

Share icon

Bookmark icon

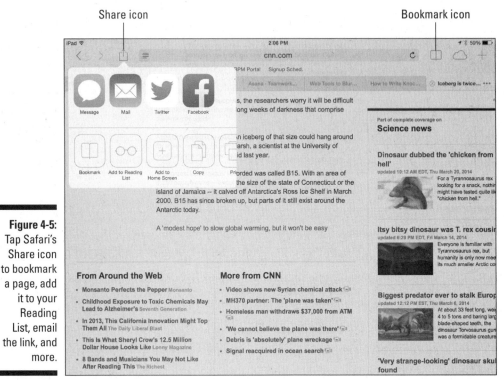

Share icon
Bookmark icon

Figure 4-5:
Tap Safari's
Share icon
to bookmark
a page, add
it to your
Reading
List, email
the link, and
more.

Bookmarks include a folder called Favorites Bar. Sites saved in that folder are displayed on a toolbar at the top of the Safari browser window. Save your most popular sites to the Favorites Bar folder for quick and easy access. Note that the Favorites Bar has to be enabled in the Safari section of your Settings app in order for it to display in your browser.

Safari in iOS 6 and later has several Share options that you can access from a number of apps, including your Safari web browser. When you tap the Share icon, you can send a link to the page to others via email, the Message app, your Facebook page, Twitter, and more.

Reading List

"So much to do, so little time." Sound familiar? It's certainly the case that there never seems to be enough time for everything you want to read on the Internet. Safari includes a Reading List function that helps you keep track of all those I'm-going-to-read-it-as-soon-as-I-have-a-free-moment articles and websites.

If you want to add a web page for later reading, tap the Share icon to the left of Safari's address bar and select Add to Reading List. When you want to catch up on your reading, tap the Bookmark icon on the right of Safari's address bar, and tap the Reading List spectacle icon in the middle of the top toolbar. You can Show All or Show Unread by tapping the menu option at the bottom of the list. Use Reading List to build your own personalized library of articles.

Adding a website to your Home screen

What if you use a website so frequently that simply bookmarking it doesn't give you fast enough access? If you have that need-for-speed, consider adding the website's link directly to your Home screen. It's as easy as 1, 2, 3.

1. **Open the web page in your Safari browser.**

2. **Tap the Share icon to the left of the address bar to display a menu of options.**

3. **Tap Add to Home Screen to add the website icon directly to your iPad Home screen.**

   You can edit the name to make the site easily recognizable, and then tap Add. Now when you tap that icon on your iPad, Safari automatically opens and displays that web page.

Adding a website directly to the iPad Home screen is a great option to use if you have a classroom website. Add the icon to all student iPads, and with one tap, they're on the class page and working.

Saving images from the web

Part V of this book demonstrates some of the tremendous potential for creating multimedia content on the iPad. You may have frequent occasions in which you'd like to use an image on the web. Tap and hold the image in Safari (see Figure 4-6), and a menu pops up with options to Copy or Save Image. Tap Save Image, and the image is added to your Camera Roll — and is available in other apps as well.

If you're using images from the web, then it might be an excellent time to discuss copyright and fair use. Make sure students are aware of when and how they can legally use images, video, music, and other web content. Note that if you use Google to search for images, you can tap the Search Tools option on the toolbar and filter results by their Usage Rights.

Figure 4-6:
Tap and hold
any image to
save it.

Searching the page

Here's a typical scenario: You do a Google search for *Philosophy Quotes Descartes.* You tap one of your Google search results and get a page that lists quotes from every famous person in history who has ever uttered a quotable phrase. That quote you want from Descartes is in there *somewhere,* but it would take you about 20 minutes and a couple of aspirin to find it. Safari has your solution: You can search the page. Just follow these steps:

1. **Open the web page in Safari that you want to search.**

2. **Tap the address field on the top of your browser, and type your search term.**

   Type whatever word or phrase you're searching in the Google search field. For example, you may type **Descartes**.

3. **Search the page.**

   A list of search results is displayed. The top section offers Google Search results. If you scroll down to the bottom of the list, you see an On This Page option. Tap the Find option to see instances of the search phrase on the current web page. As the first instance is highlighted on the page, the toolbar on the bottom of the page offers arrows to skip between any other instances.

   Now wasn't that easy?

Taking and Using Photos and Video as Learning Tools

Modern society is awash in multimedia. Movies, mobile devices, YouTube, video chat, social networking — it's all around us in work and at play. Multimedia is finally starting to make an impression within our educational spaces as well. Projects that used to consist of cardboard posters with glued pictures and articles are often now being created, edited, and delivered as sophisticated video presentations. Your iPad is well equipped with several capable tools to assist in those important multimedia communications.

Taking photos

If you have an iPad 2 or later, it comes with both a front- and rear-facing camera (see Figure 4-7). Access to the capability to take photos at any time is not only extremely convenient for classroom use, but can also be a great tool for creativity and innovation. The possibilities are only limited by your — and your students' — imagination:

- Use it to document student work and create a digital portfolio to share with parents.
- Snap an image of a busy whiteboard to record important information.
- Stage and take photos as part of digital storytelling projects.
- Document science experiments with photos.
- Take photos of real-world examples of mathematical concepts such as shapes and angles.
- Develop students' visual literacy skills by using photography as a communication tool.

To use the iPad camera:

1. **Go to your iPad Home screen and tap the Camera icon to open the app.**

   Make sure that the Photo mode is selected in the right column as shown in Figure 4-7. Slide the menus up or down with your finger if you need to change the selection.

2. **Select a camera view by tapping the Switch Camera icon to toggle between the front and rear cameras.**

3. **Aim your iPad so that your desired photo is displayed on the screen.**

   You can also zoom by pinching your fingers together to activate the zoom slide bar. Slide right to zoom in and left to zoom back out.

Camera button

Switch between front and rear cameras

Figure 4-7:
The iPad 2
and later
have front
and rear
cameras
for use in
the Camera
app.

HDR Off

VIDEO

PHOTO

SQUARE

Camera Roll

Switch between camera and video

4. **Tap the image to set the primary point of focus if required.**

   Tapping anywhere on screen tells the camera where you want it to focus.
   You can even lock the point of focus so the iPad doesn't change it automatically as you move the camera. Frame your photo and then tap and
   hold any spot on screen. A yellow box flashes around your fingertip.
   An AE/AF Lock message appears when you lift your finger. The focus
   remains locked until you take your photo.

5. **Tap the Camera icon or press the Volume button on the side of the
   iPad to snap your image.**

   The photo is captured and saved in the Camera Roll in the Photos app
   on your iPad.

Shooting video

The iPad makes the creation of video a realistic and practical option for students. If you have an iPad 2, the rear camera takes video at 720p. The third-generation and later iPad iSight cameras shoot video at 1080p. What does that all mean? If you have an iPad 2, your video quality is reasonable, but if you have a more recent iPad, the video is higher quality and includes features such as 3x video zoom and video stabilization. Either way, it's an excellent option for developing the creation of video as a core tool for learning and communication.

Shooting video is as simple as taking a photo. Here's how:

1. **Go to your iPad Home screen and tap the Camera icon to open the app.**

2. **Tap and drag the camera menu options in the right column so that Video is the selected option.**

3. **Tap the red Record icon or press the Volume button on the side of the iPad to begin shooting your scene.**

4. **Tap the red Record icon or Volume button again to stop the recording.**

   Your video is captured and saved in the Camera Roll in the Photos app on your iPad.

Remember that forward-facing camera option? You know, the camera that made you jump when all of a sudden your own face appeared onscreen! That camera can be most useful in a classroom setting when in video mode. If you teach a foreign language, or are working on an oral language learning goal, you can have students record themselves reading a passage or engaging in dialogue. This can be played back for student reflection or submitted to you as a form of assessment. And let's face it: Kids love listening to their own voices!

Importing pictures and videos

You can import photos onto an iPad in several ways:

- ✔ **Using iTunes:** Synchronize photos from applications or folders on your computer using iTunes.

- ✔ **Via iCloud:** If you have an iCloud account with Apple, it synchronizes and pushes your content to all your devices wirelessly.

- ✔ **Importing from your camera:** Apple sells an optional Camera Connection Kit, which you can connect to your iPad to copy photos directly from your camera.

✔ **Via an email, the web, or a cloud account:** Email photos to any list of recipients. With the email open, the recipients can tap and hold the image and select to save it to their Camera Roll. You can also place images on a class home page and have students tap and hold to save them to their iPads. Alternatively, use a cloud storage account such as Dropbox (www.dropbox.com) or Google Drive (https://drive.google.com). Upload any list of images to a Dropbox account, and then open and save them on your iPad.

✔ **Using apps:** My favorite app for transferring photos and video is PhotoSync (see Figure 4-8). Open PhotoSync and select the photos and video you want to transfer. It automatically detects any device on the same Wi-Fi network that has PhotoSync installed — including any laptops or desktops — and allows you to transfer the files wirelessly and effortlessly. PhotoSync can be a terrific solution for moving photos and large video files between student iPads and a teacher's computer.

Editing pictures

It happens rarely, but this time you were in just the right place to snap that perfect photo at the exact instant it happened. You open it in your Photos app only to find out the photo is too dark. Luckily, the Photos app gives you access to some handy editing tools that can clean up your image.

Tap the Photos app and select an image by tapping it. Tap the Edit option in the top right of the display, and a toolbar with five editing tools appears along the bottom of the image as shown in Figure 4-9:

✔ **Rotate:** Each tap of the Rotate icon turns the image 90 degrees counterclockwise.

✔ **Enhance:** Tap Enhance, and the photo editor analyzes the lighting, color composition, and contrast of your photo and automatically makes adjustments. You'd be surprised how much better you can look after a little enhancement!

✔ **Filters:** Select and apply effects such as Noir, Fade, or Chrome.

✔ **Red-Eye:** Follow the onscreen prompt and tap an area to remove red-eye, and tap again to Undo.

✔ **Crop:** Tap the Crop button to do the following:

- *Crop:* Tap and drag the brackets in the corners of your image to crop the desired portion of your photo.

- *Straighten and zoom:* Tap your picture with two fingers and swivel to rotate the image. To zoom, unpinch two fingers outward.

- *Aspect Ratio:* Tap the Aspect Ratio button to set the cropped image to popular proportions such as 4x6 or 5x7.

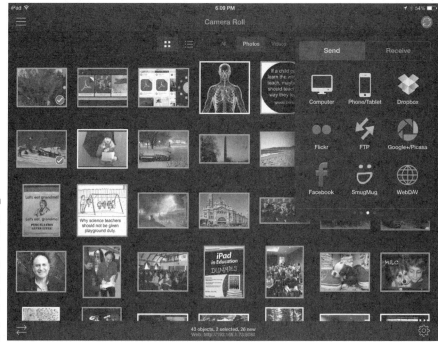

Figure 4-8:
PhotoSync
can trans-
fer photos
and video
wirelessly
between
devices.

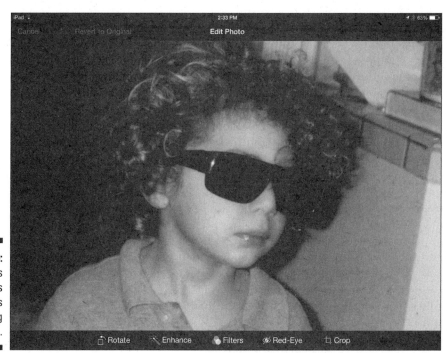

Figure 4-9:
The Photos
app includes
several tools
for editing
your photos.

You think the photo looked better before you started messing with it? No problem. Tap Undo on the top menu bar, and you can step back through your changes. Tap Revert to Original to go all the way back to the original image.

Editing video

You don't need a degree in cinematography to edit your videos. You can easily do some simple trimming of your video right in your Photos app. Tap to select the video to perform these video-editing tasks:

- ✔ **Set the start and end frames.** At the top of the screen, you'll see a bar with video frames. Drag the sliders at each end to the frames you want your video to start and end.
- ✔ **Trim.** Tap Trim on the top toolbar, and then you can choose to either trim and overwrite the original version of the video or save your edited video as a new clip.

Those last few seconds when your hair looked all messed up? Gone.

Using pictures and video in projects

The iPad puts multimedia at your fingertips and allows it to become an integral part of the learning process. You and your students have myriad ways to use media, and I devote Chapter 13 to the very important topic of *digital storytelling* — the art of creating stories and conveying knowledge through the use of media. Here's just a quick snapshot of some ideas to get you started:

- ✔ Narrate a slide show of photos to learn a foreign language.
- ✔ Create videography detailing the life of your favorite U.S. president on Presidents' Day.
- ✔ Create a regular student news video outlining what students have learned.
- ✔ Have students write and narrate a story using a slide show of images that best convey its plot and sentiment.

Refer to Part V for lots more information and ideas.

Reading and the Digital Book Revolution

As much as some of us still enjoy the feel and smell of that well-worn paperback book, there's no denying that the nature of reading is shifting. Everything from cookbooks to the Bible can now be downloaded and read in digital format. Given how quickly digital storage is becoming cheaper and the speed of data transfer is becoming faster, within a few years you will probably be able to download entire libraries of digital books to mobile devices within minutes.

The iPad represents one of the first fully featured mobile computers that also doubles as an excellent reading device. It's extremely simple to purchase and download books that can be read on your iPad and transferred to other devices. You have a selection of many excellent reading apps for the iPad, including Apple's iBooks app. Apple aptly describes iBooks as both a way to buy books and to read them. It connects directly to Apple's iBooks Store, where you can purchase and download books. Downloaded books are stored in the iBooks bookshelf on your iPad and opened for reading with a simple tap on their cover. (See Figure 4-10.)

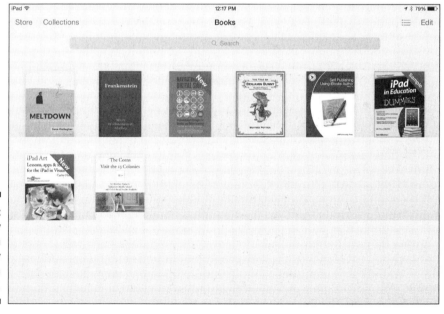

Figure 4-10:
Open any
book in
iBooks by
tapping on
its cover.

Customizing reading settings

 Tap the iBooks app icon on your Home screen and you'll see a bookshelf (refer to Figure 4-10) with any books that you have downloaded. Tap any book to open it and start reading. Now before you wiggle your way into a comfortable reading spot on the couch, let's look at some adjustments you can make in iBooks to enhance your reading experience (see Figure 4-11).

Start by tapping the button on the top menu bar marked AA, and you'll get a pop-up menu of options:

- ✔ **Selecting a color theme:** Themes change the color scheme to match the needs of different lighting settings. Select from White, Sepia, and Night.

- ✔ **Adjusting brightness:** Set the Brightness slide control to the level that makes it most comfortable for you to read.

- ✔ **Choosing font size:** Under the Brightness slider are two buttons with the letter A. As you tap the smaller A button on the left, the text gets progressively smaller. Tap the larger A and the font size increases.

- ✔ **Picking your favorite font:** Tap the Fonts button to change the text font. Experiment and find the one that makes it easiest for you to read.

iBooks remembers your settings each time you use the app.

Figure 4-11:
iBooks enables you to change reading options and jump to any page.

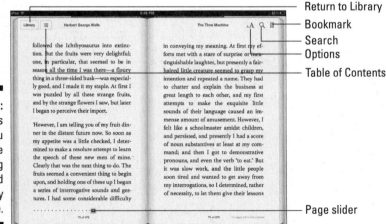

Changing pages

You can change pages in an iBook in several ways:

- ✓ **Tap:** If you want to turn the page to the right, tap or flick your finger in the right margin.

- ✓ **Swipe:** To turn the page to the right with a little more flair, place your finger in the right margin and swipe to the left.

- ✓ **Jump:** Tap anywhere near the center of the page to bring up the Navigator controls. Drag the slider along the bottom of the page and jump to any page in the book.

- ✓ **Table of Contents:** Tap the Table of Contents icon on the top toolbar, and tap to go to a specific chapter or title in the book.

If you activate the VoiceOver feature, the iPad reads the book out loud to you. It's one of the many assistive technologies that have made the iPad so popular with users who have special needs. Chapter 12 covers this topic in detail.

Using bookmarks, highlights, and notes

Don't think for a moment that all you can do with iBooks is *read* books.

- ✓ **Bookmarks:** No need to tear strips of paper to keep your place. iBooks remembers where you left off every time you open it. You can also add a bookmark to any page in the book you want to remember. Tap the Bookmark icon in the top-right corner of your page, and a red bookmark slides down. Tap it again and it disappears.

  To find your bookmarks, tap the Table of Contents icon and tap the Bookmarks tab to view the list of bookmarks you added.

- ✓ **Highlights:** I'm not sure about yours, but my memory is like a sieve. I always need to highlight text in a book so that I can browse and review the important sections I've read. Highlighting text in iBooks is similar to selecting text in any editor on the iPad.

  - *Tap and hold any word for a second.* When you lift your finger, the word is highlighted with a shaded box that has grab points in the corners. A pop-up menu offers options that include Highlight, Note, Define, Search, and more.

  - *Drag the grab points out to highlight the area of text you want to highlight.*

  - *Tap Highlight and select a highlight color from the pop-up menu of choices.*

✔ **Notes:** Are you the sort of reader who fills the margins of your favorite books with comments? Thankfully, that's a feature you can also access when using iBooks. Tap and hold to select text on the page, and then tap Note on the pop-up menu. Type your notes in the little sticky note that pops up onscreen, and your note will be saved right where you left it. It's a great way for students to gain a better understanding without defacing school property!

Access your highlights and notes in the same manner as you got your bookmarks. Go to the Table of Contents and tap the Notes tab at top (see Figure 4-12). The Notes tab includes text you highlighted throughout the book along with any notes that you added. Your Table of Contents becomes the central navigation point for everything in the book.

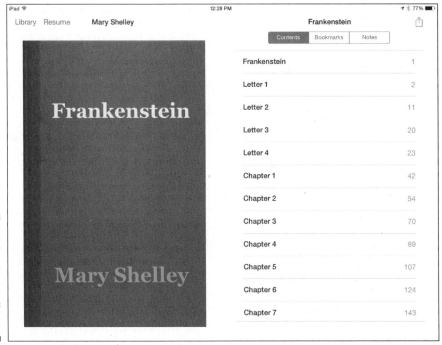

Figure 4-12: Access your Bookmarks, Notes, and Highlights in the Table of Contents.

iPad 🔋   12:28 PM   🔋 77% 🔋

Library   Resume   Mary Shelley   Frankenstein

Contents | Bookmarks | Notes

Frankenstein

Mary Shelley

TIP

✔ **Word definitions:** One of the nicest features for students using iBooks is the capability to easily access word definitions. Tap and hold to highlight any word, and select Define from the pop-up menu. That's a lot simpler than hauling around that huge and heavy dictionary, don't you think?

Note that the first time you select Define, it responds that no definition is found. You need to tap the Manage option and select the dictionary to use.

Searching

You're trying to find that page in your book that mentioned the name of Roosevelt's dog. You've scoured the Table of Contents, but it only lists general chapter headings. That's when the Search tool becomes a tangible advantage that you can use in digital books.

To search through the text of a book, tap the magnifying glass icon on the top menu bar, and type in the word or phrase you want to find. A list of search results is displayed; you can tap any one to jump to that reference in your book. Search even includes options to expand your search to the web or Wikipedia. By the way, Roosevelt's little dog was named Fala.

Purchasing books

As is the case with many people in my generation, I often find myself with one foot planted in two completely different eras. I'm an avid technologist, yet I grew up as part of the pre-Internet generation. Growing up, I loved perusing the shelves of a bookstore, and I have to confess to feeling some sadness that many bookstores are closing. On the other hand, browsing and purchasing iBooks couldn't be simpler. The iBooks Store has several hundred thousand books that I can search and sample. Finding the book I want is quick, and any book I buy is delivered directly to my device, available for me to start reading in a matter of seconds. No driving or parking. No backorders or waiting in lines to pay. Anytime, 24/7. It couldn't be more convenient.

1. **Tap the Store button in the top-left corner of your iBooks bookshelf to enter the online iBooks Store.**

2. **Browse for titles.**

   Navigating in iBooks Store is similar to moving around the App Store. Look through the top charts, review featured and new lists of books, browse based on category and genre, or search for a specific title. There's even a section with the list of *New York Times* bestsellers.

3. **Tap any book to read a description and see reviews from other readers.**

4. **(Optional) Tap to download a sample.**

   A sample is downloaded, which you can review to decide whether you want to make the investment of actually buying the book.

5. **To buy a book, tap the price and confirm that you want to buy the book.**

6. **Complete your purchase by entering your iTunes password.**

   In a few moments, the book will appear in your iBooks bookshelf, ready and waiting for you to flip open the cover and turn the pages — virtually, of course.

There are several wonderful e-reader apps for downloading and reading books on the iPad. Each has its own specific and unique features. Check out Chapter 8 for a review of some of the more popular book-reading apps.

If you have an Apple iCloud account, you can sync your iBooks content between devices wirelessly. Start reading a book on your iPad, and then when you're in the waiting room at the dentist, you can pull out your iPhone and continue reading right where you left off on the iPad (complete with the note you left in the margin reminding yourself to go to the dentist!). It's really as simple as that. And remember to floss every day and you'll cut down on those visits to the dentist.

The books that you read in Apple's iBooks app are formatted with a variation of the .ePub format that's commonly used for eBooks. Chapter 10 covers how you can create your own eBooks on the iPad. Those books and any other books that are formatted as .ePub files can be transferred to your iBooks library and read.

Adding PDF documents

iBooks is also a great way to store and organize your PDF documents. Anytime you're viewing a PDF, whether in Safari, in Mail, or in one of the many other apps that can display PDF documents, you have an option to open the document in iBooks. It's automatically added to your PDF Collection and can be saved and accessed at any time through iBooks (see Figure 4-13).

This can be an effective way to deliver content to students. Email a PDF or place it on a classroom website, and have the students open and save it in the iBooks app. Many other apps also enable you to open, save, and annotate PDF documents. Those apps are covered later in the book in Chapter 9.

Figure 4-13: PDF attachments and documents can be opened in iBooks.

Organizing collections

When you first open iBooks, you'll notice it has two collections — Books and PDFs. Think of a collection as a bookshelf. It's simply a group of books or content that you can set up and keep organized.

Tap the Collections button on top of your iBooks bookshelf to add and edit your collections. You can also move books and documents between collections by tapping the Edit button in the top-right corner, selecting the content, and tapping the Move button that pops up on the left of the top toolbar.

Using iTextbooks

The days of students carrying that 30-pound backpack filled with heavy textbooks may finally be coming to an end. Traditional textbooks are expensive, cumbersome, and come apart with increased usage. Most importantly, we live in an era that's characterized by very rapid changes and developments in information. Scientific facts are evolving, maps are being rewritten, and political leaders and systems seem to be shifting all around the world.

Can educators and students afford to be using static textbooks that are several years old? Can we continue to lean almost exclusively on traditional text-based information in education when the rest of our world is saturated in multimedia? Digital textbooks offer a significant step forward, and iBooks has features to support the use of vivid, media-rich textbooks on iPads. iBooks 2 or later can display books that contain videos and other interactive features. As with apps, textbook content can also be updated with the simple tap of an Update button.

When you go to the iBooks Store, tap the More menu on the top toolbar and scroll down to Textbooks. Many major publishers have started producing interactive content for use on iPads (see Figure 4-14). In addition, Apple has released free software for Mac computers, called iBooks Author, that enables anyone — publishers or individuals, authors, teachers, or even students — to create and publish their own interactive, multimedia textbooks. I take a closer look at iBooks Author in Chapter 10.

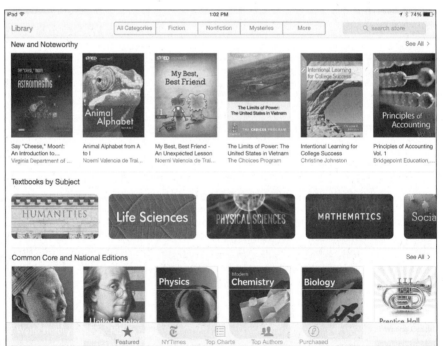

Figure 4-14: The iBooks Store now has a Textbooks category.

Getting Organized with Contacts and Calendar

My closet still has about three old briefcases that I used for carrying notepads, papers, organizers, lesson plans, and more. They've been in there collecting dust for several years. Why? Yes, because I don't clean out my closet very often, but that wasn't the answer I was looking for! Most of us now use digital tools to stay organized, and they've become an essential part of our daily lives. Of course, your iPad came with apps to help you get organized as well.

✓ **Contacts:** Your Contacts app lists the important contact information about the people you know. Add contacts manually or set them up to sync them with your computer or email account.

✓ **Calendar:** As with Contacts, the Calendar app enables you to add appointments manually or to sync them with an existing calendar.

 If you're planning on syncing your contacts or calendar to a mail account, make sure you have that option turned on in Settings. Tap and open Settings from your Home screen, and then tap Mail, Contacts, Calendars. Check your email account to ensure that the contact and/or calendar option switch is set to On.

Finding Value in Other Apps

You'll find tremendous value in the apps that come with your iPad, whether you're at work, school, or home. I discuss several of them in detail earlier in this chapter. Here is a quick breakdown of a few of the other apps you'll find when you first power up your iPad.

✓ **FaceTime:** FaceTime enables you to make video calls with other FaceTime users on iPads, iPhones, iPods, and Mac computers. To call someone using FaceTime, you need his phone number or email address. Add that person as a contact and then simply tap his name within the FaceTime app to call.

FaceTime uses the front-facing camera as its default, but you can also tap and switch to the rear iPad camera during your call and show your surroundings.

✓ **Messages:** Yet another way to avoid cellular fees is to use Messages as an alternative to text messaging. Because Messages also uses a Wi-Fi connection, you can send unlimited free text and multimedia messages to other Apple product users. And if you have more than one iOS device, Messages keeps the conversation going across all of them.

✔ **Reminders:** If you're loaded with too many things to do. then you'll appreciate Reminders helping you keep track of your tasks. It's simple to add any sort of To-Do, a due date, and time, and Reminders will alert you as needed.

✔ **Photo Booth:** Pose for a photo and add an effect with Photo Booth. Whether you take a photo of a flower with a kaleidoscope effect or a shrunken-head self-portrait, Photo Booth puts some creative fun in your photos.

✔ **Music:** Who doesn't love listening to music? Hum your way through the day with the iPad's Music app. It can sync with your other devices to ensure you always have access to all the songs you download through iTunes.

✔ **Videos:** Download videos from the iTunes Store or transfer them from a computer. Either way, they'll look great on the iPad, and you can watch them with the Videos app. You can even connect your iPad to a TV via cable or Apple TV and turn your iPad into an entertainment hub.

✔ **App Store:** Whether you want to play games with maladjusted birds or order a pizza delivered to your front door . . . as you've heard, "There's an app for that." The place you'll find those apps is the App Store. There are literally more than a million apps you can run on your iPad. I discuss how to find and download them in the next chapter. Just be forewarned that I cannot cover every last one of them.

They say that timing is everything, and that includes when you purchase your iPad. Apple is now bundling the iWork and iLife suite of apps with new iPad purchases. If you bought your iPad any time after October 2013, you're fortunate enough to get the following list of additional apps . . . free!

✔ **Pages:** Apple's powerful word processing app for creating letters, reports, resumes, and all other types of documents.

✔ **Keynote:** Create beautiful presentations with images, charts, transition effects, and more.

✔ **Numbers:** The spreadsheet app that makes number crunching easy and . . . well, almost fun!

✔ **iPhoto:** View, share, and edit your photos.

✔ **iMovie:** Apple's popular video-editing app.

✔ **GarageBand:** The easy and fun way to create music on your iPad — whether you're a seasoned professional or a complete novice.

Of course, if you bought your iPad prior to October 2013 and had to pay for all the iWork and iLife apps, I suggest you quickly move on to the next chapter before you get an iHeadache.

Chapter 5

Purchasing and Downloading Apps

. . . .

In This Chapter

▶ Perusing apps in the App Store

▶ Knowing the difference between iPad and iPhone apps

▶ Finding and selecting educational apps

▶ Deciding between free or fee-based apps

. . . .

*O*ne of the greatest features about personal computers, including iPads, is that they are tools that you can personalize. The simplest way to customize your iPad is by finding and downloading apps that align with your personal objectives. To the accountant, the iPad might provide a way to stay in touch with financial news and data. The businessman might need to access documents and create a mobile office environment. A designer could envision it as the perfect tool for delivering client presentations and portfolios. To the educator . . . well, that's where you come in.

You'll want to load your iPad with apps that fit your educational objectives and teaching style. To put it mildly, there are more than a few to choose from — Apple currently reports that there are more than a million apps in the App Store that have resulted in over 60 billion app downloads. Browsing the list of apps is like standing in an ice-cream store with a tantalizing array of ice cream flavors and toppings. So many delicious flavors, colors, and smells — which ones do you pick?

Several factors affect your choice of apps. You need to consider the cost. Some apps are free and others cost a few dollars. You may work at a school that can purchase apps in bulk at a reduced rate, or you may be paying full price for them yourself. You also clearly need to weigh the features an app offers and how it has been reviewed by experts and other users.

Select the right apps and your iPad becomes your digital book reader, personal assistant, game player, mobile office, movie theater, and more. The challenge lies in wading through the oceans of apps to find the ones that work best for you (but then, that's why you're reading this book).

Browsing the App Store

The App Store is the key to personalizing your iPad experience. You can access the App Store on either your computer or your iPad. The functionality is fairly similar on both. For the purposes of this book, I use the iPad as the platform for accessing the App Store and focus more on helping you find the best educational apps. If you'd like a more detailed step-by-step tutorial on using the App Store, check out *iPad For Dummies* by Edward C. Baig and Bob LeVitus (John Wiley & Sons, Inc.). It's an excellent introductory book, especially helpful for new iPad users.

Tap the App Store icon on your iPad to open it. You'll immediately see a row of icons on the toolbar at the bottom of the app, as shown in Figure 5-1).

Figure 5-1:
The App Store toolbar helps you browse and find the perfect app.

Each icon reflects a different way of browsing and finding apps in the store, as described in this list:

✔ **Featured:** Use this section to browse the latest and most popular releases. At the very top, you can tap to narrow your selection to a specific category. Options include Games, Kids, and Newsstand, and if you tap the More option, you see additional categories such as Education and Textbooks. Tap any category to see what's featured in each.

✔ **Top Charts:** As the name indicates, this lists the most popular apps and breaks them down by whether they are free or paid.

✔ **Near Me:** See what local apps are popular in your area.

✔ **Purchased:** Displays what you have already purchased. At the top of the screen, note the two tabs that break your purchases into All and Not on This iPad. That's a really helpful way of identifying what you've purchased that isn't on your iPad and then deciding which ones to download. You aren't charged anything additional for downloading apps that you've already purchased.

✔ **Updates:** This highlights existing updates for apps that you have on your iPad. The badge indicates the number of updates that are currently available for download. Tap the Update button next to any app or tap the Update All button. You can also set your app updates to automatically download in the background in the iTunes & App Store section of the iPad Settings app. Like your mother told you: Drink your milk, eat your veggies, and keep your apps updated as often as you can if you want your iPad to work smoothly.

Selecting Between iPad and iPhone Apps

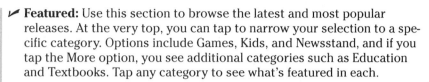

As you browse through apps, you'll quickly notice that they are often categorized by device. Some are designed for the iPad and others for the iPhone. Some are hybrids that work on both. You can use either device, but they work differently on your iPad:

✔ **iPhone (iPod touch) apps:** These apps were designed for the smaller screen space of an iPhone, but they can be used on iPads too. What you have to remember is that their native resolution (just a fancy way of saying screen size) is the same on an iPad, but they will appear to be relatively small on the larger iPad display.

✔ **iPad apps:** The interface on apps designed for the iPad takes full advantage of the complete iPad display area.

✔ **Hybrid apps:** Hybrid apps are denoted by a little + sign on the app price button and will automatically adjust to the resolution of your device. In other words, an app that works on the smaller iPhone screen also expands to take advantage of the full iPad display.

✔ **Resolution, pixels, and other mumbo jumbo:** You just want to know which apps to use. Well, here's the scoop on iPhone versus iPad apps. It's like the difference between watching your favorite movie on a 27-inch television in the bedroom versus watching that movie at a theater. To quote an old cliché, size does matter.

Apps designed specifically for the iPad simply look better. It comes down to their screen size as measured in pixels — those little invisible dots that make up the images on your screen. Here's how the resolution breaks down by device:

- iPhone apps display a resolution of up to 640 x 1136 pixels on an iPhone 5.

- Apps designed for iPhone 4 have a resolution of 960 x 640 pixels, whereas iPhone 5 apps have a resolution of 640 x 1136 pixels.

- iPad 1 and iPad 2 apps have a resolution of 1024 x 768 pixels.

- Apps designed for the third-generation iPad and later have an amazingly crisp resolution of 2048 x 1536 pixels. The second-generation iPad Mini boasts the same resolution.

✔ And then of course you have the hybrid apps that can adjust their display according to the device they detect. I know. You bought your iPad a while ago, and now you're sitting there with a terrible case of iPad envy. Don't worry. When it becomes available, you'll go out and buy the latest and greatest iPad and have the last laugh . . . well, for a few months, anyway.

Using iPhone apps on your iPad

Some apps are available in both iPhone and iPad versions. In those cases, always select the iPad app, of course. Many publishers allow you to download the iPhone version free if you have both an iPhone and an iPad and have paid for the iPad-based version.

In some cases, however, the app you really want may have been designed only for the iPhone. As an example, having grown up in Australia, I'm an avid follower of Australian football. Guess what: The app I use to follow games "down under" is available only as an iPhone app, but I can still use it on my iPad. It just displays in its smaller native resolution. See how that looks in Figure 5-2. You can also tap the little 2x button in the bottom corner, and the display doubles in size to fill the iPad screen. Be aware, however, that this doesn't increase the pixel resolution of the app. It's just displaying that resolution over the entire screen. It looks fine in most cases. It's never as sharp as an iPad app, but really, what's a guy to do when he needs the football scores from Australia?

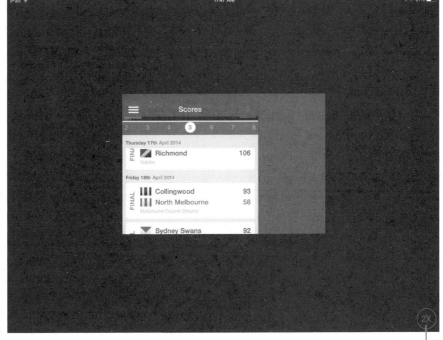

Figure 5-2:
Display
iPhone apps
at their
native size
or tap the
2x button to
enlarge.

Tap to double the image size.

Using the App Store on your iPad or computer

You can access the App Store on your iPad or on your computer. In both cases, you need an Internet connection and that all-important iTunes account (see Chapter 2). Apps that are purchased on your computer will be transferred to your iPad the next time you sync them. For a more in-depth discussion of syncing, see Chapter 3.

Have you ever tried walking into a bank where nobody knows you and cashing a check without your ID? You'll get the same cold shoulder in the App Store if you don't have your user ID and password. Make sure that you've signed up for an Apple ID, or you won't be able to download any apps. Refer to Chapter 2 if you need instructions on signing up for an account.

Finding the Golden Nuggets

Some apps are incredibly imaginative, well designed, and productive. Others may not be worth your time and money. With literally hundreds of thousands of apps to choose from, you'd be well advised to learn how to sort the wheat from the chaff. Here's some advice from someone who has had to battle a fair share of chaff.

Searching for and purchasing apps

If you have an idea of what you're looking for, then get right to the point by using the Search field in the upper-right corner of the App Store screen. Search by typing any portion of the app title or an associated keyword, and then tap the Search key on the keyboard.

Refine your search by using filters. Enter your search term in the Search field and tap the Search key on your keyboard. If you're using the iOS 7 App Store, you'll see a series of filters displayed along the top of the results as shown in Figure 5-3. The filters are for iPad or iPhone Only, price, category, relevance, and age level. Use them to help narrow your search results. Tap any one, and a menu of choices drops down. Let's say you're looking for a free app to help you learn about the elements in Science. If you type **Elements** in the Search field, you get a wide range of apps, from puzzles and arcade games to utilities. Instead, apply filters that set the category to Education and the relevance to By Rating. The results will be a shorter, more meaningful list.

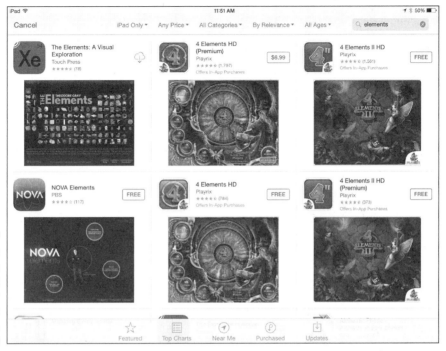

Figure 5-3:
Use Search
filters to
narrow your
Search
results.

After you've found an app that could potentially serve your purpose, tap the app name or icon to get more information about it. The information page details the app's features and includes some screenshots to give you a taste of the interface (see Figure 5-4). The description is written by the app's developer. The editors at the App Store try to keep hyperbole to a minimum, so when app descriptions use adjectives such as "fun" or "exciting," just keep in mind that they likely are somewhat biased. That's when you tap the Reviews tab and scan the opinions of users. Reviews show an average star rating from 1 to 5, along with individual ratings and comments.

Reviews are tied to a specific release of an app. Earlier releases may have been buggy and may have even crashed, so make sure you check the ratings and reviews of the current release for the latest information. Also, I wouldn't rely solely on the star ratings. Read the reviews of the app, especially if it doesn't have a lot of ratings.

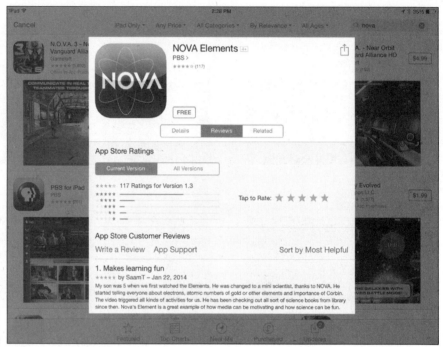

Figure 5-4:
User
reviews
and ratings
appear on
the app
detail page.

Thousands of educators, bloggers, and technical reviewers are trying out and recommending apps all the time. The better approach to finding apps is often to identify your objective, and then see what others are recommending. Some paths to consider might include the following:

- ✓ **Search Google.** Try a Google search using the app name; you often get a host of reviews from magazines, websites, and blogs. Sometimes those blogs may even be from teachers explaining how they use the app in their classes.

- ✓ **Keep reading.** After searching for and reading some information on blogs and websites that review educational apps, follow the ones you like and see which apps they recommend.

- ✓ **Join an online learning community.** iPads in Education (http:// iPadEducators.ning.com) is a place where you can connect with like-minded people and learn from them.

✔ **Follow educators on social networking sites.** Twitter and Google+ are the obvious choices here. See which apps educators are using in their iPad classrooms, and how those educators are using those apps.

✔ **Take an online course or webinar.** There are dozens of companies and professional organizations offering online learning opportunities all year long.

✔ **Attend educational conferences.** Conferences are good opportunities to learn about effective practices and network with others.

After you've decided upon an app, it's fairly simple to purchase and download it. With your iTunes account information handy, follow these steps:

1. **Tap the Price or Free button.**

   The Price button is next to the app icon on the top left of the details screen. It may also say Free if there's no fee for the download.

2. **Tap the Install button.**

3. **Enter your account information and then tap the OK button.**

   The app is downloaded to your iPad; a little animated circle icon details the download progress. The app icon is placed into the first open slot available. You can rearrange icons on your iPad screen, as I describe in Chapter 2.

Getting help finding apps

There's no lack of websites that review and recommend apps. Try a Google search for *iPad app reviews* and you'll get a list of websites. Here's a few to get you started:

✔ **Common Sense Media (`www.commonsensemedia.org/app-reviews`):** This popular site reviews different types of media, including kid-friendly apps. Filter your search by genre, age level, subject, and more.

✔ **Balefire Labs (`www.balefirelabs.com`):** Balefire Labs recommends apps that help students learn. It's a fee-based service that applies an evaluation rubric to each reviewed app.

✔ **Appitic (`www.appitic.com`):** This site features reviews and webcast videos by Apple Distinguished Educators.

Deciding Between Light and Full Apps

Many iPad apps offer a *light* version with some of the features stripped out so that you can try the app before buying it. For example, one popular educational app that is used for storyboarding and mind-mapping is Popplet (see Figure 5-5). At the date of writing, you have the option of downloading Popplet Lite free or purchasing the full version of Popplet for $4.99.

Read the product descriptions of both the free and paid versions of the app to identify the benefits of the full version and to see if it meets your needs and is worth the cost. In the case of Popplet, purchasing the full version allows students to create their projects online and then continue them outside of class on other computers if needed. Students can also share and collaborate on Popplet with others. If you want your students working in groups and outside class, it may be a good idea to opt for the paid version.

Figure 5-5:
Many apps, such as Popplet, offer free light versions and full paid versions.

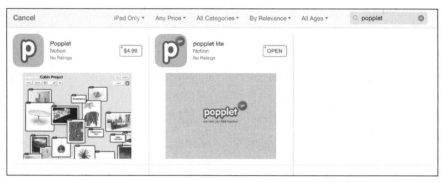

Although $4.99 may not break the bank for one copy, if you want all your students to use it, you may end up purchasing multiple copies. That said, make sure you'll use the additional features.

Apple offers a Volume Purchase Program, which can help cut costs in this arena. See Chapter 2 for more information.

Part III
Finding and Organizing Educational Content

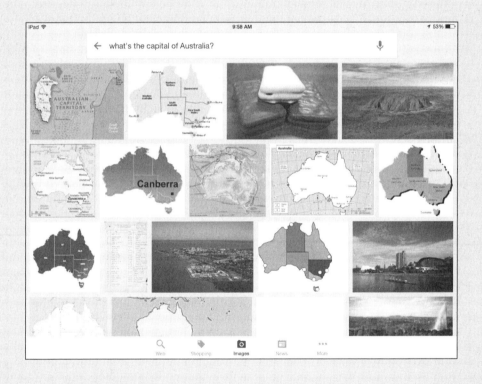

Visit www.dummies.com/extras/ipadineducation to learn how to create and access educational content on any topic in the ever-expanding course catalogs of Apple's iTunes U.

In this part . . .

✔ Find and organize educational content on the web

✔ Use a digital notebook for creating and storing information

✔ Learn through social networking

Chapter 6

Finding and Organizing Content

- -

In This Chapter

▶ Googling for information on your iPad

▶ Filing web pages for later reading

▶ Tagging, highlighting, and annotating web content

▶ Creating a custom digital news magazine

▶ Using a digital notebook for creating and storing information

- -

*W*e used to live in a world where information was controlled and "released" to us by news media, book publishers, and even schools and teachers. The majority of what we learned in school was determined by authorities who set curriculum and selected textbooks. But now, the Internet — a technology most of us hadn't even heard of just 20 years ago — has completely revolutionized information access.

Many argue that it has "democratized" the methods in which information is published and accessed. Anyone can post information online or even write and publish digital books. We don't have to wait until the evening news or the morning paper to get the latest world news. It has already been reported the instant it happens — on Twitter, Facebook, blogs, and more, and most of us first hear the news through these social networking channels. Encyclopedias and journals? How useful are they when we can increasingly access facts and opinions over the Internet at any time from a device we carry in our pockets?

How vast is the Internet? We're approaching one billion websites. That's a staggering figure considering that there are seven billion-plus people on the planet. Even more, some estimates have the size of the Internet currently growing at a rate of over 5 percent a month. That means it doubles every 15 months! The bottom line is clear. It's imperative that we become proficient in using tools for finding, organizing, and accessing all the information we come across online. It's also essential that we integrate these tools into our educational processes and that children become fluent in their use.

That's the focus of this chapter. We look at different ways to archive and organize information for later reading. As our archives start growing, we need to have tools that make it easy to sort through our digital archives and find what we need. This chapter examines different tools that aid in that process.

Googling on Your iPad

They say that Google is the ultimate arbiter of most arguments. Whenever you need information, someone inevitably pulls out a mobile device and uses Google to search for the answer. When students are allowed to use mobile devices at school, they're constantly using them to search during class discussions. Google has become such an integral part of our lives that we use it as a verb in our everyday vocabulary. You don't search for an answer to a question any longer — you "google" it.

One of the very first apps you should download on your iPad is the free app from Google. Chapter 4 looks at how to use Google as your default search tool in Safari. The Google Search app puts that search capability right on your iPad Home screen along with some very handy additional features. (See Figure 6-1.) Other than Mail, it's probably the app I use most on my iPad. Along with the regular Google search, you can also search using voice or even an image you take with your iPad camera.

Tap the Google icon to start the app, and you immediately get that familiar-looking Google Search page (refer to Figure 6-1). Type your search term and the Google app presents your search results in its integrated browser — just as it would in a regular web browser. You even have the standard Google search options along the top of the results page that enable you to restrict your search to images, videos, news, and more. Tap any of the results and the browser displays the page. One handy feature is that results are presented on a separate tab right within the app itself. You can simply swipe the tabs left and right to switch between the results page and your Google search as shown in Figure 6-2. Whenever you need, tap the Google logo and left arrow in the top-left corner at any point to start a new search.

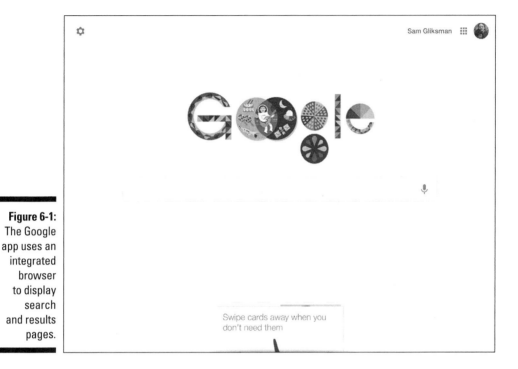

Figure 6-1:
The Google app uses an integrated browser to display search and results pages.

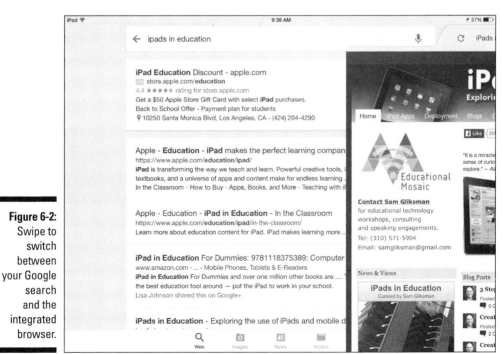

Figure 6-2:
Swipe to switch between your Google search and the integrated browser.

You'll also have access to popular Google search functions such as the following:

✔ **History:** I have to confess that my memory is like cheesecloth. It's bad enough that I forget the results of my searches, but I get really annoyed when I can't even remember what I needed. Well, tap anywhere in the empty Google search bar and it drops down a short list of your latest search terms. The Google app also has one really cool feature that's hidden from view. Close the doors and blinds while I tell you about it . . . swipe your finger from left to right on the search page and it displays a visual history of your search terms and the pages that you selected (see Figure 6-3). Pretty amazing isn't it? Now go open the doors and blinds — you don't want people thinking you're a geek.

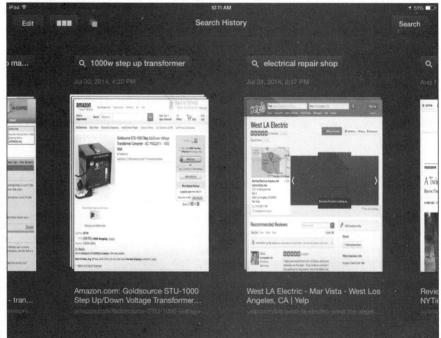

Figure 6-3:
Swipe right on the Google search page to get a visual history of searches and results.

It was an innocent mistake. You were searching for "Capistrano." One simple typo and Auto-Correct jumped right in and changed it to "campus tramp." You know the next term you'll immediately search is "how to delete search terms from Google history." Let me help you out. Tap in the search bar to drop down a list of your recent search terms.

Simply swipe left from the right side of any search term in your history and a Delete prompt appears. Tap in an empty search bar (delete the text if there's anything in it) and a View All History option displays at the bottom of the list. Tap it to get a complete history of all your searches, and then tap the Clear All option to erase your entire search history.

✔ **Voice:** Having trouble maneuvering those greasy fingers over the virtual keyboard while eating that grilled cheese sandwich? Don't worry. Google also allows you to search using your voice. Tap the microphone icon on the right of the search bar and speak clearly into your iPad microphone. Google does an excellent job of interpreting your search request (especially in light of the fact that your mouth is filled with cheese).

✔ **Search options:** Tap any of the icons on the bottom toolbar to select search categories such as Web (default), Shopping, Images, News, and More (see Figure 6-4).

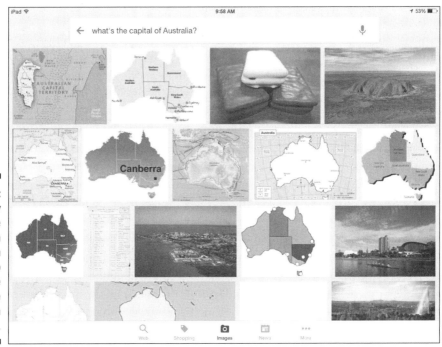

Figure 6-4: Tap any of the options in the bottom toolbar to change the Google search category.

Evaluating Google Search results

We tend to place way too much importance on the ranking of Google search results. I've heard statistics ranging from 50 to 80 percent of users clicking one of the first three results on a Google search result page (after the advertised links). Couple that with the fact that students have a tendency to believe everything they read on the Internet, and that can sabotage effective learning. Google uses an algorithm to determine the ranking of its search results. It takes factors such as presumed relevance and popularity into account. Often, the Google algorithm delivers very pertinent results; however, there are times that it doesn't. That may be because of a badly framed search term. It might also be because many website owners play the SEO — search engine optimization — game. They create their websites with content and links that manipulate Google's search engine and push their sites up the rankings for the desired search terms. On occasion, the Google search results can even be downright scary, presenting users with websites that try to sell products or display offensive opinions and images by tricking the Google algorithm into thinking results are something that they aren't.

Educators have traditionally adopted the role of information curators, carefully weeding and selecting textbooks and articles for students to read. We now live in an age where anyone can post information on the Internet for all to access and read, and Google is often the key used to open the door to that kingdom. It's a fantastic search tool, but you can never rely on any search tool or website to deliver accurate information. Help children navigate the Internet. Teach them how to frame their searches using terms and conditions that deliver the most accurate results. Ensure they know how to identify owners of a website and to research and evaluate the information presented. Most importantly, teach them to always use a critical eye when reading anything, whether that be on the Internet or elsewhere.

Saving Web Pages for Later Reading

So much to read and so little time. I find myself needing to read more and more every day and am increasingly left with less time to do it. Fortunately, you have some excellent tools on the iPad that enable you to keep a list of the things you come across and want to read later. Here are a couple:

Reading List

Let's start with the more recent entry: Apple's own Reading List that comes included in Safari. When you come across any web page that you want to revisit later, simply tap the Share icon at the left of the address bar and select Add to Reading List from the menu. Your page is saved. Whenever you want to go back and read anything in your Reading List, tap the Bookmark icon in Safari, and then tap the Reading List menu item at the top of the menu. Simple. It basically creates your list as a separate category in Bookmarks. Reading List also categorizes your saved pages into Read and Unread tabs, which it updates every time you open and read a saved page. Safari used to only save a link to the page, and you'd need a live Internet connection to read it. If you have iOS 6 or later, however, Safari saves the page itself to your device complete with text, images, and layout. You can also opt to sync that list with your other devices using your iCloud account. Add a page on your iPad, and then read it later on your iPhone.

As nice as it is to have the Reading List built right into Safari, you can't access it in other browsers. For example, if you use the Chrome browser on your iPad, you won't be able to use or access your Reading List. Also, Reading List lacks other features, such as being able to see what your friends are reading.

Reading List is, however, a great place to start saving pages. See Figure 6-5.

Now let's look at another option that offers even more features.

Add to Reading List option

Figure 6-5: Adding pages for later reading is simple with Safari's Reading List feature.

Pocket

Pocket is one of the most popular of a slew of programs for saving and reading content from the web. For people who need to stay updated on the latest web content, Pocket belongs in your toolkit of essential apps. If you're trying to empower students to use the Internet to gather, evaluate, and use information, a tool such as Pocket is indispensable for keeping that content organized and available as needed.

Among its many features, the following are some of Pocket's most striking benefits:

- ✔ **Any device or platform:** Pocket is available on most computers and devices. It's an app that works on your Apple iOS devices as well as Android phones. Pocket is also web-based, so you can use it on any computer that has access to the Internet — Apple, Windows, or otherwise.

- ✔ **Organization:** Create folders for easy filing and organization of your articles.

- ✔ **Offline reading:** Save articles for offline reading. This is great for those times when you're in a car, plane, or anywhere that you may not have Internet access.

- ✔ **Easy viewing:** The Pocket app offers a variety of ways for browsing and reading your content.

- ✔ **Integration:** Pocket not only works with Safari but is also integrated into a host of other iPad apps, such as Twitter and popular social news apps such as Flipboard, Zite, and others. When you find a link to any article in those apps, you can simply tap a link within the app to send it to your Pocket account.

- ✔ **Favorites:** Tag articles with a "Like" to store them in your Favorites list and share them with others.

- ✔ **Networking:** As covered in the next chapter, you can connect with your friends and share articles with each other.

Pocket has a variety of methods for saving articles. Follow these steps to install and use it:

1. **Go to the App Store on your iPad, search for the Pocket app, and download the iPad version.**

2. **Tap the icon to start the app. The app prompts you for your account information.**

3. **Either tap to open an account within the app or go directly to** `www.instapaper.com` **and open your account there.**

It's a good idea to have an account so that you can log in on any device and access your Pocket content.

4. **Install the bookmarklet or email contact.**

Most of us using an iPad also use a laptop or desktop. After you have your Pocket account, ensure that you can save pages from any device or computer. Installing a bookmarklet in your browser — a button that sits on the browser toolbar — is the simplest way to save pages on your laptop or desktop. It's a little more complicated on your iPad, but you have some alternatives there as well.

- **Desktop browser:** Go to `www.getpocket.com` and log into your account. Click the How to Save link on the top menu bar. Follow the instructions in the Save to Pocket from Your Computer section to add an icon on your browser's toolbar.

- **Mobile Safari:** Open the Pocket app and tap the Pocket menus icon — the lined icon in the top left of the display — and select Help. Tap How to Save and scroll down until you see the From Mobile Safari option, as shown in Figure 6-6. You can install the bookmarklet in Safari by tapping the Install button. It starts your browser and steps you through the process.

- **Saving via email:** Add Pocket's `add@getpocket.com` email address to Contacts. Go to the Help menu, tap How to Add, and you see Save Via Email as one of the categories. Tap the Learn How button and follow the directions to add Pocket's email address to your address book.

5. **Add pages to your Pocket library.**

You have several options:

- *Using the bookmarklet:* If you've installed the bookmarklet on your browser toolbar, simply click the Save to Pocket button when you're on any page you want to save for later reading and it's added to your Pocket library. It couldn't be easier.

- *Save from other apps:* Over 300 apps connect to Pocket. Tap icons to save content to your Pocket account from within apps such as Twitter, Pulse, Zite, Flipboard, and more.

- *Using email:* You can email any page to Pocket's `add@getpocket.com` email address. Pocket recognizes your email address as the sender and files the content in your account. If you have added the Pocket email address to your Contacts as described in Step 4, tap the Share arrow on the top menu in Safari and select Mail. An email message pops up with the URL of the page in the body. Start typing **Pocket** in the To: field, and Mail recognizes the Pocket email address and offers it as the default addressee. Send the message, and the page is added to your Pocket library.

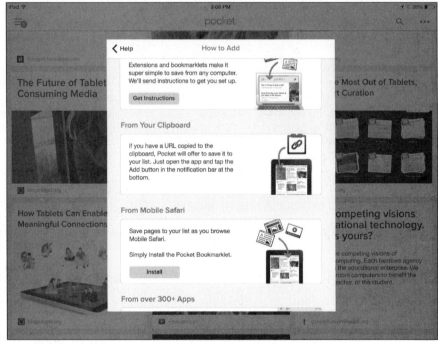

Figure 6-6:
Email any
web page
to Pocket,
and the
app adds
it to your
account.

6. **Tap to open the Pocket app and browse through your library as shown on the left side of Figure 6-7.**

   Your list of articles is displayed along with the opening text for each.

7. **Select any article by tapping it.**

   The integrated reader presents the article in a clean format after stripping it of ads and distractions as shown on the right side of Figure 6-7.

Many additional options are worth exploring. Here's a synopsis of the best ones:

- **Tag Articles:** Swipe across any item with your finger, and it reveals a menu of options. The first option allows you to tag the article for easy retrieval. For example, if you saved a recipe for Sweet and Sour Chicken, you may want to add tags such as *Food, Recipe,* and *Chinese.* Tap Tags in Pocket's menu later, and select any tag from your list to view all the articles related to it.

- **Like or Archive:** Swipe across any item and tap the star icon to "like" it and add it to your Favorites list. Tap the Trash icon to delete the article, or tap the Check Mark icon to save it into your Archive folder for later reference.

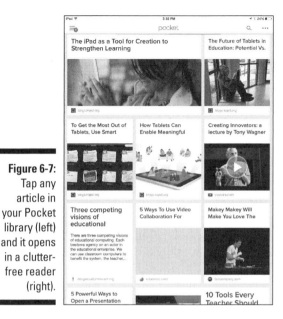

Figure 6-7:
Tap any article in your Pocket library (left) and it opens in a clutter-free reader (right).

- **Share:** Your mother always told you to share, didn't she? When you find an interesting article, it's easy to let others know about it. Swipe across any item and tap the Share icon. Share the article via Twitter, Facebook, and a host of other social networking services. You can also send the article via email using the Send to Friend option.

- **Search:** Tap the magnifying glass on the top toolbar and type your search term. Pocket does a full text search through all the articles in your list.

Use Pocket for simple, collaborative content curation. Open a class account for Pocket with your email as the primary account holder. Each student can log in to the class account and add a Save to Pocket icon on their web browser toolbar per the instructions listed above. You can also enable students to add content via email. Open your desktop browser and log into your account at www.getpocket.com. Click the down arrow next to the Pocket logo at the top of the screen and select Options from the drop-down list of menu choices. Click Email Accounts and add the email addresses of students. Emails sent from any of those accounts to add@getpocket.com will automatically be added to the content in your group account.

Creating Custom News Feeds

The quantity of available news, articles, and information is escalating at a rapid rate, and no single website or source can possibly keep you updated with all the information you need to access. A host of new apps seek to use the iPad's wonderful interface for reading to combine multiple sources into an integrated magazine format. In this section, I show you a couple of excellent choices.

Flipboard

Flipboard describes itself as the "social magazine." The topic actually belongs in more than this chapter, which discusses finding and organizing content. The next chapter focuses on sharing. Flipboard performs both functions very well.

Download the Flipboard app, and then select your news and information sources. Flipboard creates a personalized magazine out of everything you've selected. Flipboard combines your list of news websites, blog posts, social networking feeds, images, and more into a beautifully displayed layout of articles that mimics the digital equivalent of flipping through the pages of a magazine. The latest versions even enable you to add video and audio feeds to your multimedia Flipboard magazine. Using Flipboard requires a few short steps:

1. **Select some content and create an account.**

   Tap to open the Flipboard app, and tap the little flip arrow on the right side of the display to get started. Create your Flipboard magazine by selecting some of the content categories. You can integrate content from social networking accounts such as Twitter, Google+, and LinkedIn. Just tap the icons and sign into your account. When you're done, tap the Next button, and you're prompted to create a free Flipboard account so that your preferences can be saved. Flipboard drops you back into its beautifully designed magazine layout, now filled with content from the various categories you selected.

2. **Customize your Flipboard content sources.**

   After you get started, you'll probably want to edit and customize your Flipboard content. Tap the red ribbon in the top corner to open the Content Guide as shown in Figure 6-8. Browse through the categories in the left menu and tap any to see the suggested sections and sources. For example, tap the News category to get a list of sections such as Business, Politics, and Sports. Scroll down, and you can also select from the list of sources such as BBC World News, CNN, and more. Tap the Bookmark icon next to any of the sections to subscribe to it and add it to your custom Flipboard magazine.

3. Customize the news from your social networking accounts.

Tap Accounts in the left menu of the Content Guide to connect to your social networking accounts. You can customize the news you receive even further by tapping the account and selecting any of the filtering options. For example, if you connect to your Twitter account and tap it, you can subscribe your entire Twitter timeline, your Twitter favorites, saved searches, and more.

Tap Accounts to link to Twitter, Facebook, and others

Figure 6-8: Create a Flipboard magazine by selecting sources and linking to web accounts.

4. Read and enjoy.

When you open Flipboard, you get the latest news from your selected sources. Turn the page by flicking it to the left or right. Tap any source to open it, and you see all the latest articles presented in a beautifully designed magazine format. Tap on any article that interests you and read further. Your custom news is updated every time you open Flipboard . . . and you don't even have to train your dog to bring it in from your front doorstep.

5. Share, comment, save.

When you open an article, you see that familiar Share icon in the bottom-right corner. Tap it to share the article via email or on social networking accounts such as Facebook and Twitter. Add your comments to it, and even save it to that Pocket account you opened when you read about it a few pages back in this chapter! Another Share option is the Flip This into a Magazine option. Tap it, and you can also save articles to a custom magazine that you can share with other Flipboard users.

Flipboard is great for personal use, staying up with the news, and professional development. It also has a place in your classroom. Consider having students build a custom magazine with categories that track news events for class discussion and opinions on the web about specific topics they are studying.

Diigo

Diigo is my favorite tool for cataloging, archiving, and sharing information that I find on the web. You're probably familiar with the process of bookmarking a website. Most browsers come with a simple mechanism for saving bookmarked sites, and I discuss Pocket earlier in this chapter as a way of saving and organizing bookmarked content for later reading. Diigo also works on desktop computers and mobile devices, but it takes a very different approach to saving, organizing, and sharing content.

As you browse the Internet, Diigo offers tools for taking notes, highlighting, and tagging web pages that you'd like to save for later reference. Learning deepens when you connect new information to your existing knowledge and see ways to apply it. There's that "aha" moment when you read something and the light goes on. Diigo lets you capture those moments with highlights, annotations, and notes. That would be reason enough to use Diigo, but where it really distinguishes itself is as a "social bookmarking" tool — a tool that enables cataloging and annotating of web pages along with the sharing features that are so popular with social networking sites. It's the perfect tool for collaborative research because it allows groups of Diigo users to pool and share their content and notes. Chapter 7 has a deeper exploration of the social networking aspects of Diigo.

To see if you like Diigo as much as I do, install it and start using it by following these steps:

1. **Go to www.diigo.com and sign up for a free account.**

Diigo offers a free upgrade to premium accounts for educators. Diigo Educator accounts have additional features, such as a Teacher Console that gives you the capability to create student accounts for an entire class and to automatically set up the class as a Diigo group so students can share bookmarks and annotations. It's a terrific way for students to compile, annotate, and share content.

2. **Install the Diigo desktop bookmarklet or download the Diigo app for your iPad.**

   The process for using Diigo varies depending on whether you're using a desktop browser or a mobile device:

   • *Desktop browsers:* After you have created an account, your account name appears with an arrow in the top-right corner of the page. Click the arrow and select the Tools option. Select the Diigolet option under Bookmarklets; follow the directions, and drag a button to your browser's toolbar.

   • *iPad (and mobile devices):* Start by downloading the free Diigo Browser app from the App Store. After you've installed it, tap to open it and sign in with your username and password. Use the Diigo browser to read web pages, just as you would use any other web browser. When you find a page you want to save or share, you can use Diigo's tools for highlighting, annotating, and tagging the content by tapping the "d" icon in the toolbar as shown in Figure 6-9.

3. **When you find a page that you want to save, tap the Diigo button in your browser toolbar.**

   Tap the "d" Diigo icon on the browser toolbar and tap the Save option. You see a window with options that include adding a description, tagging the page, and sharing it with your groups. You can add multiple tags; just separate them with a space. Create multi-word tags by using a character such as a dash between the words or by enclosing them in quotation marks. As you start typing a tag, Diigo prompts you with any similar tags you've used in the past.

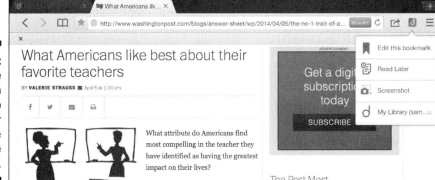

Figure 6-9:
Tap the "d" icon in the Diigo Browser to save and share content.

The social networking wave that has swept over the Internet has enabled collaborative learning in ways we never previously imagined . . . and Diigo is a great example. Set up a group for your class and have students sharing resources and notes. Create a group for your department so teachers can pool information and ideas. Don't stop there — join some existing Diigo groups. Go to www.diigo.com and select the My Groups option in the top menu bar. Whether you're interested in astronomy or dog training, simply browse or search for an appropriate group and join it. Remember, two heads are always better than one, and the group you join likely has many members sharing and learning together.

4. **When you finish typing your tag, tap Save.**

5. **(Optional) Select any text in the article to highlight it.**

   Select any text on the page and a menu pops up. Tap the Highlight option, and Diigo adds a colored overlay, as shown in Figure 6-10. It's as if you used a marker to highlight it. That's a nice tool to help you scan the main points of the article when you come back to it later.

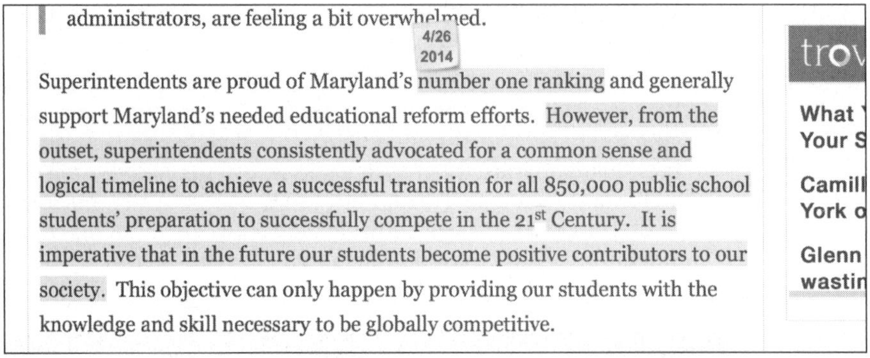

administrators, are feeling a bit overwhelmed.

4/26
2014

Superintendents are proud of Maryland's number one ranking and generally support Maryland's needed educational reform efforts. However, from the outset, superintendents consistently advocated for a common sense and logical timeline to achieve a successful transition for all 850,000 public school students' preparation to successfully compete in the 21st Century. It is imperative that in the future our students become positive contributors to our society. This objective can only happen by providing our students with the knowledge and skill necessary to be globally competitive.

tro

What
Your S

Camill
York o

Glenn
wastin

Figure 6-10:
Highlight
text and add
notes to
pages saved
with Diigo.

6. **(Optional) Tap the Web Highlighter button, and then tap the Note option.**

   An onscreen yellow sticky note opens.

7. **Type your notes in the body, and tap Save when you're done.**

   Diigo leaves a little yellow icon on the page that represents your note and opens it whenever you tap it.

Whenever you come back to that page in the future, whether on your iPad or any other computer, Diigo remembers your highlights and notes and presents them to you when you tap the Diigo button.

8. **Go to My Library in Diigo to search your archives.**

   If you're using a desktop browser, go to www.diigo.com, sign in, and click the My Library option in the top menu. If you're using the Diigo Browser for the iPad, tap the Diigo button and select My Library.

   You'll see all the tags you've used in the left column and how many times each has been used.

9. **Tap (or click, if you're on a computer) a tag, or type it in the search field next to the My Library Tagged heading on the top left.**

   All the articles that use that tag immediately appear, complete with any highlights and notes that you've added to them. Figure 6-11 shows where I have searched for my "edreform" tag.

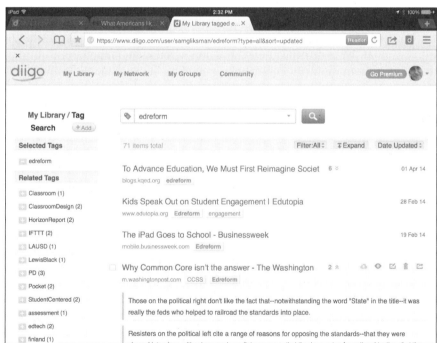

Figure 6-11: Diigo displays content related to a tag, complete with highlights and notes.

Organizing: Folders or tagging?

What's the difference between tagging content and organizing it in folders? Folders use a linear, top-down tree structure for storing content. It's like keeping papers in a filing cabinet in which you organize in separate drawers, folders, and files. The problem is that our lives are flooded with information these days, and it doesn't always fit neatly into a single category. For example, you just read an excellent article about the Great Depression. Do you file it under a folder for Economics, History, Politics . . . or maybe Prohibition? Probably all of them. That's why tagging is such a great way of archiving articles. It uses the computer's capability to search content quickly and compile results for you. You save content with tags that trigger your association to it, making it that much easier to find. When I search for *Prohibition*, Diigo presents me with a list of all the articles I tagged with that keyword — complete with any highlights and annotations I made on the page.

Another part of the magic of Diigo is that it's a social bookmarking tool. That means you can follow other Diigo users and what they are saving, and you can also share with them the content that you're tagging. I take a closer look at the wonderful sharing features of Diigo in Chapter 7.

Keeping a Digital Evernote Notebook

When you were a kid and prepared your school supplies the week before school started, one of the first things you likely packed was your notebook. Evernote is the digital equivalent of that notebook, with an impressive list of features that lend themselves to a variety of creative uses.

As with Pocket and Diigo, Evernote (shown in Figure 6-12) is a web-based service that can be used across all your devices. Having tools that work on both mobile devices and computers is indispensable when you use your iPad while you're out and about and then need to continue your work on a laptop or desktop. Evernote is a blend of digital notebook and all-purpose filing cabinet. You can use it to create and keep information or to store and organize all types of digital content. In fact, Evernote is so multi-dimensional that it's difficult to pin down a simple description.

Evernote keeps digital content in notes that you organize in notebooks. The Evernote publishers describe their product as a way to "help you remember everything across all of the devices you use. Stay organized, save your ideas, and improve productivity."

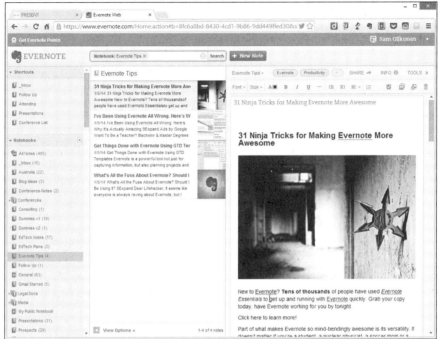

Figure 6-12:
Access
Evernote in
a browser
(as shown
here) or with
the Evernote
software or
app.

It's easier to describe Evernote by what you can do with it. The following list highlights just a few examples:

- ✔ **Take notes.** Type class notes, meeting notes, to-do lists, ideas, and more. Just set up notebooks in Evernote and create notes as you need them. Take Evernote with you on your mobile device wherever you go and use it to remember everything. Your notes will be waiting for you on your desktop or laptop when you sign in.

- ✔ **Record audio.** Notes don't have to be text. Use the microphone on your iPad or mobile device to record audio in your notes. Record a lecture. Have students record themselves reading or speaking in a foreign language. Record a snippet of a song you want to remember. Record voice reminders.

- ✔ **A picture is worth 1,000 words.** Take and record photos with the iPad camera. Whether it's the cover of a book you want to read or the whiteboard in your class, open a new note, tap the camera icon, and snap your pic.

✔ **Collect content from the web.** Evernote can be used to archive web pages, images, or any other portion of a web page. Using a tool called Evernote Clipper, you can cut out any portion of a page for archiving.

✔ **Archive anything you can email.** You don't need to have Evernote with you to archive your digital content. Every Evernote account has its own unique email address. As long as you can email anything, you can save it to your Evernote account.

✔ **Share.** Share folders with others so that you can collaborate and access content together.

Some software tools have a well-defined, but limited, scope of use. Evernote is at the opposite end of that spectrum. As you start using it, you'll begin discovering imaginative new ways to create and store digital content. Let's get you going.

1. **Sign up for an account.**

   As with every web service that synchronizes content across devices, you need an account so that you can access your files from any location and computer. Go to www.evernote.com and select the Create Account option in the top-right corner of the Evernote home page (or download the Evernote app on your iPad and select Create an Account on the opening screen of the app). You can sign up for a free account or opt for the Premium account, which gives you additional storage and features. In most cases, it makes sense to start with the free account and assess your ongoing needs after you start using the service.

2. **Create notebooks.**

   Think of how you intend to use Evernote, and create the notebooks that represent the different categories of usage. For example, you may want a notebook for taking notes in class. You may want a separate notebook for a project you're researching. I was looking for a used car recently and set up a notebook for storing car advertisements. Don't worry; you can always come back and edit your notebooks at any time.

   As you use Evernote more and create more notebooks, you may want to consider creating notebook "stacks." A stack is essentially a notebook with other notebooks nested underneath it. For example, you may have a notebook for Classes — let's call it the "category" notebook — and a list of separate notebooks nested under it for each class that you attend. Create the notebooks you'll use (for example, Math, Science, English) and then create a notebook that represents the category (such as Classes). Open Evernote in your desktop browser and then click and drag each nested notebook until you can drop it on the category notebook. The category will have a little arrow next to it which, when clicked, reveals a list of all the nested notebooks. Note that this adopts a fairly traditional approach to content organization where items are grouped by their physical location. Tagging content, which is described later in this section, can be a more effective method of organization, but ultimately you should use whatever works best for you.

3. Download the Evernote app and sign in.

Tap the App Store icon on your iPad, type Evernote in the search field, and download the Evernote app. After it's downloaded, tap the app icon and sign in when prompted on the opening screen. You're in!

Evernote offers a number of different tools for using your account. Aside from the Evernote iPad app, you'll also use Evernote extensively on your laptop and desktop. Access your Evernote notebooks by signing in at the Evernote website (www.evernote.com). In addition, you can download an Evernote software program for Mac and Windows computers. Open the web browser on your computer, and go to www.evernote.com/evernote to download the Evernote software. You can also download it from the Mac App Store.

There are many different ways to add and edit notes in your Evernote notebooks.

✔ **Add a new note within Evernote.** Click the New Note icon on the Evernote account page in your web browser or the downloaded software on your Mac or Windows computer, or tap the app on your iPad or mobile device. They all work the same way.

Type a subject line and fill out the body with your text, images, or media. You can upload and attach any documents or images, and don't forget that if you're using your iPad, you can take a photo by tapping the camera icon or record sound by tapping the microphone. Select a folder for filing your new note, and add some keywords in the Tags field to enable you to find the note easily. Separate your tags with a comma.

Note that anything you add to your Evernote account, no matter where you added it, is automatically stored in your Evernote account and synced to all your devices.

✔ **Save web content with Evernote Web Clipper.** Save content from the web to your Evernote account with the Evernote Web Clipper, as shown in Figure 6-13.

If you're on a laptop or desktop, open your browser and go to http://evernote.com/webclipper. Select your browser from the list, and follow the download instructions to add a button to your toolbar. Save entire pages or highlight any part of the web page you're viewing, and click a button in your browser's toolbar to save it.

You can install a bookmarklet in your iPad browser and use the Web Clipper there as well, but it's a lot trickier and takes a little fussing to get it working. If you're brave enough to give it a whirl, open your browser and go to www.support.evernote.com. Type **clipping web pages in iOS** in the search field and follow the instructions on the page. It's worth the effort.

Evernote Web Clipper

Figure 6-13:
Highlight any web content and use the Web Clipper to save it to a notebook.

✔ **Email content to Evernote.** Every Evernote account is given a unique email address. To find your Evernote email address, tap to start the Evernote app on your iPad, and then tap the Settings gear icon. Tap General, and scroll down and select Evernote email address under Settings. Now here are a couple of nifty little tricks that will make emailing content really simple.

First, select the option to copy your Evernote email address to your Contacts. Make sure to call it something simple like "Evernote." You've now created a new contact for your Evernote account.

Most apps on your iPad have functions for emailing content, whether it's photos from the Photos app, web pages in Safari, or documents in Pages. When you email the content, start typing **Evernote** in the To field (or any other name you gave the contact), and your Evernote email address pops up as the default.

Here's the second tip. In the subject line of the email, add an @ symbol and the name of the notebook you'd like to use for the note. For example, Let's say you want the content to be filed in the Research notebook. At the end of your subject line, type **@Research** and send the email. Magically, when you open Evernote, you see a new note in your research notebook with the content you emailed. If you're feeling particularly wild and adventurous, you can even try adding a hashtag and the name of a tag to attach to the note. For example, adding **#holidays** at the end of the Subject line would add "holidays" as a tag to the note you email.

Most web pages can be difficult to read because they're cluttered full of advertisements and links to additional articles and content. Chapter 4 discusses Safari's wonderful Reader function – the little lined icon at the left of the browser's address bar. Tap it, and Reader removes page clutter, leaving you with clear text on screen. If you're saving a web page to Evernote, I'd recommend using the Reader function to strip out all the extraneous content before you send it to your Evernote account. Your Evernote note will contain a link to the original page URL, followed by simple, distraction-free text.

There are a host of ways to search your Evernote content. The more you start saving content, the more you'll want to become proficient in different ways of finding what you need. Of course, we all have to walk before we can run, so here I show you a few simple ways of searching:

- **Browse by notebook.** Tap Notebooks in the left menu of the iPad app, and Evernote presents you with your list of notebooks, as shown on the left in Figure 6-14. Tap to select and browse the notes in that notebook.

- **Browse by tags.** If you were diligent about adding accurate tags every time you saved a note, then this is a breeze. Simply tap Tags in the left menu of your iPad app, and Evernote displays your list of tags used, as shown on the right in Figure 6-14. Tap any tag and browse all the notes associated with it.

If you're creating notes with a mobile device with GPS such as an iPad, Evernote automatically tags your notes with the location in which they were created. Want to take a break from work and see the notes you created when you were on holiday in Hawaii? Scroll down the left menu column in the iPad app, tap Places, and select Honolulu . . . then hurry up and get back to work before you get in trouble.

- **Use the Search box.** Type a search term in the Search field, and Evernote searches through the text of all your notes and presents you with a list of results. It even searches for text in any images you've saved in notes! For example, let's say you liked a particular jam and snapped a photo of it as a reminder to buy it later. Search for the name of the jam, and Evernote finds it in the photo, as shown in Figure 6-15. Impressed? The jam was pretty good, too.

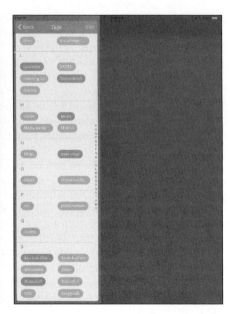

Figure 6-14:
Evernote
groups
notes by
notebooks
(on left) or
Tags (on
right).

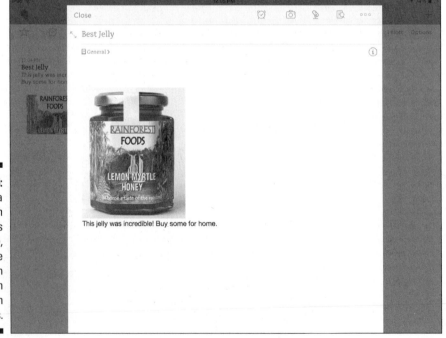

Figure 6-15:
Type a
search term
(such as
rainforest),
and Evernote
can even
find it within
images in
your notes.

Using Evernote in your classroom

Evernote is the Swiss army knife of tools for your iPad classroom. There are a variety of ways to use Evernote. Once you start using it, I can guarantee you'll think of many more. Here are just a few ideas to get you going:

✔ **Taking class notes:** Students can take class notes and organize them in notebooks for each subject. Even if they don't take the iPads home, they can access their Evernote accounts and notes on any computer with an Internet connection.

✔ **Creating shared notebooks:** If you have a Premium account, you can set up notebooks and share them with anyone — even if they have a free account. Create and share a notebook for each student in your class. You can monitor their progress and offer advice and feedback on their notes.

✔ **Sharing notebooks for group work:** Notebooks can be shared — a point we look at more closely in Chapter 7. Sharing a notebook is a great way for students to work collaboratively on a group project and share research and information.

✔ **Distributing content to class:** Teachers can share a notebook with students. That's a very simple way to distribute information to the class. Just create a note in the shared notebook, add the content, and it's available for all students to open and access.

✔ **Submitting work to the teacher:** Sending content via email to your Evernote email address is a fantastic way to easily create notes on an iPad. It can also be used creatively to create a class "dropbox" where students can submit work to a teacher. You can have each student add the teacher's Evernote email address to the Contacts on his or her iPad. Students then send their work to the teacher's Evernote email address and bingo — it's automatically filed as a new note in the teacher's Evernote account. Also, by simply giving the email address to students, you don't give them any access to see or open any notes in the teacher's Evernote account. It won't guarantee that students submit their work on time, but each note will indicate the exact time each student submitted it.

✔ **Blogging:** Get students to set up a notebook and keep it as a writing journal or blog. They can share it with you so you can access it and add comments.

✔ **Foreign language:** Use the recording feature, shown in the figure, in notes as a tool for students to record themselves practicing their foreign language skills. ¿Es muy increible, no? Or something like that . . .

✔ **Reading and speaking:** Use the recording feature in notes as a method for students to record themselves reading or speaking. Notes are kept as a way of gauging progress through the year.

(continued)

(continued)

Chapter 7

Social Networking and Sharing

In This Chapter

▶ Connecting, sharing, and learning on Twitter

▶ Sharing your web findings with groups in Diigo

▶ Watching and sharing videos with Showyou

*T*he future of learning is evolving from the traditional one-to-one exchange between teacher and student to a dynamic model that thrives on networking, collaboration, and sharing. This chapter focuses on how you can start learning with social networking services. That applies whether you're a teacher recognizing the need to continually be learning, a professional updating his or her expertise with new discoveries and practices, or a student working on a school project. You look at learning with Twitter, collecting and sharing information with social bookmarking services such as Diigo, and sharing videos with Showyou. So go ahead and sit back, relax, and invite the world to your living room. It's okay; you won't have to provide dinner.

Teachers typically have been the curators of information in schools, selecting and presenting information, and specifying articles and books for students to read. Then came the Internet. The fact that we can connect to people and information anywhere has raised the very important issue of how we can expect to filter the wheat from the chaff. What sources do you use, who published them, and how do you know the information is reliable and accurate? These questions form the basis of an important new capability that many are calling "information literacy." Children have a tendency to believe everything they see and read on the Internet. We can't just metaphorically throw them out into the midst of a vast information jungle and expect them to navigate their way to the sources they need. If we want them to Google for information, it's vital they receive training and guidance on how to filter, verify, and analyze anything they find. Information literacy needs to become a staple in the diet of every child's education.

Learning with Twitter

Everyone knows how Twitter is used. It's where you tell everyone about the lousy movie you saw last night and what you ate for breakfast, right? We've all heard the stories about celebrities with millions of followers making the most outrageous comments and politicians who have been caught publishing things they later regretted — no details required. What you haven't heard enough about is that there are millions of users sharing news, opinions, and important information in every field of knowledge, especially education.

I'm an avid Twitter user and I could easily devote several chapters to using Twitter for learning and professional development. The concept is pretty straightforward. *Tweets,* as they are called, are messages of up to 140 characters that Twitter subscribers post on their accounts, as shown in Figure 7-1. When you have an account, you *follow* people who talk about topics you find interesting. The latest messages from those users show up on your home page for you to read. Don't underestimate your opinion. People will follow you and want to hear what you have to say as well!

Tweets

Figure 7-1:
Use a desktop browser (as shown here) or mobile device to read tweets from people you follow.

Hashtags

Finding people to follow on Twitter

There's no question that celebrities tend to be the one group of Twitter users with the largest followings. That's unfortunate considering the wealth of important people and information you can access through Twitter. *Time* magazine listed 140 people you should consider following on Twitter. The list includes scientists, historians, political analysts, and yes, even some comedians and entertainers. If you'd like to see the list, search for *Time magazine 140 best Twitter feeds* and you'll get the link to the article and list.

Twitter users include a hashtag symbol (#) before a relevant keyword (refer to Figure 7-1) or phrase in their tweets to categorize them and make them easy to find in a search. For example, users include the hashtag #edtech to indicate that a tweet is about educational technology. If you click or tap the hashtagged keyword, you'll get the latest list of tweets from all users who have used that keyword. It's a great way to find relevant information and additional people to follow.

 You can set your Twitter account to be private or public. Your Settings page has an option to protect your tweets. If you select that option, other users will need to request your permission to view your tweets. There are good arguments for and against making your tweets public, and you should select this option if you decide to keep your account private.

The following steps get you started with an account and using it to find and learn from other users:

1. **Open any web browser and go to www.twitter.com.**

2. **Tap or click the link to sign up for an account.**

3. **Tap or click and register for an account.**

4. **Look for people you know, news sources you read, and so on, so that you can follow them.**

   You'll get information from Twitter users whom you *follow*. You follow them by finding their accounts and tapping or clicking a Follow button on their pages.

   You don't need to find too many to start; it tends to snowball. You can see the people they follow and get information from people they "retweet" — when they quote information that someone else posted on their Twitter accounts.

5. Follow hashtags for topics that interest you.

As you begin to use Twitter, you'll run into common hashtags that represent your areas of interest. For example, #iPadEd is often used for messages about using iPads in education (as shown in Figure 7-2), #mlearning for mobile learning, and so on.

6. Post a message with a link to an interesting article or your opinion about an important topic.

Add a relevant hashtag keyword, if you know it.

Get involved. Remember that sharing works best when it flows both directions.

7. Go to the App Store and download the Twitter app for your iPad.

You can also add your Twitter account information in the Settings app (scan the left column for the Twitter menu item), and it automatically installs the Twitter app with your account.

There are Twitter apps for your iPhone, iPad (see Figure 7-3), and most other mobile devices, so you can connect and access your Twitter account and feeds whenever needed.

When you start using Twitter, you'll be amazed how much important information starts literally landing in your lap every time you access your Twitter page. Opinions, links to articles, debates, latest news . . . it's all there. The more you use Twitter, the more you'll develop additional connections and get even more information and knowledge. You'll also be making important contacts and friendships within a community that you follow.

And of course I'd love to hear from you as well. Sign up for your account and you'll find me on Twitter as @samgliksman. See you there!

Connecting through Twitter

You wouldn't believe how easy it can sometimes be to connect with someone through Twitter. Here's one example: I was working with an English teacher whose class was reading a book by a contemporary British novelist. We decided to try to locate the author. Sure enough, a quick search on Twitter revealed that he had an account, so we sent a message

inviting him to videoconference with the class and discuss the book with the students. Within the next couple of weeks, the author spoke to the students via Skype. They experienced and related to that novel from a completely new perspective — all through the magic of social networking and Twitter. And the author never once told us what he ate for breakfast.

Figure 7-3:
The Twitter app for the iPad displays your Twitter account feeds.

Twitter, a great tool for personal, professional development, can be used effectively in a classroom setting. Here are a few ideas to get you thinking, including some hashtags you might use. (I'm appending a unique identifier such as ms6 to the hashtags as an example for a fictitious 6th-grade class in Venice Middle

School.) By the way, always check that any hashtag you want to use isn't already being used for some other purpose. You can use Twitter's search function to check whether there are existing tweets that already reference the hashtag you'd like to use.

✔ Create a special hashtag phrase for your class and use Twitter as a classroom discussion forum for communication after school hours (#discuss-vms6). You can review the hashtag discussions the following morning or at any other time.

✔ Use Twitter as an easy way for students to post questions and comments during lectures and field trips (#comments-vms6).

✔ Have students adopt the character in a historical event or book and get them to tweet as that character with other students/characters. Don't forget to use a hashtag to group the tweets into an easy-to-follow discussion (#civilwar-vms6).

✔ Post a question of the day that requires your students to practice their information literacy skills and search for the answer online (#infolit-vms6).

✔ Ask children to read something and summarize it in a string of 140-character Twitter posts. The skill of condensing issues to their essential core is important to all forms of communication (#novel-vms6).

✔ Learn vocabulary by having students submit a sentence a day (#vocab-vms6).

Twitter is such a popular service that it has spawned an entire industry of Twitter add-on services. One such app that can be great for educational *or* recreational use (hey, all work and no play . . .) is Twitterfall. Use a standard desktop browser to access www.twitterfall.com and get a current stream of all tweets on anything you search. For example, say that you're debating the politics and issues regarding gun control. You can type phrases such as *gun control* and *nra* as searches, and Twitterfall will give you a stream of tweets as they are being published on the web. It's amazing to see the stream flowing down your screen. You can even look at the difference in opinions within different geographic areas by using the geolocation option and only displaying tweets within a specific geographic area.

A word of warning about using Twitterfall, and for that matter, any public Twitter search: They are not filtered. That said, you may run across all forms of profanity and objectionable opinions. Exercise some reasonable amount of caution when using these tools, especially when you are using them with your students.

Group Sharing with Diigo

Diigo is a wonderful tool for organizing and archiving web content. Diigo is often referred to as a social bookmarking tool. Chapter 6 focuses on its bookmarking prowess, but it's that social component that I explore further in this chapter.

If you think that something you find on the web is worth archiving, then there's a good chance that your friends and colleagues will consider it helpful as well — and vice versa. Diigo enables the sharing of content in a number of ways.

- ✔ **Public and private bookmarks:** You can set any Diigo bookmark listing to be private or public. Private bookmarks are still very helpful for archiving and referencing content, but only public bookmarks can be shared and viewed by others.

- ✔ **My Network:** You can certainly learn from what other people are reading and bookmarking — especially people you know and respect. Diigo has a My Network feature that enables you to add friends and colleagues and see what they are bookmarking. Access your account on any web browser and tap or click the My Network item on the top menus. Look for the link to Browse and Edit your friends and then add more. After you have added some people to your network, you'll see everything they have publicly bookmarked in your My Network section.

- ✔ **My Groups:** Start or join a Diigo group. Groups are formed around a common theme, and members can share their findings with each other.

  Tap or click the My Groups menu item on the top of the web browser page and browse for groups with which you share a common interest. Groups exist for everything from teaching mathematics to scuba diving. You can also type a term in the Search box and Diigo drops down a menu of options, one of which is to find groups that are interested in your search term. Tap or click on any group in the search results, and it takes you to the group page. You'll see a large button to apply for membership in the group.

  As Groucho Marx famously said, "I don't want to belong to any club that would have me as a member" . . . and if you feel so inclined, then go ahead and start your own group! Just tap or click the Create a Group button on the My Groups page, define your group's topic of interest, and start inviting members. (Just don't grow one of those Groucho moustaches!)

- ✔ **Sharing with a group:** Whenever you save a bookmarked page, Diigo offers you the option to share it with a group. Select any one of your groups, as shown in Figure 7-4 taken from the Diigo Browser iPad app. Your finding will be shared and available to all the members of the group.

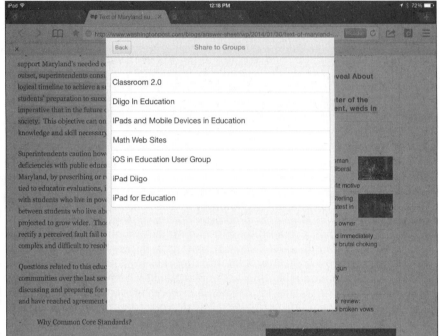

Figure 7-4:
Use Diigo to
bookmark a
page so you
can share it
with any of
your groups.

✔ **Sharing in class groups:** If you upgraded to an Educator account
(described in the last chapter), then you can set up a private group that
includes your students. That's a great way to create and organize class
research and to build a knowledge base for your course. You can also
create subgroups that can share findings when working on collaborative
projects.

Remember, effective teachers are also learners. Create a Diigo group for members of your faculty department and encourage them to tag and save content
to the group. Join other groups of educators that share similar interests. Two
heads are always better than one, and the group you join likely has many
members contributing and learning together.

Sharing Videos with Showyou

So much of our modern communication is gravitating toward multimedia
that it helps to have a simple, dedicated method for sharing and accessing
video with your friends. That's the singular objective of Showyou, shown

in Figure 7-5. Unlike other social sharing services that accommodate a variety of media, the Showyou app does one thing only — and it does it with style. Showyou is a "social video" app that enables you to browse through all the different videos your friends have shared on social networks such as Facebook, Twitter, YouTube, Tumblr, and more.

Video categories   Currently popular videos

Figure 7-5:
Showyou
enables you
to browse
videos
friends
share on
social
networks.

As you can see from the figure, Showyou presents you with a grid of some of the more popular videos referenced by Showyou members on their social networking sites. Slide the grid to the right with your finger to open the left menu panel that categorizes the video content by subject matter. Tap any topic in the left menus, and Showyou presents the videos in that category. Tap any video in the grid to open and play it. Nice, but Showyou can do so much more.

After you download Showyou from the App Store, you can create a profile that enables you to make connections, find friends, and search for shared videos. Just follow these steps:

1. **Tap the Showyou icon on your iPad Home screen to start the app.**

2. **Follow the prompts to sign up for a Showyou account and set up customized social network channels.**

   After you have signed in, you can start connecting with your friends and colleagues. During the sign-up process, you're prompted to connect to social networking services such as Twitter, Facebook, and Tumblr. You can also edit these connections in Settings at a later time as shown in Figure 7-6.

   As you select any of the options, Showyou asks you to sign in to that service and verify that you're allowing it to connect.

   Now that you have given Showyou access to your accounts, it can look at your connections and suggest some of your friends who are using Showyou.

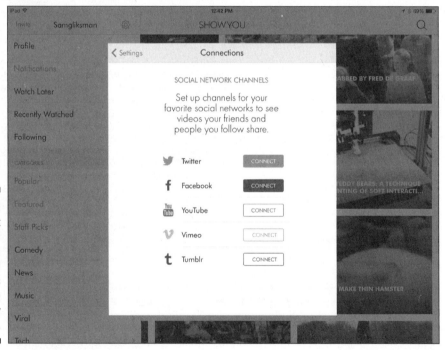

Figure 7-6:
Connect
to social
networking
services and
add friends
to see
videos they
share.

3. **Tap the Find Friends menu option in Settings to get a list of friends whom you can follow.**

4. **Tap the Follow button next to any name, and the videos they share through Showyou show up on your video grid.**

   It's as if you are creating your own social networking video channel.

5. **Search for videos shared on Showyou by tapping the magnifying glass and entering a term in the Search field on the upper right of the screen.**

Part IV
Reading, Writing, and 'Rithmetic in the Digital Age

Find helpful articles and videos on all sorts of topics at www.dummies.com.

In this part . . .

✔ Read documents and eBooks on your iPad

✔ Use apps to create and annotate documents

✔ Create eBooks that enhance text with different media

✔ Utilize the iPad for learning in math and science

✔ Examine built-in accessibility features on iPads

Chapter 8

Reading on the iPad

*I*f you're old enough to be parenting or educating, then you probably love the smell of printed paper just as much as I do. Printed books won't be disappearing quite yet, but there's no question that the whole publishing industry is in a period of transition. Many large retailers have closed, and the number of digital reading devices and e-books sold continues to rise dramatically. The popularity of e-books is partly due to their convenience factor. Browse books online, read samples, and with the tap of a button, order a book that arrives on your device within a minute or so. However, convenience alone wouldn't explain the degree of change currently taking place in the book publishing industry. We've had books in digital text format for a few years, and their adoption has been relatively slow. Two major factors are now contributing to the growth of e-books:

✔ E-reading devices are becoming more sophisticated. Their displays are crystal sharp, books are easier to browse and deliver within seconds, and devices are decreasing in price. All that allows users to carry around libraries of digital books in devices that weigh less than a single paperback.

✔ The nature of what we call a "book" is evolving; e-books are increasingly including elements of multimedia and interactivity. Also, they're being read on devices that integrate the experience of reading with search tools, dictionaries, highlighting and annotation features, and even elements of social networking.

We all develop an attachment to familiar things from our past that we loved. I still love walking down the aisle in a bookstore and browsing the titles on the shelves . . . but that experience is becoming increasingly rare as more and more traditional bookstores are closing. In contrast, reading digital books on a mobile device continues to grow rapidly in popularity.

In this chapter, I take a look at different approaches to using your iPad for reading — from book subscriptions to the purchase of individual books, book apps, and even ways to access free e-books. I present different ways to access books for young readers and adults. Finally, I take a peek down the road at the emerging market for e-textbooks that is finally beginning to materialize. Read on!

Digital Reading for Younger Students

It's one of the more commonly asked questions you hear about children using iPads: Should we encourage them to read e-books or paper books? The answer is fairly simple. As long as they are enjoying reading, does it really matter? I vote for an extra hour a day reading either a digital or paper book instead of more time wasted with a mindless video game.

Some children love the extra "perks" that come with reading e-books. Some of the common features include

- **Interactivity:** Touch objects and they react. Turn your iPad and things move.

- **Dictionary:** Touch words and their definitions pop up.

- **Audio and soundtracks:** Characters talk. Background music plays. Sound effects play as events occur in the book.

- **Read to me:** Younger children — and those that have vision problems — can have the book read to them.

- **Change languages:** Select the language for text and/or audio.

- **Record:** Record yourself reading the text and play it back as the audio narration.

- **Games and activities:** Coloring pages, puzzles, and more are often included in the books.

It's difficult to keep up with the rush of new digital books (or electronic books, known as e-books) being released for younger readers. The range of options is expanding rapidly as new books are being released.

E-books

E-books can be read on a number of digital devices including the iPad. They're available for download from numerous sources including the Apple iBooks Store, which delivers them directly to the iBooks app on your iPad. There are also a variety of other e-readers and e-reading apps for the iPad such as Kindle, Nook, Kobo, and more that can also be used for reading e-books from other sources.

Apple has a Children and Teens section in its bookstore, as shown in Figure 8-1. You can also access the list of bestselling books by tapping the Top Charts icon in the bottom toolbar of the Bookstore and selecting the Children and Teens category. Any book that you purchase is automatically added to your e-books library and available on other iOS devices you own.

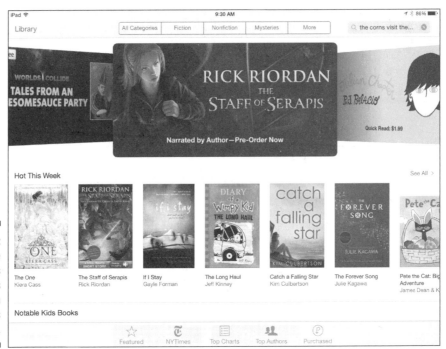

Figure 8-1: The Apple iBooks Store has a Children and Teens category.

 If you tap the Top Charts icon in the bottom toolbar of the Apple iBooks Store and select the Children and Teens category, you see the top sellers divided into Top Paid Books and Top Free Books, as shown in Figure 8-2. It's an excellent way to find a wealth of good, free e-books for your child to read!

Figure 8-2:
Top-selling
books are
divided into
Top Paid
and Top Free
Books.

Book apps

Many book publishers prefer the flexibility of creating their own book app. Book apps function in much the same way as the books you read in iBooks; however, in creating their own app, publishers are free to use additional functionality outside the framework of the regular e-book or ePub formats. They aren't read within an e-reader such as iBooks. Instead they function as apps and are purchased through the App Store. For example, the book *Al Gore — Our Choice: A Plan to Solve the Climate Crisis* by Push Pop Press is in the App Store and not the Apple iBooks Store. It opens as its own app and not within an e-reader. Pick objects up and move them around, pinch to open and zoom around images, and interact with objects such as windmills that simulate the generation of power when you blow into the iPad microphone!

The quality of many of these e-book apps is outstanding. You find them listed in the Books section of the App Store. They feature beautiful musical soundtracks, top-quality narration, and amazing illustrations and effects. Reviews of these books are all over the web, and even institutions such as *The New York Times* now occasionally feature reviews of e-books and book apps.

The list of quality books is too long to mention, but if you want a sampling of what's out there, consider the following book apps:

- ✔ ***The Three Little Pigs* by Nosy Crow:** Featuring excellent graphics and sounds, this book is an excellent choice for younger readers. It tells the traditional tale of the Three Little Pigs . . . with a few twists. It offers lots of interactive surprises and sophisticated animations, and you can listen to the story narrated by children or read it yourself. One of the highlights of the book is that you can help the wolf blow down the houses by blowing into the iPad's microphone!

- ✔ ***The Fantastic Flying Books of Mr. Morris Lessmore* by Moonbot Studios:** This beautifully designed book app (see Figure 8-3) is based on a story by William Joyce that was also an award-winning animated short film. The animation sequences in the book are stunning, and the interactive elements keep the reader entertained and engaged. The story revolves around a man infatuated with books. One day, he's blown away in a storm and finds himself in a remote country house filled with books. It's a poignant story about the power of books and the people that love to read them. The book is also filled with games that children will love, such as spelling in a bowl of alphabet cereal and playing "Pop Goes the Weasel" on a piano.

Figure 8-3: *The Fantastic Flying Books of Mr. Morris Lessmore* illustrates the potential of e-books.

Walking slowly inside he discovered the most mysterious and inviting room he had ever seen. It was filled with the fluttering of countless pages, and Morris thought he could hear the faint chatter of a thousand different stories, as if each book was whispering an invitation to adventure.

✔ *Unwanted Guest* **by Moving Tales:** This is a stunning book app (see Figure 8-4) adapted from a traditional Jewish folk tale. It tells the story of a poor old man living in an old, dilapidated house. He's visited by an unwelcome house guest, and the story details his attempts to rid himself of his surprising visitor.

This book is beautifully produced. The illustrations are gorgeous and it also includes sophisticated 3-D animations, original music, professional narration, and sound effects. It's a book that children and adults alike will enjoy.

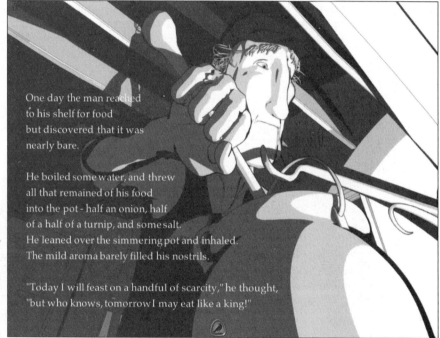

Figure 8-4:
Unwanted Guest is an iPad book app that's beautifully produced.

E-book subscriptions

Given the ease with which e-books can be delivered to any computer or mobile device, it makes sense that some companies would start offering subscription services that have you sign up and get e-books delivered directly to your device as needed. At the risk of repeating myself, this sector is evolving and new options are springing up all the time. In this section, I highlight two existing services.

Storia

Scholastic is a leading publisher of children's books in the USA and is now producing e-books as well. Storia is Scholastic's e-book management app designed to download, store, manage, and read e-books (see Figure 8-5). Storia comes with five free e-books. Sign up for a Storia account online, and you gain access to a growing catalog of e-books that include picture, chapter, read-to-me, and enriched e-books that contain a variety of interactive activities. Scholastic's books are targeted to children from early readers to teens. The company offers popular and reasonably priced books ranging from the Harry Potter series to *Clifford the Big Red Dog* and *The Hunger Games*. Set up a separate virtual bookshelf for every child. As you purchase e-books, you can assign them to the bookshelf of any child.

To purchase and add books to your Storia library:

1. **Use your Internet browser to go to the Scholastic Storia website (www. scholastic.com/Storia).**

2. **Select the Shop for e-Books option.**

   You can select books by age, grade, reading level, price, and character or series. Follow the prompts and purchase your book. You need to sign into your Storia account to complete the purchase.

3. **When you have completed the purchase, open the Scholastic Storia app on your iPad.**

4. **Tap Create Bookshelves and specify how many bookshelves you want to create.**

   You can create one bookshelf for each child.

5. **Tap Assign eBooks and then download the e-book and assign it to the appropriate bookshelves.**

You can track an individual child's progress through each e-book, see what new words he learned, how many pages he read, and how long he spends reading each day.

Figure 8-5:
Storia is an e-reading app with links to Scholastic's library of children's books.

Reading Rainbow

You probably remember *Reading Rainbow*, the TV series hosted by LeVar Burton that ran on PBS for more than two decades. Reading Rainbow is now an app that offers subscription-based downloads of books for children ages 3 to 9.

Children tap a themed island (see Figure 8-6), such as Animal Kingdom, My Friends, My Family, or Genius Academy, which takes them to a selection of books they can browse. Each island also has a selection of "field trip" videos, some of which come from the original series. As was the case with the TV show, many of the stories are read by celebrity actors, and you can elect to turn the narration on or off. Books feature light animations and activities to enhance the story. Reading Rainbow currently contains a library of 150 interactive e-books; monthly subscriptions range in price depending on the term of the subscription. They're also in the process of introducing special pricing structures for schools and libraries.

Figure 8-6:
The Reading
Rainbow
app is based
on the
PBS series
hosted
by LeVar
Burton.

Reading Documents with GoodReader

You aren't limited to reading only e-books on the iPad. You often need access to all sorts of documents when you're on the move. Thankfully, the iPad makes it easy to download and read them.

I discuss how to get content onto your iPad in Chapters 3 and 6. Options include using a cloud storage service such as Dropbox or Google Docs/Drive, and, of course, moving content directly onto your iPad by syncing it through iTunes. One of the issues you may encounter, however, is that documents come in all formats, sizes, and types. The spreadsheet that looked just great in Excel on your Windows desktop computer either doesn't open or looks like a jumbled mess on your iPad. One of the better apps for handling content from a variety of sources is GoodReader.

GoodReader is an iPad app that enables you to download, read, manage, organize, access, and annotate just about any file you have stored — locally or on the web. Many have described it as the all-purpose, "Swiss army knife" of document readers.

GoodReader can download and synchronize content from a variety of sources. It reads and displays most common file types and is equally comfortable with your 100-page manual as with a 1-page letter or a 30-slide PowerPoint presentation.

GoodReader is extremely versatile in the ways it enables you to connect to the different locations where documents might be stored, as I describe in the following list:

- **Open In:** When you tap and hold a document in most iPad apps, such as Mail, the Open In function menu pops up. GoodReader usually appears as an option to open most types of documents.

- **Connect to cloud services:** Tap the Connect to Servers pane, and you can add your account on any of a long list of storage and file synchronization services such as Dropbox, Google Apps, Box, SugarSync, and more. Tap any option and then type your account name and password to establish a connection. Now you can view and download any files you have in that account.

- **Connect to a computer:** Transfer files to GoodReader from your desktop or laptop. Just connect your iPad directly to the USB port of your computer, or tap the wireless icon on the bottom toolbar and follow the instructions to connect GoodReader to your desktop or laptop.

- **Connect to the web:** Tap the Browse the Web pane and use GoodReader's internal browser to locate any page or document on the web and download it to your iPad for reading. Tap the Sync button on the Web Downloads pane to update your downloaded document with any changes that may have occurred since you downloaded it.

Remember that GoodReader does more than just download a document to your iPad. Tap once on the Sync arrow, and GoodReader synchronizes a file or folder that updates and incorporates any changes that have been made since the last time you downloaded it.

The Manage Files pane, shown on the left in Figure 8-7, enables you to move and delete files, create folders, e-mail files, and more. Tap the Preview pane, and you can preview any file you have downloaded before opening it.

GoodReader built its reputation as being the file reader you wanted on your iPad. Simply tap any document in the list of downloaded files on the left pane, and GoodReader opens it for reading. It doesn't stop there either. If your document is a PDF, GoodReader includes a full palette of tools for editing and even annotation as shown on the right in Figure 8-7. Chapter 9 covers annotating documents on the iPad in more detail.

Figure 8-7:
Tap a document in the GoodReader downloaded list to open and edit it.

Reading Books Electronically: E-Reader Devices and Apps

You can read electronic books two ways: on a portable electronic device designed as a dedicated e-reader — such as the Amazon Kindle or Barnes & Noble Nook — that can store and display e-books, or on a device like the iPad, which serves many different functions, including acting as an e-reader via an e-reading app. Using the iPad as an e-reader is a great thing, especially with the high-resolution display of the third-generation and higher iPad (if you're lucky enough to have one).

You can read e-books using your choice from a variety of e-reading apps on the iPad. Each has a unique set of features and often its own store for buying the books. In this section, I compare a few. You can decide which ones to use and when.

iBooks

iBooks is the native e-reading app for the iPad and the most popular book-reading app for users of any Apple iOS device. A new version of iBooks is now also available for Mac computers using the Mavericks OS or later. I discuss the functionality and interface of iBooks in Chapter 4. One of the app's strengths is that it's the only one on the iPad that has a built-in bookstore for browsing and in-app ordering of books. In most cases, you can download samples to read before buying the book. To be fair, some of the other major e-reading apps had in-app purchasing in earlier versions; they were required to remove it in their iPad versions.

iBooks has improved steadily with new releases and is a solid choice for reading on the iPad. The capabilities to change color schemes, increase and decrease font sizes, keep notes, annotate text, and more have made iBooks the standard e-reading app on the iPad. It also works across your devices. Start reading a book on your iPad and continue reading later on your iPhone or MacBook. Go to Settings⇨iBooks and you can even toggle options to sync Bookmarks and book Collections.

Kindle

Amazon (www.amazon.com) offers e-reading devices — its Kindle models — and an e-reading app — the Kindle app — that can be used on other devices. Amazon has the advantage of offering the largest selection of paid e-book content available, with more than a million titles in its inventory. Download the free Kindle app to your iPad (see Figure 8-8), and then when you purchase an e-book on Amazon.com, you have the option of downloading it directly to the Kindle app on your iPad. You can also purchase hundreds of newspapers and magazines and download them to your Kindle device.

The Kindle app is available on a variety of devices, including Androids, Windows Phones, iPhones, Windows PCs, and Mac PCs. In addition, the Kindle's WhisperSync feature saves your last page read, bookmarks, and notes so that you can pick up any other device and synchronize to where you left off on another device. Amazon also offers free samples for download so you can review books before buying them.

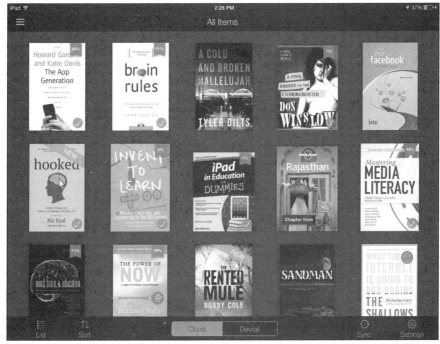

Figure 8-8:
Amazon's
Kindle offers
the widest
selection of
e-books for
purchase.

Nook

Barnes & Noble (www.bn.com) offers an e-reading device — the Nook — as well as an e-reading app that can be used on iOS and Android devices. Barnes & Noble created the Nook app to promote and bolster its sales of e-books.

Barnes & Noble offers a large selection of paid and free e-books as well as magazines and newspapers. The free Nook app is also available for your Mac, PC, and smartphones, and it syncs your reading status between devices. Unfortunately, the Nook does not yet have a way to deliver a hot cup of coffee and pastry with the book, but at the rate technology continues to advance, you can probably expect that sometime soon as well.

Kobo

Kobo (www.kobo.com/ereaders) has various models of e-readers, and its e-reading app shares many features with other e-reading apps. You can purchase books from Kobo's online store; it has apps for several devices (including the iPad and iPhone); the app synchronizes your account between your devices. You also can change text size, add notes, annotate text, and more.

What really distinguishes Kobo from other e-reading apps, though, is its *Reading Life* feature. Reading Life is an example of a new trend called *social reading*. You're probably familiar with social networking — possibly the most powerful phenomenon sweeping the Internet — and it has reached the world of reading. You may think of reading as a rather solitary activity, but book clubs have been around for a long time. Book club members meet in someone's living room and, over a drink and some snacks, discuss a book everyone has read. The advent of social reading is born out of book clubs . . . except in a social reading club, you can meet any time of day you want, at any place you happen to be, and discuss books with countless readers from all across the planet. You just have to bring your own tea and snacks.

Kobo is one of a new generation of e-reading apps that is moving the social networking experience into the realm of book reading. Some of Kobo's social reading features include the following:

- Tap the cover of any book in your library and share what you're reading with friends on Facebook and Twitter. (See Figure 8-9.)

- Select any text in the book and then post and share it — along with your comments — on your social networking sites.

- Select text and attach notes for your own reference or that you share with the community of Kobo readers.

- Tap the icon on the top left of the menu bar on your Kobo Home screen or bookshelf to reveal additional options:

  - Stats displays statistics about your reading: how long you have been reading, the average pages per hour, time to read a book, and more.

  - Tap the Friends option, sign in with your Facebook account, and see what your Facebook friends have been reading and recommending.

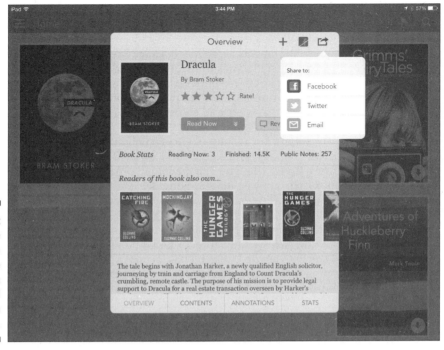

Figure 8-9:
Tap the
cover of a
book you're
reading in
Kobo and
share it with
others.

Social reading with Subtext

Kobo's Reading Life feature was cited earlier as part of a new *social reading* trend. Another leading social reading app is Subtext. Open a Subtext account as a teacher, create a group, and add or invite members. Groups may be kept private or public and can include students from your class. Consider adding and reading together with students in other classes, schools, or even countries. After you have your group, the next step is to assign a book or PDF document for the group to read.

Subtext enables readers to select portions of the text and add notes. Those notes can be shared with group members. Teachers embed instructions or pose questions for students to consider as they read. Students can highlight text and ask questions of other group members. Responses may be sent privately to an individual or posted for the entire group to access and discuss. If you elect to get a paid, premium account, you can monitor each student's reading progress and access an educator community to share assignments and plan curriculum.

Getting Free E-Books

There's no such thing as a free lunch, right? That may be true with regard to eating, but when it comes to reading, there actually are a few ways to get your hands on lots of free e-books. One of the best ways to access thousands of free e-books is through the Project Gutenberg website (www.gutenberg.org). Just download, read, and enjoy.

Project Gutenberg is a volunteer effort to digitize, archive, and distribute public domain books. The project was founded in 1971 and offers more than 40,000 free e-books that you can download or read online. They are primarily older books, the copyrights of which have expired, and include many of the classics you grew up reading. Downloading them to your iPad is simple: Go to www.gutenberg.org and browse the books in the archives, or type your search term in the Search field at the top of the page. You can search for a complete title, any part of a title, or an author. (For example, searching for *Oscar Wilde* lists all the books he has written.) You have various formats to choose from for the download, but select EPUB to view items in iBooks (see Figure 8-10).

Figure 8-10:
Download
free books
from Project
Gutenberg
and open
them in
iBooks.

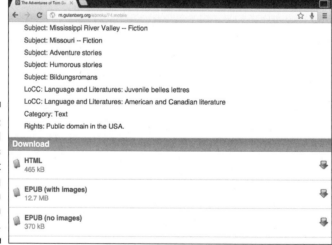

Another website I'd recommend checking is `www.baen.com/library`. It also has a nice selection of free e-books that you can download and read on your iPad. Remember to select the ePub format.

Goodreads (`www.goodreads.com`), which has an iPad app, is a great way to keep track of your reading lists and preferences and share them with friends. Keep track of what you have read and want to read by adding books to your shelves. Check what your friends are reading and read their book reviews. It's a great way to discover new books to read. And as an added bonus, Goodreads also has a library of more than 2,000 free public domain books you can download.

Many public libraries now offer users the option of downloading eBooks with a mobile app. You usually need an app to sign in with your online account, and then you're able to download books or reserve them until they become available for loan. As with physical books, eBooks can only be borrowed for a specific period of time, after which they automatically expire. Check with your local library for specific details.

Entering the E-Textbook Era

How many of us see our children leave for school in the mornings carrying backpacks filled with heavy textbooks that could break a lumberjack's back? We've finally reached a period of transition where many traditional publishers are recognizing the need to publish and promote e-textbooks. In addition, smaller publishers and even individuals now have the technology to create and distribute their own textbooks — something that wasn't possible when textbooks had to be mass produced and sold through traditional sales channels.

The dust is still settling and there's a variety of e-textbook formats in the market. In the case of the iPad, Apple has released a free software program for the Mac (requires 10.7.2 or later), called iBooks Author, which I discuss briefly in Chapter 10. iBooks Author was released with the specific intent of enabling authors to create e-textbooks for the iPad and distribute them through the Apple iBooks Store. The iBooks Store now has a Textbooks category (see Figure 8-11), and the content in it is growing rapidly. Other publishers are also releasing interactive textbooks as standalone apps. That gives them more capability to add features such as monitoring and reporting on student progress. Sites such as Inkling (`www.inkling.com`) focus solely on interactive textbooks and have apps for a variety of platforms, including iPads.

Figure 8-11: The iBooks Store now includes an iBooks Textbooks category.

Chapter 9

Creating, Editing, and Annotating Documents

*Y*ou may tire of hearing me talk about the fact that modern communications have progressed from being primarily text-based to an evolving mixture of multiple digital media formats. If we want school to remain relevant, students need ample opportunities to express themselves in all forms of media. Pushing education into the 21st century doesn't, however, mean leaving all 20th-century skills behind entirely. You could theoretically sit through a long business meeting sketching everyone around the table and recording audio of all the conversations, but it would probably be a lot simpler to jot down the important points and create a quick list of tasks to complete. Even longer reports may include references to the web, images, and links to video, but they often still require a substantial amount of writing. So let's not throw out the baby with the bathwater: Taking notes, creating documents, and editing or annotating text all remain vitally important. They also are what this chapter focuses on.

If you're an adult who just started using an iPad, I won't need ESP to mind-read your first complaint: "I can't type on this thing!" You might use slightly more colorful language, but you get the point. I agree. Whether you use the onscreen virtual keyboard or go out and purchase a physical keyboard that works with the iPad, it does take time to get accustomed to creating text on your device. I mean, did you pick up a pencil when you were a kid and immediately start writing a 50-page thesis? New skills take time and practice. You need to determine how and where you want to use your iPad, and then decide how best to use the appropriate apps and skills. As you'll see, you have many options that range from simple note-taking apps to full-featured word-processing and hand-writing apps. There are literally hundreds of excellent apps for creating and editing text on the iPad. Yes, even for those of you who still insist you did write a 50-page thesis when you first picked up that pencil as a kid.

Determining Your Objectives

I'll be honest. If you look in the satchel that I take to work most days, you'll find both an iPad and a MacBook Air. They are neatly slotted in the section next to the cheese sandwich I forgot about last week. I take both because there are days I need to attend meetings and take brief summary notes; the touch interface and virtual keyboard on an iPad (see Figure 9-1) are ideal for this task. Other times I have time to sit somewhere quiet and really write. At those times, I prefer having the full-sized keyboard and larger screen that the MacBook Air provides.

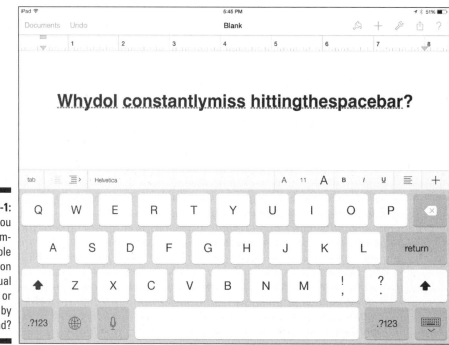

Figure 9-1:
Are you more comfortable typing on the virtual keyboard or writing by hand?

Some days I have to jot notes in my lap because I'm taking a long plane ride, and the big guy with the stained, blue-checked shirt next to me in seat 26B insists on spreading out and monopolizing the armrests while slurping that soft drink (you know who you are . . .). Other times I have access to a desk and lots of space to stretch out. There are times I can complete all my notes in a quick session, and times I'll need to finish writing later at home. You get the point. As they say in Australia, "Different horses for different courses," meaning that what's suitable for one purpose may not be for another. So let's ask a few pertinent questions:

- ✔ **Are you usually taking short notes for a class or meeting?** If so, look for a simple note-taking app without a lot of frills.

- ✔ **Do you need to share notes with others or file them somewhere that will give you access on all devices?** That will require that your app connect to a *cloud storage* service such as Dropbox (www.dropbox.com) that stores your files on the Internet and enables sharing of folders and files with other users.

- ✔ **Are you more comfortable typing or do you prefer handwriting?** If handwriting is your preference, then consider trying an app that supports note taking by writing with a stylus.

- ✔ **Are you writing something that's longer and may be continued later?** You'll require a more robust word-processing application, and cloud storage is important.

- ✔ **Will you continue the file on a device other than your iPad?** If that's the case, you need to make sure that you use an app that has the capability to save or export the file in a format you can use in other software applications (Word document, Pages file, and so forth).

- ✔ **Do you often need to access files for review and editing?** You'll need cloud storage and annotation features.

I review solutions for all those situations later in the chapter. Determine your priorities and you can mix and match the various options as needed.

Taking Notes

Whether you're sitting in class, meeting with clients, or attending a board meeting, there are times you want to create short notes as a synopsis of the event for later referral or study. You could create documents and store them somewhere for later retrieval, but a good note-keeping app would satisfy the following requirements:

- ✔ **Simple and quick:** It needs to be quick to open and get to the point at which you can start taking notes. You don't want to always be leaning over, asking the person next to you to repeat what was just said. Typing should be simple without the need to work out complex margin settings, hanging paragraphs, line spacing, and more. You need to get that text down quickly and easily.

✔ **Organized:** You're usually taking notes as part of some ongoing process. Ideally, the system or app you use has a built-in format and flow for organizing your notes. Set up one folder for Biology and another for English. Set up a folder for one client and subfolders for individual projects. Notes should easily fit in the right category and have a simple flow so that everything you need is there in sequential order.

✔ **Always available:** Apps that have an accompanying website service and interface are always my preference. I like to know my notes are available in a common location that every device supports. These days, every computer and device has a web browser, so I need an app that provides secure web access.

✔ **Cloud storage and backup:** Back in the day, if you lost your folder with months of notes, you'd more than likely start hyperventilating. Digital storage is simple these days. Don't use an app that uses the iPad as its primary storage location and relies on you to synchronize your files in order to create a backup. Select a solution that allows simple and automatic cloud storage.

✔ **Search:** An added bonus is the capability to tag your notes with keywords and an effective search function to find whatever you need easily.

✔ **Images, sketches, sharing, and more:** You're using an iPad! Your note-taking app should take advantage of the capabilities it provides. It's helpful to use that camera to add a quick picture of a document or a whiteboard to your notes. Sketch something in your note with your finger or stylus. Record a snippet of important audio. Email your note to someone else who needs it, or, even better, share it so that groups of people can have access.

Following are some of the best apps for simple, quick note taking, whether you're a student in class or summarizing discussions at an executive board meeting:

✔ **Evernote:** I discuss Evernote in significant detail in Chapter 6. For my money, Evernote has all the features you want from a note-taking app. It excels in organization, storing notes into Notebooks that you can create and share while also allowing you to add all types of digital content within your notes, including audio, images, and even websites. Your account is also available from any device and through the Evernote website.

✔ **Google Docs:** Google released a Google Docs app that integrates with your Google login and Google Drive account. If you are already an active user of Google Drive or your school uses Google Apps for Education, this approach may make sense. Your documents are automatically stored online and available across all your devices. Also, it's easy to share documents and collaborate with others.

✔ **iA Writer:** iA Writer (see Figure 9-2) is a fantastic app for simple text editing — but it's text and only text. One huge feature is a much needed extended keyboard (hello, Apple?) that adds keys for those simple functions such as moving through text letter by letter or skipping through it word by word. Dropbox and iCloud integration is provided as well.

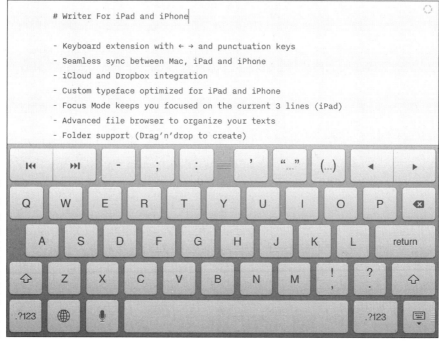

Figure 9-2:
iA Writer's
focus is
simple text
with an
extended
keyboard
to simplify
editing.

If you prefer creating handwritten notes, don't panic. I discuss some great apps for that later in the chapter.

Blogs are online web pages where users post ongoing narratives that others can read and comment upon. Many teachers have come to recognize the educational value of having their students maintain a personal blog. It's a great way for students to develop writing skills within an online framework that offers them the freedom to write about topics of interest. Their posts are shared so they can both give and receive peer feedback.

There are many excellent blogging platforms, such as WordPress (https://wordpress.com), Edublogs (http://edublogs.org), and Kidblog (http://kidblog.org). Most blogging platforms aimed at schools give teachers a web-based "dashboard" for creating and managing student blog accounts and moderating their posts and comments. Students can write and publish their posts on the iPad. I'd recommend checking out the iPad apps from the three blogging platforms mentioned here as well as other blogging apps such as Blogsy (http://blogsyapp.com/) and Easy Blog Jr (www.easyblogjr.co/). Whichever app you decide upon, make sure that it has the following features:

- ✔ It connects to the blogging platform you selected and therefore enables students to log in and access their accounts.
- ✔ It has simple features for creating and editing posts.
- ✔ Media such as images and video can be used in blog posts.
- ✔ Students can read and comment on posts by other students.

Word Processing with Pages

There are many full-featured word-processing apps for the iPad, but if I have to choose only one, it would have to be Pages (shown in Figure 9-3).

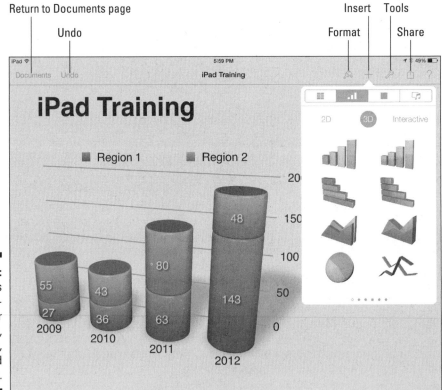

Figure 9-3: Pages has full support for text styles, charts, images, and more.

Return to Documents page

Undo

Insert   Tools

Format   Share

Pages is packed full of functions you expect from a word processor — adapted for use with the touch interface of the iPad:

- ✔ Templates with preselected formatting of colors, backgrounds, and fonts to get you going

- ✔ Full page and paragraph formatting options, such as margins, line spacing, columns, bulleted and numbered lists, and more

- ✔ Support for text and paragraph styles

- ✔ Easy addition and formatting of images. Options for editing photos are simple to use, and you can add 3D charts and tables as well. Set text to wrap around your image automatically.

- ✔ Full support for multitouch gestures such as pinch to zoom in and out, touch to select, and swivel to rotate images and more

- ✔ Step back through changes with Undo even after you next open the document

- ✔ A Page Navigator that allows you to browse and change pages by tapping on thumbnail previews

- ✔ Automatic document saving

- ✔ Tight integration with iCloud. You can set options to synchronize documents across devices, even to the point that you can continue from the point at which you left off on another device.

- ✔ Pages is Microsoft Word and PDF friendly. Open Word and PDF files and edit them in Pages. You can also export your document as a Word doc, a PDF, or even as an ePub file, which is used for e-books.

If you're lucky enough to have purchased an iOS device any time after September 1, 2013, you're eligible for a free copy of Pages along with Apple's other iWork and iLife apps. On the other hand, if you're like me and bought your iPad before November 2013 . . . well, if you don't have something nice to say, it's better to just smile and remain silent.

If you've used a word processor before, using Pages will come pretty easily. Tap the Pages icon to start the app, and then just stick with me through the following sections as I hit the highlights of using Pages.

Using Pages with iCloud

I strongly recommend that you open an iCloud account if you haven't already. You can automatically store the latest versions of all your Pages documents online in your iCloud account and sync your files and data between all your devices and computers. I am keeping one Ace up my sleeve, though. Check out the later Tip section about syncing Pages with other cloud services for a fabulous alternative. I believe that's called a "teaser" in the book business.

Backing up to iCloud

If you're using Pages frequently, you'll probably want your documents backed up and synchronized with your iCloud account. Here's how to make that happen:

1. **Open your Settings app and then scroll down and select iCloud from the menus on the left.**

2. **If you're not already signed into your account, sign in using your Apple ID.**

3. **Tap Documents & Data, and then turn on the Documents & Data option at the top of the list.**

This allows apps to store documents and data in your iCloud account.

4. **Grant permission to certain apps to store their data in iCloud.**

5. **Scroll down the list of apps and turn on the option for Pages.**

6. **Scroll all the way down the left menus in your Settings app and tap Pages.**

7. **Turn on the option to Use iCloud.**

Starting or opening a document

You start on your main documents page, which contains any files and folders you have created. If you have any documents on your iPad that you'd like to open and edit, you can simply tap them.

To create a new document, tap the + sign in the top-left corner and select Create Document. Tap the blank template option to start from an empty page, or select from the library of preformatted templates. Tap the Show Categories option on the right of the top menu bar to display templates in a specific category such as Reports or Newsletter.

Editing documents

Tap anywhere in the document to enter editing mode. The keyboard slides up with a ruler and formatting toolbar. I strongly suggest turning your iPad to landscape orientation because it makes the keyboard larger and easier to use. You can also consider using it in portrait mode if you are using an external keyboard. Some of the main editing features include the following:

✔ **Font size and style:** Adjust the appearance of your document using the text formatting options in the toolbar on top of the keyboard. Pages allows you to adjust font style and size using options along the top of the keyboard. Other options such as text style and color can be set by tapping the Format icon (paintbrush) on the top toolbar.

- Tap the font name (such as Helvetica) on the left of the toolbar and a pop-up menu displays a list of your different font options. Tap any font to select it.

- Font size options are displayed as a large and small A on the toolbar with a number size in between them. Tap the number and select a font size from the pop-up menu, or change the size one point up or down by tapping the large A or the small A.

- Tap the toolbar icons for Bold, Underline, or Italic to change text formatting accordingly.

✔ **Text selection:** Double-tap to select a word. Triple-tap to select a whole paragraph. Tap and drag the selection handles to select a block of text.

✔ **Replacements and definitions:** Double-tap a word for options of Cut, Copy, Paste, Delete, Replace, Define, Highlight, Comment, and Style (you'll see them by tapping the More button on older versions). Replace gives you the option to replace your misspelled word with a choice of similar words. Definition brings up the dictionary definition, and Style gives you the option to copy the style. Tap Highlight on selected text and it will . . . umm, highlight it.

✔ **Text styles:** Select any block of text, tap the Format button, and then choose format options from the menu that appears (see Figure 9-4).

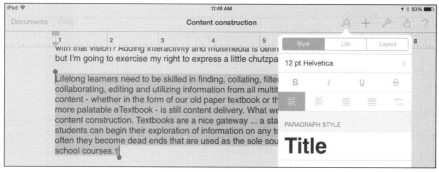

Figure 9-4: Triple-tap to select a paragraph, and tap the Format tool to change styles.

The menu has three tabs:

- Tap the Styles tab for preset styles that you can use to ensure titles, headings, body, and captions match throughout your document. You can also change text alignment and font selections and style.

- Tap the List tab for bulleted or numbered list options.

- Tap the Layout tab to create columns or tweak line spacing.

✔ **Ruler:** Tapping and dragging the arrows on the Ruler adjusts the margins of your page or the width of your columns. Tap and drag the flat button to adjust the paragraph indentation on the first line.

✔ **Document Setup:** Tap the Tools icon (the wrench) and select Document Setup (as shown in Figure 9-5) to make changes that apply to every page in the document:

• Tap to add or edit headers, footers, and page numbering.

• Tap and drag the double arrows to adjust page margins.

• Tap the + Insert icon to add logos and images.

• Tap the Format icon to set the formatting of a selected object on the page.

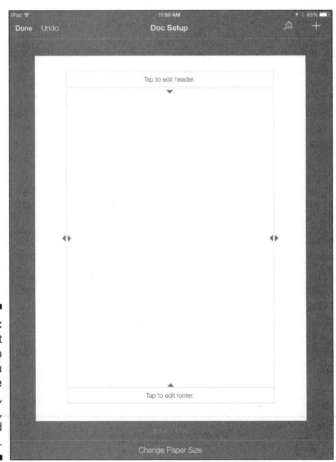

Figure 9-5:
Document
Setup
allows you
to change
headers,
footers,
margins, and
more.

✔ **Page Navigator:** To find and jump to any page, tap and hold your finger anywhere against the right edge of the screen until the navigator appears, displaying a thumbnail image of a document page, as shown in Figure 9-6. Drag up or down to view the thumbnail images of any page in the document. When you get to the page you want, lift your finger straight up from the screen to jump to that page. To release the navigator without leaving the current page, swipe to the right.

Page Navigator

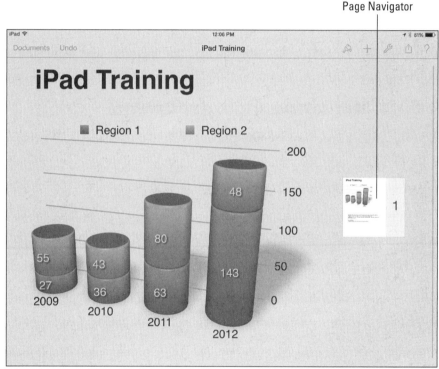

Figure 9-6: Tap and hold the right edge of the screen until the Page Navigator appears.

✔ **Image insertion:** Tap the Insert icon to select and insert photos from your iPad.

• To resize photo, tap and drag the selection handles in the corners.

• To move, tap the image and drag it to any location.

• To rotate, tap and select the image and then rotate it with two fingers.

- Tap and select the image, and then tap the Format icon for Style options such as borders and effects. You can also tap the Arrange tab to move the photo in front or behind other objects and set the way text wraps around it.

- Double-tap to mask the image and determine which portion of it appears. Slide the image within the masked area and tap outside the picture to save your new cropping.

✔ **Tables, charts, and shapes:** Tap the Insert icon to select and insert tables, charts that map data visually, and different shapes.

✔ **Printing, protecting, and more:** Tap the Settings icon on your toolbar to send your document to a printer, add password protection, and more.

Managing your documents

Your Documents screen displays thumbnails of all the documents on your iPad.

✔ Rename a document by tapping and holding the document name, and then type the new name in the text field that pops up.

✔ Group documents into folders by tapping and holding on a thumbnail image until the documents start to jiggle, and then drag one document onto another. That automatically creates a folder and prompts you for a folder name. Tap outside the folder area to close it.

✔ Remove a document from a folder by tapping the folder to open it. Touch and hold until it jiggles, and then tap, drag, and drop the document outside the folder.

✔ Delete a document by tapping Edit, tapping to select the document(s), and then tapping on the Trash icon in the top toolbar.

Sharing documents

When you're ready to present your work to the world, open a document and tap the Share icon (the rectangle with an arrow) on the top toolbar. Share a link via iCloud, or send a copy of the document via email to your iTunes account or a WebDAV server. Don't forget that Pages gives you the option of sending the document as a Pages, Word, PDF, or ePub document. Of course, if you have an iCloud account and set it to synchronize documents, your document will automatically find its way floating up to the cloud and to all your other devices without your having to do anything.

iCloud versus ALL cloud

iCloud is a wonderful service, but many other options are out there when it comes to cloud storage services. I love my Dropbox account, and I also use Google Drive extensively. I could sync my Pages documents with iCloud and create another, third storage location, but I'm a "keep it simple" sort of guy: The idea of having to organize all these different storage accounts just makes me nervous. Of course, you know I wouldn't bring it up unless I had a great solution, right?

Otixo gives you access to all your cloud accounts from a single location. So I recommend that you run to the Otixo.com website (www.otixo.com) and open an account. As with many other web services, what was initially free now comes at a price, but you'll get great value out of your account if you use multiple cloud services. Whether you use any combination of Dropbox, Google, Box, CX, and something else, just add them all to your Otixo account and let it be the single access point for all the files in those accounts. Download the Otixo app or use it through the website, and you can access files in any of your cloud accounts from the one location. You can even move files between one cloud account and

another. Here's the great part . . . it's accessible right from within Pages.

To save your Pages document, follow these steps:

1. **Download the Otixo app on your iPad.**

2. **Share your document.**

   Within your document in Pages, tap the Share icon and select Open in Another App. Then select Otixo from the list of apps.

3. **Tap to select a file format.**

   Your choices are to save the document as a Pages, Word, PDF, or ePub document.

4. **Select the Otixo app.**

   Select Otixo from the list of available apps.

5. **Select a cloud account.**

   The Otixo app will open onscreen and prompt you for a save location. If you have already added all your different accounts at Otixo.com, they are all now available to you. In my case, I get my Dropbox, Google Docs, and SugarSync storage accounts as options for saving the copy of my Pages document.

Microsoft Office Arrives for the iPad

Those of you who have been waiting patiently to use Microsoft Office on the iPad will be pleased to know that Microsoft finally released long-awaited versions of the Microsoft Office suite of apps for the iPad in March 2014. The Office suite includes Microsoft Word (see Figure 9-7), PowerPoint, Excel, Outlook, OneNote, and more.

The Office apps are available for free download through the App Store on your iPad. Seriously! OK, there's one catch. Download Word, Excel, and PowerPoint free and you can view your documents, spreadsheets, and presentations. If you want to create and edit documents on your iPad, you need a current subscription to Microsoft's Office 365 service. Annual fees start at $99 for home users, but that gives you access to the full Office suite of apps on up to five PCs or Macs in addition to five mobile devices. You also receive an account with Microsoft's OneDrive online storage service. Your OneDrive account starts with 15GB of free storage to keep your files backed up and synchronized across all your devices.

There are also various plans and pricing structures if you want to get Office 365 for your educational institution. Contact Microsoft for details.

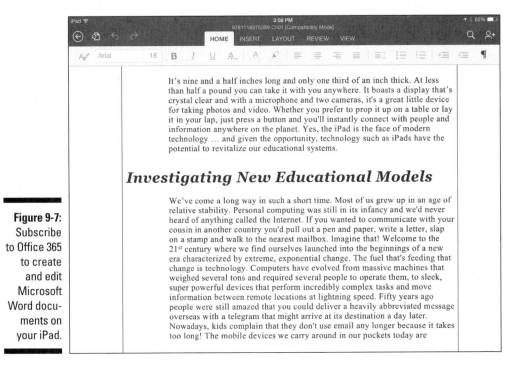

Figure 9-7:
Subscribe
to Office 365
to create
and edit
Microsoft
Word docu-
ments on
your iPad.

Annotating PDF Documents

Here I am, supposed to be providing you with all the answers, and yet I spend so much time asking questions. If you want to look into marking up and annotating PDF documents, I have to ask you, "What's your objective?" Depending on your answer to that question, I do have apps to suggest:

✔ **Filling out forms? Consult the PDF Expert** (`http://readdle.com/ products/pdfexpert_ipad/`): If your primary need is to fill out forms and sign them, then I recommend looking at an app called PDF Expert. As with most PDF annotation apps, it links to your cloud accounts so that you can download documents easily.

PDF Expert reads most document types and provides standard highlight and annotating functions. Use the keyboard or write on the form with your finger or a stylus. Annotations are saved within the document in PDF format.

The app excels in its support of PDF form fields and functionality created in Adobe Acrobat. Special fields such as text fields, check boxes, radio buttons, and other form elements all function as needed, and all information you enter is saved inside the form — including, of course, any signatures.

✔ **Serious, heavy-duty annotations? Try iAnnotate PDF** (www.branchfire. com/iannotate): If you're looking for a robust annotation app that can be used for everything from grading papers to marking up important business documents, then take a look at iAnnotate PDF (shown in Figure 9-8).

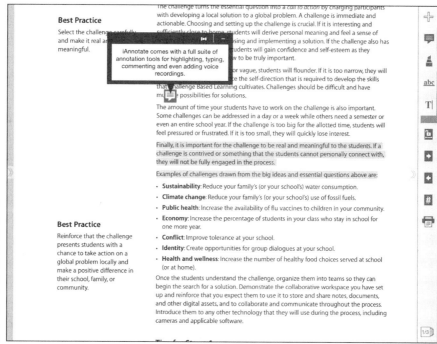

Figure 9-8: iAnnotate provides a robust set of features for heavier annotation needs.

iAnnotate provides a wide range of annotation features, including annotation tools such as a pen, highlighter, typewriter, stamps, notes, underline, strikethrough, photo, date stamp, and even voice recording.

- Read, mark up, and share PDF files, Word documents and more.
- Create custom stamps, including one for your signature.

- Organize, insert, and delete pages.

- Organize files with the graphical file manager.

- Use the navigation and search tools to find any text you need anywhere in your library.

✔ **Simple and effective? PDFpen is what you need** (`http://smilesoftware.com/PDFpen/index.html`): PDFpen (shown in Figure 9-9) lacks the organization and management features of apps like iAnnotate, but it provides all the features you'd need for annotation within a simple and effective interface. You can add text boxes, notes, comments, highlights, and strikethrough, for instance, and many other features make it simple to mark up any document you retrieve from the cloud.

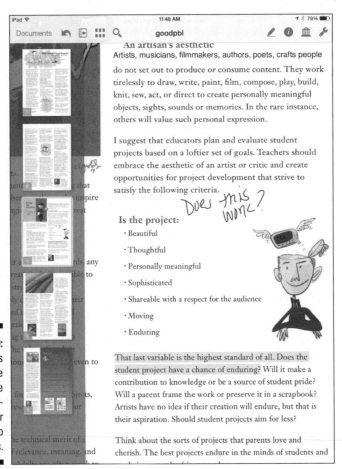

Figure 9-9:
PDFpen has a simple interface with powerful tools for marking up documents.

Looking for a free option for annotating PDFs? Adobe has released a version of its popular Acrobat Reader program for the iPad. In addition to opening and reading any PDF document, the free version also contains a number of helpful tools for annotating and highlighting text, adding comments, and inserting text. It even includes a freehand drawing tool for handwriting. Whether you need to fill out forms or mark up a document, Acrobat Reader will prove to be an excellent solution . . . at a price you can't beat!

Writing and Sketching

That virtual keyboard may not be a good fit for you. Maybe you tried using a Bluetooth keyboard. Some people still feel more comfortable writing, and when you start to look at the features included with the leading handwriting apps, you'll realize they offer so much more than just doodling a few squiggles on a page.

Touring Notability

When comparing the features of multipurpose handwriting apps, it's difficult to look past Notability (www.gingerlabs.com). Notability is a note-taking app for the iPad that gives you the power to integrate handwriting, typing, drawings, audio, pictures, and PDF annotation all into one document. It's easy to go from typing to sketching and then adding media to your page.

One of the killer features of Notability is the capability to add audio recordings that automatically link to your notes. Tap the microphone icon on the top toolbar to keep an audio track as you take notes. When you read your pages back, just tap a word to hear what was said at that very moment you were writing that note. How many times have you looked at your hastily scribbled pages, trying to decipher what you'd written? Was it exogenous zones or erogenous zones? Tap to listen to the audio, and it's easy to find out. You can also use the recording feature to add your own voice to notes and memos.

It's a wonderful tool for students in middle school through college and into the workplace. Whether you want to take notes, keep memos, or capture your own ideas, Notability has a rich set of features (see Figure 9-10) for any note-taking objective. And Notability can be an especially effective tool for people who have difficulties taking notes.

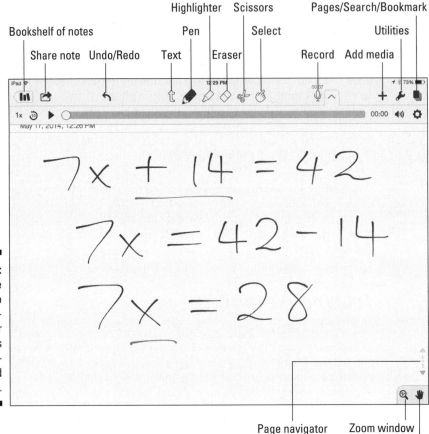

Figure 9-10:
Use
Notability to
take hand-
written or
typed notes
with syn-
chronized
audio.

Notability offers the following:

- ✔ **Full-featured handwriting:** Select from different paper and pen styles. Use the palm rest to make handwriting easier and prevent unwanted marks and smudges. You can even set handwriting to left-handed mode.

- ✔ **Zoom capability for more detail:** The zoom window helps you clearly draw every detail or take detailed notes. Change pen colors and widths easily.

- ✔ **Document markup:** The same tools that help you take beautiful notes in Notability equip you to annotate PDFs. You can import pictures or PDF files, and then you can highlight or take notes directly over them.

- ✔ **Word processing:** Notability isn't just for handwriting. Use your keyboard for typed text as well. It has many word-processing features such as font size and selection, spell check, bullets, numbering, bold, italic, underline, and more.

✔ **Flexibility:** Create notes that are as vivid, visual, and informative as required by the occasion.

- A scissors tool lets you move and even restyle objects.

- Enhance your notes by adding pictures from your photo library or iPad camera.

- Insert web clips, figures, or drawings to complement your notes. Don't worry; your text automatically flows around the images.

- Crop, resize, and draw on your images to make them more detailed.

✔ **Organization:** Organize your notes into subject folders. Within any note itself, tap the Page Navigator icon to scroll through your pages in a pop-up sidebar, rearrange them, or add and delete pages as needed.

Using Notability

I'm just as eager as you are to start using the app. The following sections break down using Notability into a four-step process.

Getting started

To create a new note, tap the Compose (pencil) icon on the right of the top toolbar in the Library. Tapping the Bookshelf icon within a note at any time returns you to the Library, and your note is automatically saved.

Choose a paper background by tapping the Utilities icon on the top toolbar and selecting the Paper option. Examples include graph paper, lined paper, canvas, colored paper canvas, and so on.

Writing, typing, sketching, and recording

Notability has a powerful set of tools that can accommodate all your note-taking needs and preferences. In the following list, I review some of your options:

✔ **Text:** You can type text notes using the following techniques:

- Tap the Text icon in the top toolbar, and then tap in the document wherever you want to type; the keyboard slides up.

- Tap the Font name icon to select your font, and use the icons to the right of it to change the color, size, and style.

- Create a text style by setting the font size, style, and color, and then tapping and holding a font preset button (the heart icons with an A, B or C).

- Tap the Bullet icon on the right of the toolbar to format items in a bulleted or numbered list.

✔ **Keyboard toolbar customization:** You can customize your keyboard toolbar (see Figure 9-11) by tapping and holding the toolbar above the keyboard to open the tool window. Simply drag the tools onto the keyboard toolbar to create your ideal tool set, including font presets, bold, italic, underline, cursor controls, and bullet or numbered outline styles. Press Done when you're finished.

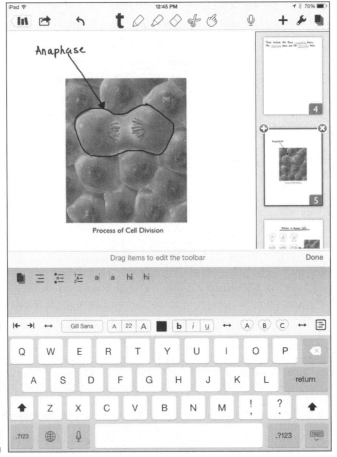

Figure 9-11:
Customize
the Notability
keyboard
toolbar with
your favorite
functions.

✔ **Finger or stylus writing:** Select the Pencil tool by tapping the Pencil icon on the top toolbar. Tap it a second time to select color and line width, and then proceed to write with your finger or stylus.

Notability improves the look of your handwriting, giving you smooth and organic-looking strokes, as shown in Figure 9-12. It mimics the way a marker writes by creating lines with varying thickness that give you the tapered look of a natural marker stroke.

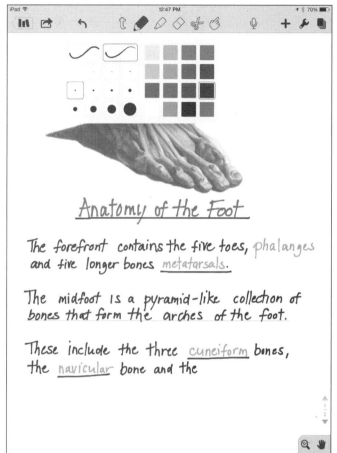

Figure 9-12:
Double-tap
the Pencil
icon to
select the
color and
line width.

- ✔ **Highlight:** Tap the Highlighter icon to draw attention to information in your note. As with the pencil, tapping it a second time displays options for color and width.

- ✔ **Eraser:** Tap this icon to erase handwriting or drawings. It removes whole strokes as a single object, which makes it quick to erase but doesn't allow fine control.

- ✔ **Scrolling:** Use two fingers to scroll through a note.

- ✔ **Palm Rest:** Tap the Palm Rest icon to lay the heel of your hand on the iPad without making marks on the page. See Figure 9-13. One superb addition to this tool is that you can adjust the palm rest to a height that suits you by tapping and dragging the icon with three horizontal bars on the top right of the palm rest.

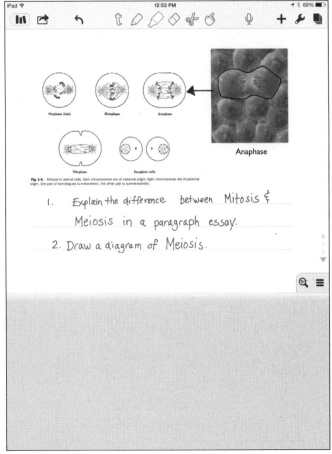

Figure 9-13:
Adjust the
palm rest
height by
tapping and
dragging the
horizontal
bars icon.

✔ **Zoom:** Tap the Zoom icon to open the Zoom window and a zoom *target box* (see Figure 9-14) that you can move around the page to magnify any area. Write or sketch in the magnified zoom window to gain finer control over handwriting, sketching, filling out forms, adding notes or details on a drawing, or writing small captions. Resize the zoom target box by dragging the lower-right handle.

✔ **Cut/copy/paste:** Tap the scissors icon and circle an area with your finger or stylus to cut, copy, paste, and restyle content you have handwritten or sketched. Move the selected object anywhere on the page, or tap it to display menus with options to cut, copy, or change styles such as color and line width.

✔ **Left-hand capability:** Don't fret if you're a lefty — you haven't been forgotten. Tap the Library icon, and then tap the Settings icon on the bottom toolbar. Scroll down to the Other Settings section (using two fingers, of course) — and smile as you turn on Left Handed Mode.

Figure 9-14:
The Zoom box magnifies areas of your note that require finer details.

✔ **Synchronized audio recording:** The audio recording feature really makes Notability stand out from many other handwriting apps. It's a simple way to listen to important audio that's synchronized with the notes you were taking at the very same time!

• Tap the microphone icon to start recording at any time, and tap it again when you're ready to stop the recording.

Any notes taken during a recording are synchronized to the audio taking place at the same time.

• Tap the Playback button to listen to the recording. After recording, you can tap the down arrow next to the microphone and hear what was being said at any point in your notes. I know I'm repeating myself, but I'm awed by the possibilities this feature presents. Whether you have attention deficit problems, difficulty hearing or processing audio, or just plain don't understand anything being said during an important class, you'll absolutely love the recording option.

Playback options include volume control, fast forward, rewind, and deletion of recordings.

✔ **Page Navigation:** Tap the Pages icon on the right of the top toolbar to open the Page Navigation tool, as shown in Figure 9-15. A window slides open along the right of your screen, with thumbnails of all the pages in your document. Add, delete, or reorder pages, or simply tap to go to a specific page.

Figure 9-15: The Page Navigator slides open to display thumbnails of all your pages.

✔ **Media insertion:** Tap the Insert Media + icon on the top toolbar to insert web clips, photos, figures, and sticky notes into your document.

- You can write or draw over the top of any media. It's a great way to add notes and little captions for additional detail on images.

  Text automatically wraps around images.

- Tap any media object to select it and display the menus. Tap Edit to enter the figure editor, where you can crop, or use a pen to edit your media. Tap the caption field at the bottom of the image to insert your caption text.

- Tap Stickies and insert a sticky note anywhere on the page, or tap the Figures option and use the image editor to create and insert shapes.

- Tap the Web Clip icon to open a browser and select a page to insert into your notes. After you've inserted it, tap the clip and select Edit to add notes and highlights.

Insert a Sticky and select the Typing Sticky as a great way to fill out forms, annotate PDFs, or add text that you can easily move around anywhere on the page. Tap the Insert Media + icon, and then tap to select Stickies and then Typing. You can tap anywhere on the page to insert your text box, and then start typing in it. Grab the corner handles if you need to make it larger or smaller, and tap and drag the lined handle icon to drag to an exact spot on your page.

Importing, annotating, and sharing notes

From the Library, tap the curved arrow Import icon on the right of the top toolbar to bring in an existing file from a connected cloud service.

Use Notability's tools for annotating your document, including writing, typing, highlighting, and adding media.

To share from within a note, tap the curved arrow Share icon, and choose whether to email, print, or upload to a cloud service, where you can select the specific folder and file type. To share from the Library, select the notes to share by tapping them and follow the same process.

Organizing your notes library

I could go into mind-numbing detail on this topic, but you probably need a break and a cup of tea as much as I do. Tap and hold, drag, and look for the Edit button in the top-left corner of the Library. Here's a short breakdown that you can read while your tea water is boiling:

✔ All the organization takes place in the Library, as shown in Figure 9-16.

✔ Set up Categories that contain Subject folders. Your notes are stored in the Subject folders. Add and delete as needed. Your subject folders are listed and color coded in the left column. Tap the Edit option in the top-left corner above the list of Subjects to edit their settings. Tap the gear icon next to a Subject to rename it, change background color or icon, or even to password-protect it.

✔ Notes are filed in folders and listed on the right side with thumbnails.

✔ Add, delete, file, sort, rename, search, move . . . it's all there and pretty intuitive to use.

On that note (pun intended), it sounds like the water is boiling. Enjoy!

When the iPad first came out, many critics used to proclaim that whatever was created on the iPad stayed on the iPad. Backing up content from different apps was quite a painful procedure. Thankfully, that's become a lot simpler as the technology has matured, and Notability provides several options for securing content and accessing it on other devices. Tap the Settings icon on the bottom toolbar under your list of Subjects. Select and turn on the iCloud option to save your content to your iCloud account and synchronize it to your other devices (note that you have to turn on iCloud saving in your Settings app and select Notability under Documents and Data). You can also tap the Manage Accounts option to connect Notability with cloud services such as Google Drive and Dropbox, and then use the Auto-backup option to save your files to those services in Notability format or as PDF files.

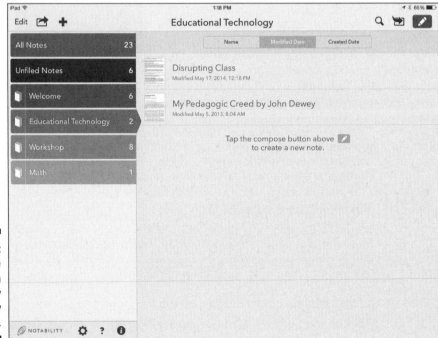

Figure 9-16:
Notes are organized in the Library by category and subject.

Chapter 10

Becoming a Digital Author

*R*emember those days you'd come to school with your assignment on a large sheet of cardboard, little pictures stuck randomly around it and punctuated with large headings you wrote with bold markers? If you think I am going to dissuade you from encouraging your students to create those types of projects, you are wrong. There's always a place for such hands-on work, and you should continue to encourage it wherever appropriate. As parents and educators, however, it's also important for us to recognize that the landscape is changing at a rapid rate and that there are some compelling, digital alternatives that need to be incorporated into education.

The whole notion of writing is changing. Being an author used to mean having an agreement with a book publisher to distribute and sell your book. Don't get me wrong: It's still a good idea for those of us in that situation! The publishing market, however, is in a period of transition: We're seeing a range of tools that make it simple to create and publish your own digital content. Those tools range from simple blog formats where you can post opinions and articles to full-blown book authoring tools that enable any prospective author to create a book and use online publishing channels to sell and distribute it.

Anyone, of any age, can now create and distribute books — textbooks, storybooks, personal accounts, class assignments, and more. The whole notion of publishing is changing with the amazing growth of the Internet and technologies such as social networking. These days, anyone — even the students in your class — can express herself to a worldwide audience. Tools exist to make the process simple and to incorporate digital publishing into any grade level and academic discipline.

This chapter focuses on the different ways you can use these book authoring tools — from the simpler apps that empower young children to create and distribute their work to the more robust tools that can create full-blown interactive and multimedia experiences.

With a little enthusiasm, creativity, and resolve, today may be the day you start helping your students develop their voices as expressive writers. In the immortal words of Mark Twain, "Apparently there is nothing that cannot happen today." (Well, he also said, "Cauliflower is nothing but cabbage with a college education," but I couldn't find a way to work that quote into the paragraph.)

Choosing an E-Book Format

I admit. It's confusing. You have Pages documents that won't open in Microsoft Word. Then there are Microsoft Word documents that don't open in older versions of Word itself. You have HTML files that look all messed up wherever you open them. And, of course, PDF files . . . well, nobody wants you messing with their formats.

You're already having a hard enough time handling the different programs and files you have on your computer, and now I start tossing in new terms such as *e-books* and *iBooks*. Well, don't throw this p-book (yes, that stands for *paper book)* at me quite yet. Give me a moment to take a stab at explaining the various terms to you.

It's important to understand the difference because it helps determine your options in creating e-books — and other digital files — and the apps you'll use when reading them. I'll take a stab at clarifying some of the common terms:

- ✔ **Documents:** Unless they are very basic text files, most documents are associated with editing software. The most common formats include Word documents and, to a lesser degree, Pages documents. They are primarily designed to be opened and edited within the software that created them — a fact we all encounter when we get that all-important email attachment we can't open.

- ✔ **PDF files:** Also known as Acrobat files, they share a common formatting standard used by the Adobe Acrobat software. Generally, anything that can be printed can be turned into an Acrobat document. PDF files are easily distributed and read by anyone who has the free Acrobat reader on her computer.

Both word-processing documents and PDF files are essentially designed to be printed on paper. Of course, they can be read onscreen, but the paper size and formatting options are directed at printed output. Then along came e-books.

✔ **E-books:** An e-book can simply be the digital version of a printed book, or it can be a lot more. The defining element of an e-book is that it's designed to be read on a computer or mobile device. E-books can normally be purchased and/or distributed online.

Many e-books are PDF files or in the ePub format, which is an open standard designed to work across a variety of reading devices. Traditionally, e-books were just text and images; many now incorporate multimedia and interactive elements. They provide a pleasant screen reading environment, with tools for changing colors, text size, searching, bookmarking, and more.

✔ **iBooks:** Apple's e-book reading app, iBooks opens books made with iBooks Author, ePub books, or PDF documents. Of course, it also links to the iBookstore, where you can purchase and download e-books.

So if you want to create e-books, you have a variety of options. You can turn an existing document into an e-book, or you can use a variety of apps to create e-books — from the very simplest levels you might use in lower grades all the way up to sophisticated multimedia and interactive books that older students or teachers might consider. Options abound.

Distributing Documents for E-Readers

One simple way to distribute content is to create any document and convert it to a PDF file. Distribute it via email or the Internet; just about any e-reader will open it.

Add your PDF documents (and ePub) books on to your iPad in the following ways:

✔ Drag and drop them into the Books Library in iTunes on your computer. Select your device in the sidebar and then click the Books tab. You see your content listed there. Check the books you want to sync and click Sync to move them onto your iPad.

✔ Use the Open In function on your iPad to open the document in iBooks from any email or app. Tap and hold the attachment for a few seconds and then choose Open in iBooks (see Figure 10-1) from the pop-up menu that appears.

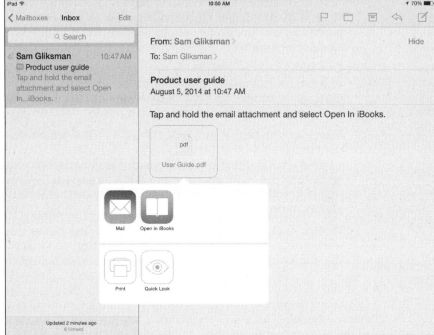

Figure 10-1:
PDF files
can be
opened and
added to
your iBooks
library.

Creating a standard text document and turning it into an e-book is quick, simple . . . and sooo 20th-century. Take a little stroll on the wild side and try some more adventurous alternatives. A growing number of apps are designed specifically to create e-books that integrate interactivity and multimedia. I review a couple of the most popular ones in the following sections.

Becoming a Book Creator

Book Creator is one of the simplest iPad apps for creating your own e-books. It's a great solution for a range of projects from children's picture books to cookbooks, storybooks, and more. Your completed book can be read in iBooks and sent to family and friends, or you can even submit it to be published in the iBookstore. Maybe the next J.K. Rowling is sitting at the back of that second-grade class you're teaching!

Book Creator, shown in Figure 10-2, is a simple app to use, and it's a great tool for school projects. It uses a fixed-layout format for its e-books. In practice, that means that the author controls the exact design and position of every element on the page. You create each page with elements that have a fixed position and size that cannot be changed. The reader can usually zoom in and out but can't change settings such as the text size and have elements reformat and flow onto other pages. It's well suited to shorter books with a lot of images.

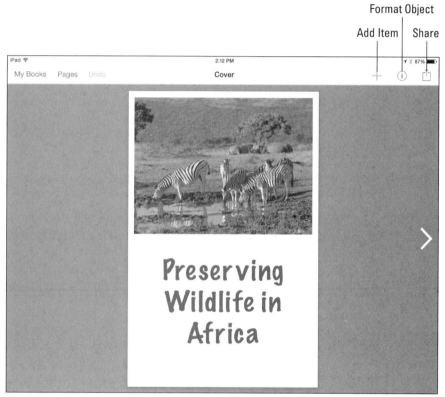

Format Object

Add Item | Share

Figure 10-2:
Students of all ages can use Book Creator's tools.

The basic steps involved in creating a book are simple; just follow these steps:

1. **Tap the + sign on the opening screen.**

2. **When prompted, choose a portrait, landscape, or square size for your new book.**

3. **Book Creator starts you on the cover page of your new book. Tap the Add Item icon (refer to Figure 10-2) to insert text such as your book title or an image or video from your photo library.**

4. **(Optional) Insert a soundtrack or record an introduction by tapping the Add Item icon and selecting Add Sound; tap the red Start Recording button (shown in Figure 10-3), and then begin your narration.** The Add Item menu also offers a Pen tool that you can use for writing or sketching on the page.

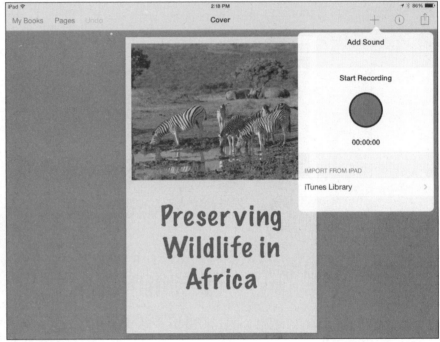

Figure 10-3:
Record a narrative for your book or add music from your iTunes library.

5. **Tap the Next button on the right side of the screen to start editing your pages.**

The Pages button on the top left of your display enables you to add, edit, and organize your pages as needed:

- *Pages can contain text, images, video, sketches, or embedded sound.* Insert them anywhere on the pages by tapping the Add Item icon on the top toolbar.

- *Format objects.* Simply tap and select an object such as text; then tap the Format Object button (refer to Figure 10-2) to change the font, color, alignment, and more. You can also move, resize, and rotate objects on the page.

- *Record any sound or narration directly, using the app's built-in audio recorder.* It drops a little speaker icon on the page, which plays when tapped. You can also import audio from your iTunes library.

- *Guidelines and snap positioning help you lay out and align objects on the page.*

- *Reorder pages.* Tap the Pages button and tap Edit; then drag pages by their lined icons in the right column.

Your book is automatically saved on your iPad.

6. **Tap the My Books button (in the top-left corner of the Book Creator interface).**

   You're returned to the My Books page (your Book Creator library). As you scroll through your books, notice the row of icons under each one.

7. **Tap the Share icon to see the Export options (shown in Figure 10-4):**

   - Email your books.

   - Print using AirPrint or a printer app.

   - Send it to iTunes on your computer as an e-book or PDF.

   - Open it in any of a slew of other apps as an e-book or PDF document.

   - Export your book as a PDF document. Remember, however, that your PDF document cannot support any video or audio elements.

Figure 10-4:
Export options for Book Creator books.

REMEMBER

Book Creator uses a fixed layout format. For example, you can't create a text box on one page and have the text automatically flow to a box on a different page. Readers won't have the flexibility to change colors and fonts. It's targeted primarily at the creation of shorter books with images and short blocks of text rather than longer, text-based books.

ScribblePress for Beginning Authors

ScribblePress is an app that gives kids the tools to author, illustrate, share, and publish an e-book. When you open the app, note that it is divided into three sections: My Books, My Drawings, and Gallery, as shown in Figure 10-5. My Books and My Drawings include your unique creations, whereas Gallery is stocked full of books created and shared by others that you can download and read. Who knows — maybe you'll decide to share some of your own.

Figure 10-5:
Scribble-
Press is
divided into
sections
for My
Books, My
Drawings,
and Gallery.

It's similar to Book Creator in the sense that it uses fixed layout pages that include text and image elements, and you can add and edit pages as needed. It doesn't have the audio capabilities included in Book Creator, but it does offer the following features:

- ✔ **Story templates:** When you start a new book, you can create your own story from a blank book or select among 50 story templates — as shown on the left in Figure 10-6 — to get you started.

- ✔ **Drawing tools:** You can create and save your own drawings in the My Drawings sections or draw within the pages of your book as you create it. The app contains a cool set of drawing tools, including markers of various colors and types, as shown on the left in Figure 10-6.

Figure 10-6: The Scribble-Press drawing tools enable you to add sketches to your story.

✔ **Stickers, stamps, and photos:** Select and add images from a collection of stickers and stamps. Take photos or choose one from one of your existing photo albums.

✔ **The capability to add a book summary and short author bio:** Write a short synopsis of the book to let potential readers know what to expect, and include a short biography of yourself as well.

When your e-book is finished, you can

✔ **Send it to iBooks:** When you tap the icon to Send to iBooks, the app converts your book to an ePub file. You then can open it in iBooks or any other e-reader app that supports ePub.

✔ **Share it or print it:** You can upload your book to the Gallery for others to read or order printed copies from ScribblePress for a fee.

When sharing a book, you're presented with a Sharing Policy form onscreen. You're required to select one box to verify that you're either over 13 years old or the parent/guardian of the author. A second check box asks you to agree that you have verified that there's no personal information or photos included in the book. It's obviously important to take precautions whenever sharing anything in a public forum, but it's also simple for anyone to select the boxes and upload the book. I recommend using it as an opportunity to discuss important issues of privacy and public sharing of information on the Internet.

Publishing with iBooks Author

Now it's time to bring out the heavyweights. Apple released its iBooks Author software in January 2012 as a means for creating and publishing a new generation of e-books that integrate different media, interactive elements, 3D objects, and more. It's designed to differentiate e-books by including compelling, interactive content that was never possible on the printed page. It's no coincidence that Apple announced the release of iBooks Author at the same event that introduced the new iBookstore category for e-textbooks. One of the more popular applications of iBooks Author is intended to be the creation and self-publishing of textbooks for the education market. The software works on Mac computers running the Mac OS X operating system (10.7.2 or higher) and is available for free download in the Mac App Store.

Creating interactive multimedia e-books could certainly be the subject of a book all its own — an e-book of course. I only scratch the surface of it in this section. The interface will be somewhat familiar to anyone who has used word processing or presentation software, and it's particularly close in nature to Apple's Keynote presentation software, as you can see in Figure 10-7.

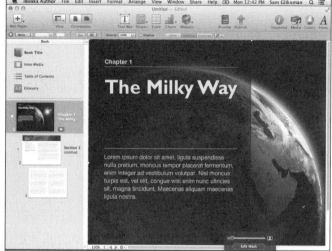

Figure 10-7:
The iBooks
Author
interface is
similar to
the Keynote
interface.

The highlights of iBooks Author include the following:

✓ **Templates:** Start by selecting a template (see Figure 10-8) that has predesigned layouts you can select and adapt.

Figure 10-8:
Start author-
ing your
e-book by
selecting a
style in the
Template
Chooser.

✔ **Text import feature:** You can import text from any Word or Pages documents directly into the Book Navigator.

✔ **Image implementation:** Drag and drop any images on to the page, and your text automatically flows around the object.

✔ **Widget power:** Including widgets for interactive photo galleries, movies, keynote presentations, animations, interactive images, and 3D objects (see Figure 10-9), this feature gives users the capability to create truly customizable objects in books. If you know some coding, you can even get your hands dirty creating HTML widgets that display custom content.

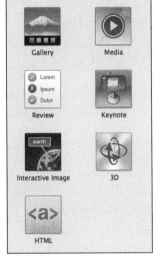

Figure 10-9:
The power
of iBooks
Author
comes from
the use of its
interactive
widgets.

✔ **Chapter reviews:** Add chapter reviews for readers to measure their understanding. Question types include multiple choice, choose the correct image, label the image, or a mix of all three. What's more, authors can include up to six alternative answers to each question.

✔ **Publishing:** Preview your e-book on your iPad. When you're ready to publish, you can submit it to the iBookstore for purchase or free download. You can also export and share your e-book on iTunes U or give it to anyone with an iPad. You can review the conditions and common distribution questions on the Apple support website at `http://support.apple.com/kb/HT5071`.

Chapter 11

The Mathematical and Scientific iPad

*W*e tend to split science and humanities as though they were separate branches of life. But no matter what profession we choose — artist, plumber, historian, or salesman — we all use some form of scientific inquiry in our daily lives. We learn about the world around us through the same vehicles of experimentation, trial, error, and experience. We use methods of scientific inquiry to learn experientially.

Today's interconnected world demands that the doctor, engineer, pharmacist, and scientist increasingly master skills that used to be classified within the domain of the arts. Skills such as communication, presentation, effective writing, among others, are now vital to all walks of life. In addition, scientific inquiry, critical thinking, exploration, and experimentation have never been more important skills than they are today. If we expect to produce independent learners who can thrive in a society that's constantly changing, it's vital that we educators search for opportunities to hone those skills in our students at every turn.

More than any other academic disciplines, science and math draw their meaning by relating to life in the "real" world outside the classroom. They seek to understand the world by inquiry, observation, and investigation. Giving children ample opportunities to develop sound investigative skills at an early age is essential to nurturing their ability to think critically and scientifically as they get older. Reading and learning about plants in a book doesn't really measure up to the experience of planting seeds and watching them grow. If you discuss the various needs of plants and then hypothesize and experiment with differing amounts of sunlight and water, you create an environment of experiential learning that imbues children with firsthand observation and understanding of what it takes for a living organism to grow.

Granting students the freedom to inquire and explore makes them the investigators of life's mysteries. In the process, they're sharpening their all-important critical and creative thinking skills. Technology offers fantastic opportunities for the examination and analysis of real-world phenomena. Students can apply critical-thinking skills by asking questions, then using technology to test and gather data that can be analyzed to arrive at appropriate answers. Technology becomes the enabler that facilitates student exploration and learning.

That's the focus of this chapter. You can find numerous apps that deliver factual content about botany or drill for understanding of rules in algebra, but I'd like to focus on how you can use technology to have students experience that knowledge from the inside out. The chapter focuses less on apps and instead discusses the "application" of mobile technology within a more inquiry-based approach to science and math education. It should be fun!

Whether it's geometry, physics, or chemistry, scientific method starts with research, discussion, and the development of a hypothesis about the phenomenon being examined. A substantial amount of space in this book is devoted to research, communication, organization, and sharing of information — all important elements in the research and development stage. You start by jumping to the next step: using the iPad for investigating and gathering data for analysis.

Exploring Tools for Scientific Inquiry

The iPad is an ideal tool for investigation. The capability to be mobile and communicate over a Wi-Fi or Bluetooth connection makes it possible to gather data with external sensors that send data to an app on the iPad. Here's a small sampling of some of the possibilities.

SPARKvue HD and PASCO Probes

Integrate sensor-based data collection into the learning experience with the SPARKvue HD app for the iPad, which communicates with any of the 70 sensors from PASCO (www.pasco.com). The connection between the sensor and iPad is facilitated by PASCO's AirLink 2 Bluetooth interface, which enables you to connect a sensor; then it wirelessly sends data to the SPARKvue HD app on your iPad. See Figure 11-1.

Measure a wide range of phenomena, including pH, temperature, force, carbon-dioxide level, and much more. Use sensors in experiments — anything from weather to cellular respiration, from sound levels in an elementary school classroom to advanced optics in physics. In addition, you can capture images with the iPad cameras and use SPARKvue HD's image analysis capabilities. Or collect and display live acceleration data with the iPad internal accelerometer.

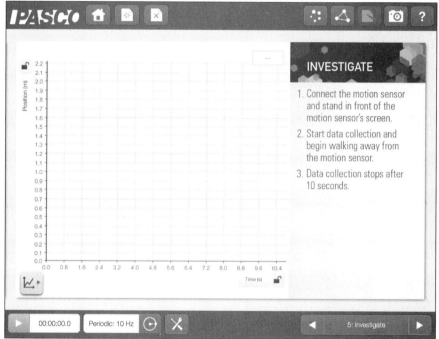

Figure 11-1: PASCO probes collect and transmit external data to the SPARKvue HD app.

ProScope Mobile

ProScope Mobile is a wireless hand-held digital microscope for iOS devices (www.bodelin.com/proscope/proscope-mobile). ProScope sends live video and captured stills to multiple iOS devices simultaneously via Wi-Fi. Use ProScope in the field, classroom, or lab to zoom in on any object of interest and project it to a host of devices. ProScope lenses vary from 0–10X to 400X.

ProScope Mobile creates its own Wi-Fi network and can be used simultaneously with up to 254 iOS devices. ProScope Mobile works with the AirMicroPad app on the iPad.

Users can view live images, freeze them, and capture them. Imagine a classroom filled with iPads. Each student would simultaneously see what the teacher is showing with the ProScope Mobile. When the teacher taps the Capture button on the ProScope Mobile, that image is captured in the photo album of each student's iPad at the same time. Students can then study and mark up that image.

Cameras, apps, and more

Your iPad comes equipped with perfect tools for investigating and recording phenomena:

- ✔ Use the camera to snap events and video processes.
- ✔ Record notes in any of the many note-taking apps.
- ✔ Record live observations and images as students gather data out in the field and use the iPad's GPS capability to log the information in a navigation app such as MotionX GPS.
- ✔ If you're using any of the sensors or hardware listed earlier, they generally come with their own iPad apps to record, analyze, and present data in multiple representations.
- ✔ If you're using the old tried-and-true methods of observation and documentation of data, you'll want a way to record and analyze the data you collect. Use a spreadsheet such as Numbers to record and statistically analyze the data. Use the charts feature to present your data visually.
- ✔ Presentation apps such as Keynote, Explain Everything, and iMovie are ideal for presenting a dynamic and media-based summary of your findings.

The Investigative iPad Classroom

This section includes a few short samples of how iPads were used in science and math classrooms to research and construct knowledge. They are cited less as specific lesson plans to follow and more as examples of how the iPad can be integrated as a tool into processes of research and scientific method. I'm sure one or two may inspire you to come up with your own ideas.

I'm extremely grateful to the wonderful and talented group of educators that have contributed to this list of sample lessons. Special thanks to Dr. Randy Yerrick and his team at State University of New York at Buffalo for the wonderful work they're doing and the projects they have submitted. I'd also like to thank Julie Hersch at Temple Israel; Leah LaCrosse at Huron City Schools; Julie Garcia at Innovation Middle School; Mary O'Brien at Manchester Elementary; Michael Mohammed at Brookfield Central High School; Bridget Mahoney at William Green Elementary School; and Jane Ross at Sinarmas World Academy.

Engineering a solar oven

Submitted by	Leah LaCrosse, Huron City Schools, Huron, OH
Grade level	5th- to 6th-grade Math
Objectives	Design a solar oven that would best conduct and retain heat
Apps/tools	PASCO temperature sensor, SPARKvue HD app
Materials needed	Alternative recycled materials for building a solar oven

Students were given various energy forms (light, sound, heat, electricity) to explore through demonstrations, text, videos, and apps. After gaining background information in the energy forms, students designed investigations to test various related concepts. With some guidance in establishing variables and gathering materials, students used the PASCO sensors with the SPARKvue HD app to test their questions. One question they explored related to finding the most efficient materials for conducting and retaining heat in a solar oven.

Students created different solar ovens using a variety of recycled materials. Their goal was to create an oven that would heat up quickly and stay warm. They were exploring insulation and energy transferring, and designed test conditions that would return valid test data while controlling the variables in their investigations.

Students decided to shine two large lights directly on the solar oven for three minutes. A PASCO sensor was placed in the oven to record the increase in temperature. The data was transmitted wirelessly to the SPARKvue HD app, which was running on an iPad and projecting on a large screen for all students to observe. The students then turned off the lights and recorded the oven's temperature for three minutes to evaluate the rate of cooling. The experiment was repeated for each solar oven. The SPARKvue HD app generated a simple graph that demonstrated changes in temperature. This provided students with a visual basis for the comparison of their test results.

Students wrote about their experiments in their personal Science blogs and used the class Twitter account to share the results.

Finding the effect of watering solutions on germinating beans

Submitted by	Sam Gliksman
Grade level	4th- to 6th-grade Science
Objectives	Learn to measure and collect data about botany and plant growth, and learn simple techniques for statistical mapping and mathematical analysis.
Apps/tools	iPad 2 (or higher), time-lapse photography app such as Animate It!, iPad stand, Numbers app
Materials needed	Packet of mung beans, four glass jars or beakers filled to 75-percent capacity with sterilized potting soil, tap water, salt, dish detergent, coffee powder, four 100-mL beakers, one measuring cylinder, one digital weighing scale, black marker and/or labels

This experiment utilizes time-lapse video (see Figure 11-2) to test how different solutions used to water plants impact their growth. The results are measured and recorded by students while also being captured on video.

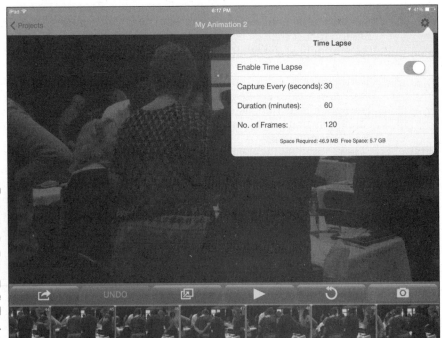

Figure 11-2:
Use the time-lapse feature in Animate It! by setting the time interval and duration.

The following points outline the process:

- ✔ The independent variable is the solution used to water the plants — plain water, coffee-and-water mixture, salt water, and water-and-detergent solution.

- ✔ The dependent variable is the growth of the mung-bean plants. This is determined by measuring the height of the plants every day.

- ✔ The constants (control variables) are the size of the container, the amount and concentration of the various solutions added daily, the amount of sunlight, and the temperature of the environment (room temperature).

The following steps outline the process:

1. **Prepare the jars.**

   Fill the four glass jars or beakers three-fourths full with the sterilized soil. Plant 12 mung beans in each pot, and allow them to germinate for five days, using the same amount of water on each plant. (You need ten seeds to germinate; add two extra just in case some don't germinate. When you are ready to record your data, make sure you have only ten germinated beans.)

2. **Set up the iPad and the app for recording the plant development.**

   Plug in the iPad, mount it on a stand, and set up your time-lapse app. Set the time lapse to take one picture every five minutes. For the first five days, you may choose to do a close-up of just one of the plants to capture the mung-bean germination in full close-up. The resultant time-lapse movie is truly magical.

   After the first five days of germination, you need to have a clear view of all four plants so that you can compare the growth of the plants and the effect of the different solutions. Make sure that you are looking at them from the same angle so that perspective will not be a factor.

3. **Water the plants.**

   Water the four plants with only tap water for the first five days, allowing the seeds to germinate. After five days, record the average heights in a spreadsheet in the Numbers app. Discuss the meaning of "average" growth and how it can be calculated in the spreadsheet. Obtain the average height by measuring the height of the ten plants in each pot, adding them up, and dividing by 10.

4. **Prepare the variable solutions.**

   Prepare your four solutions in the 100-mL (milliliter) beakers. For the coffee mixture, add 10 g (grams) of coffee to 100 mL of water, and label it Coffee. For the detergent mixture, mix 10 mL of detergent to 100 mL of water, and for the saline solution, add 1 g of salt to 100 mL of water. Label each beaker accordingly. (You could also prepare enough solution in advance for all ten days by preparing a liter of each of the mixtures.)

5. **Use the variable solutions on the plants.**

Label the four plants Water, Coffee, Detergent, and Saline. Over the next ten days, water the pots once a day with 100 mL of each solution, according to the labels on the pots. Make sure you turn the plants halfway through the experiment period to ensure that each side of the plant is getting adequate sunshine. Check to make sure that the soil is not too soggy and there is no water pooling at the bottom of the container. Adjust the quantity of liquid if need be, but be sure to give each plant the same amount of liquid as the others.

6. **Measure and calculate the average height of the mung-bean plants every day for the next ten days.**

Record all calculations in a Numbers spreadsheet.

7. **Discuss linear graphs and their meaning; then have the students use the different growth rates to create a linear graph.**

Hunting for geometric treasure

Submitted by	Julie Hersch, Temple Israel of Hollywood Day School, Los Angeles, CA
Grade level	3rd- to 4th-grade Math
Objectives	Learn about the properties of concentric circles by relating them to objects in the real world.
Apps/tools	iPad 2 (or higher); presentation app such as Keynote, iMovie, or Explain Everything
Materials needed	Anything in the immediate environment

Using visual prompts, students broke into groups to discuss the properties that distinguish and define concentric circles. When they arrived at a consensus, students were sent on a scavenger hunt in pairs to find examples of concentric circles around campus and take photos of them. They came back with examples that included sink drains, door knobs, cart wheels, clocks, and more. Each group prepared a narrated presentation of the images they found. One interesting departure was that some students wanted to create a quiz with their images, some of which looked like concentric circles but weren't. As one example, there was a series of hula hoops hung up on a wall that looked like concentric circles but didn't actually have the same central point. It's interesting how students were able to deepen their knowledge of a concept by presenting patterns that actually didn't match the required definition.

Measuring projectile motion in Angry Birds

Submitted by	Michael Mohammed, Brookfield Central High School, Brookfield, WI
Grade level	11th- to 12th-grade Physics
Objectives	Apply and test the rules of projectile motion for a projectile launched at a given velocity and altitude.
Apps/tools	Vernier Video Physics app, Vernier Graphical Analysis app, Angry Birds app, Pages, Comic Life app
Materials needed	Tennis balls

The guiding question for this unit was whether the Angry Birds game accurately represents the physics behind projectile motion. The initial phase of the project familiarized students with the concepts of horizontal and vertical projectiles and the physics behind projectile motion. Students discussed alternative test conditions and settled on studying the motion of tennis balls thrown through the air as an example of how projectiles behave on Earth. The balls were thrown straight up to represent vertical projectiles, rolled off of a table to represent horizontal projectiles, and thrown up at an angle to represent angled projectiles.

To analyze the motion of the tennis balls on Earth, the students took video of the motion of the balls when thrown. Using the Video Physics app, they analyzed the motion in the video. They set up the scale and origin, and tracked the position of the ball by marking its position in the video as it moved. The program uses the tracking of position to create a position versus time graph for the students. Students further analyzed these graphs in the Graphical Analysis app where students created best-fit lines or curves and then generated the equations for these lines/curves. Upon analysis of the three videos, they developed their basic rules for projectile motion on Earth.

The next step was to see if the Angry Birds game followed these rules. The students re-created the vertical, horizontal, and angled projectile trials within the video game. While one student was conducting the trials, a second student took video of the trials (see Figure 11-3). It was important that the video was well framed to get results that could best be tracked and analyzed. Students again used the Video Physics app to track the motion of the bird in the game and the Graphical Analysis app to generate and analyze the graphs.

The students were required to produce a final product that answers the question posed at the start. They provided their hypothesis, their rules for projectiles on Earth, and the data/graphs that led to these rules. Next, they answered the guiding question and provided the evidence to support their conclusions. Students documented their work in apps such as Pages, and some even produced comics using the Comic Life app. Depending on the target audiences that students selected for the piece, projects ranged from articles in a professional science journal to storybooks for elementary school children.

Figure 11-3: Students track and analyze the rules of projectile motion used in Angry Birds.

Expressing learning through graphical representation

Submitted by	Julie Garcia, Innovation Middle School, San Diego, CA
Grade level	7th and 8th grades
Objectives	Understand and explain graphing, intercepts, and slope through the real-world application of eating a Tootsie Pop.
Apps/tools	Camera, Numbers, Explain Everything, and Clock

This lesson was broken down into four steps:

✔ **Data collection:** Students ate a Tootsie Pop, measuring its circumference after several one-minute intervals. After each minute, students documented the change by using dental floss and a ruler to measure the decrease in circumference of the Tootsie Pop. While collecting data, students used their iPads to gather photos that documented the process. Pictures were taken before, during, and after the process.

✔ **Data organization:** Students used the Numbers app to organize data and create a graph. Students generated a t-table and scatter plot.

✔ **Screen capture:** They took a screen shot to save the t-table and graph to the photo roll.

✔ **Screencast:** Students used a screencasting app such as Explain Everything (see Chapter 17) to display their images, interpret the chart/graph, and explain their observations and conclusions.

Using Minecraft to demonstrate area and perimeter

Submitted by	Mary O'Brien, Manchester Elementary, Manchester, ME
Grade level	3rd-grade Math
Objectives	Demonstrate understanding of the mathematical concepts of area and perimeter by independently creating 3D models in Minecraft Pocket Edition
Apps/tools	Minecraft Pocket Edition
Materials needed	Planning sheet

Many 3rd-grade students are avid players of Minecraft. In this project, 3rd-grade students demonstrated their understanding of the mathematical concepts of area and perimeter by independently creating 3D models using Minecraft Pocket Edition. The students were instructed to create a rectangular garden with an area of 24 square units and a pen for their animals with a perimeter of 20 units. Before beginning in Minecraft PE, the students used math manipulatives to find and list possible rectangular arrays for both given values. Once in Minecraft, students created a garden and a pen with the given area and perimeter. They created signs displaying the measurement of their gardens and pens, and then captured and submitted a screen shot of both projects upon completion.

Exploring properties of human-made materials

Submitted by	Dr. Randy Yerrick, professor of science education, State University of New York at Buffalo
Grade level	2nd- to 7th-grade Science
Objectives	Learn to collect microscopic data with tools, recognize patterns in human-made materials, develop hypotheses regarding why things are soft, and compare predictions of softness and observed patterns to offer explanations for why some objects are soft and others are not.
Apps/tools	ProScope Mobile for the iPad, AirMicroPad app
Materials needed	Tissues

Children are rarely asked to explore their own ideas in science. In this activity, students explored their own personal theories and offered supporting evidence through the digital microscope.

This activity began with a discussion surrounding the question "What makes things soft?" Students openly discussed their ideas and compared drawings and explanations. Then students were asked to predict what a softer tissue (Kleenex or Puffs brands) will look like compared to others. Students were sent around the school to collect samples and images of tissues from teachers' purses (with said teachers' permission, of course!), restrooms, and elsewhere.

To gather data, students needed to turn on the ProScope Mobile and entered the IP information into the AirMicroPad as they selected the new network. After launching the app, ProScope Mobile broadcasted live images (see Figure 11-4) to any iPad within range of its network.

To save time and necessary equipment, tissues can be gathered in advance, and students can log in to the ProScope Mobile network through the AirMicroPad so that all the children can take their own photos broadcasted live from ProScope.

After the photos were collected, a blind softness test was conducted by students to rank the tissues for softness. Students should see features such as consistency of fibers, size of fibers, and distance between fibers. They should see evidence that some of the common predictions have no basis. For example, students regularly predicted cottony and poofy tufts for soft tissues, for which there is rarely evidence. Students also predicted finding oils or lotions they had heard from advertisements, but there was rarely evidence of these qualities.

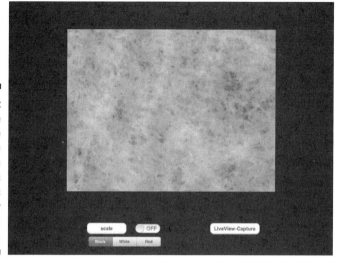

Figure 11-4:
The
ProScope
Mobile
microscope
broadcasts
live images
to any
iPad within
range.

Students should see that highly uniform, regular, and small threads make for soft tissues. This is analogous to thread count for sheets.

Designing dream-house blueprints

Submitted by	Bridget Mahoney, William Green Elementary School, Lawndale, CA
Grade level	5th-grade Math
Objectives	Apply Math concepts such as area and volume by designing a house.
Apps/tools	Notability app

This project was introduced after the completion of decimal, measurement, data, and geometry units in order to integrate and apply these math skills in a real-world scenario. Students were required to design a blueprint for a house, labeling the rooms and calculating dimensions, area, volume, and the cost of flooring and other costs (see Figure 11-5).

The teacher presented a model house design in order to demonstrate and explain the first steps: choosing a grid pattern and unit of measurement, designing and labeling rooms, color coding types of flooring, making a key, and labeling dimensions. Students worked at their own pace to create a wide variety of rooms and homes representing their interests. It was useful to point out and remind students to be as careful as possible when tracing lines for accuracy because most used their fingers, not styluses.

For the second part, the teacher modeled how to organize the information and calculations into a table. Students used scratch paper and pencils to calculate the area and volume. They recorded their answers in the table, being careful to use the correct units of measure. The color coding was replicated in the table as well, so they could tally total areas for each type of flooring and the volume of any water spaces.

Last, teacher and students searched the Internet to gauge the average price for each type of flooring. Students used scratch paper to figure out the various costs and, ultimately, the total flooring cost for their houses.

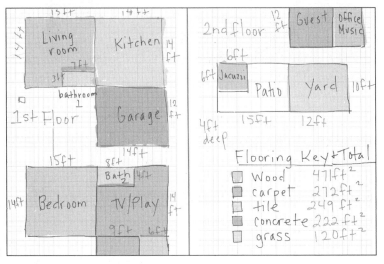

Figure 11-5: Students learn about volume and area by designing a blueprint for their dream house.

Exploring celestial mysteries

Submitted by	Dr. Randy Yerrick, State University of New York at Buffalo
Grade level	4th- to 12th-grade Astronomy
Objectives	Navigate the sky for recognizable celestial objects; identify and name constellations, stars, galaxies, and planets.
Apps/tools	Star Walk HD app

Some of the best science apps created for the iPad are those geared toward the teaching of Astronomy. An example is the Star Walk HD app, shown in Figure 11-6. One benefit of these apps is the integration with the built-in accelerometer and GPS information systems that enables users to simply point to the sky to obtain vast updated information about where they are looking. Celestial navigation is made simple through the interactive interfaces that allow the user to turn on and off the available layers of information when pointing at the night sky.

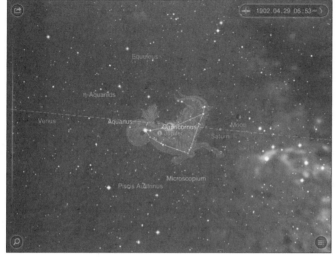

Figure 11-6: Explore the night sky with Star Walk HD, an interactive astronomy app.

Teaching with the Star Walk HD app can be as easy as taking an independent evening stroll with the self-lit app in hand and noting the relative positions of the objects in the sky. At the same time, this app adds a robust environment to explore important questions such as

✔ Does the sun really rise in the east? Does that change?

✔ Where do all the planets appear in the sky? How can you tell a planet from a star or galaxy?

✔ Can people in the Southern Hemisphere see the same stars as people in the Northern, Eastern, or Western hemispheres?

✔ Where do stars go during the day?

The power of this app can be seen in a very simple activity for children up through adulthood. Ask students, "How many planets are there? More important, how do you know?" Have students point out any objects in the sky that they think are planets, and before they use Star Walk, ask them to point to any they can see. Ask them to draw where those objects would appear at night, and explain what they would look like.

Creating narrative e-books to explain the body system

Submitted by	Jane Ross, Sinarmas World Academy, Banten, Indonesia
Grade level	4th-grade Science
Objectives	Demonstrate understanding of the human body system by creating a narrative story.
Apps/tools	Book Creator app, Keynote

Students were asked to show their understanding of a human body system by creating a narrative story that tells how a part of their chosen body system works. The students developed characters and learned to make cartoon characters that look like the different body parts. The story they created was narrative but based upon scientific fact.

The first part of this project was spent creating life-size displays of each body system. The students were asked to label all the parts of each system and create a personal definition of it by using two different resources. Next the students asked open-ended questions about their systems. These questions gave the teachers an understanding of the student's initial knowledge. Students were tasked with finding the answers. After the answers were found, the students were asked to write a formal explanation of the system and list their resources. They used movies, books, websites, and partnered with upper-grade students on some hands-on activities to further their understanding. All work was documented on class blogs.

Next the students watched the movie *Osmosis Jones* as an example of how a body system can be portrayed in a narrative. After watching the movie, they learned how to draw cartoons. Each student created three main characters and drew their cartoon images on paper. They learned how to accurately draw the different body parts yet make them cartoon-like by adding eyes and a mouth.

Story drafts were written and checked by a peer. A second draft was checked by teachers for grammar, language, and scientific accuracy. When the draft was approved, students divided up the story into slides in Keynote. The students created hand drawings, which were scanned for each character and page and layered together in Keynote. Finally the finished artwork was exported as images and imported into the Book Creator app (see Figure 11-7) on the teacher's iPad. Students took turns typing their text and recording themselves reading each page and added "About the Author" and "Behind the Story" sections. The books were published to the school online library and to the Apple iBooks Store.

Figure 11-7: Students create an e-book with a science-based narrative about the body system.

Exploration of invasive species

Submitted by	Dr. Randy Yerrick, State University of New York at Buffalo, Dr. Joseph Johnson, Edinboro University
Grade level	8th- to 12th-grade Science
Objectives	Learn that some species of plants and animals have a relatively recent history in some ecosystems and that native species can be edged out by certain selective traits that make them thrive over more established species. Learn to recognize invasive species and invent remedies and learn the consequences of some attempts to remedy the ecosystems.
Apps/tools	Leafsnap, iBird Lite, Google Earth, Dropbox, Keynote or Explain Everything, MyWorld GPS, ESRI database

Students should begin with a general photo shoot of different living environments around their school, home, and local parks. These photos should be posted in a shared folder accessible to all students. Students then use the iBird Lite and Leafsnap apps to look up the species of birds and trees local to their region. They should be able to find at least a few examples of invasive species with the help of the teacher or local environmental expert. Leafsnap has a built-in server connection to upload and identify leaf samples simply by their morphology. Using only the shape of the leaf as a clue, Leafsnap generates several suggested identifiable species and also uses the location services on the iPad to suggest local native species (see Figure 11-8). Other species are explorable through the database and reference book in Leafsnap. Leaf "collections" can be made and identified in this way without damaging trees and removing leaves. Only photos of leaves are required.

The following questions are discussed:

- ✔ What invasive species are most abundant? Plants, birds, or insects?

- ✔ What make a species invasive to this habitat?

- ✔ Do some invasive species do better in different parts of the United States?

- ✔ What invasive species cause the most trouble? What kinds of trouble/imbalances can they cause that are threatening to the ecosystem?

- ✔ Consider the example of the invasive species of chewing bark beetles common in the United States.

- ✔ Which survive better and which reproduce more than native species? Which are easier to exterminate? What other options are available to scientists/conservation experts?

- ✔ What are the natural consequences of each remedy?

Leafsnap has a built-in map system to map the number of species sampled and the density representation. Density is important in examining the threatened species. The Google Earth app allows a different view of flora from above, which may look different depending upon the date of the picture. MyWorld GPS, MotionX GPS, and ESRI offer layers, databases, and downloadable maps of different resolution to compare images over time. From these images, students can look for patterns of tree populations and make hypotheses about similarities and differences among the trees in different areas. Students should then follow up by actually visiting the area observed from above. Sample a variety of trees, identifying them via the Leafsnap app and recording numbers and density of the tree types. Different classes and groups of students can maximize their impact by looking at different areas and combining their data. Findings can be shared via a Keynote or Explain Everything presentation.

iBirds also has a database of photos, maps, bird calls, and songs from all over the U.S. and includes migratory maps as well. Students can use these to find that many common birds like finches, sparrows, and grackles are actually invasive species and opportunists.

Figure 11-8:
Take photos of leaves and use the Leafsnap app to help identify the plants.

Testing how sound travels through different mediums

Submitted by	Leah LaCrosse, Huron City Schools, Huron, OH
Grade level	5th- and 6th-grade Math
Objectives	Measure how different mediums affect the transmission of sound.
Apps/tools	PASCO sound sensor, SPARKvue HD app
Materials needed	Kitchen timer or metronome

Students explored how sound travels through different mediums, designing and controlling variables within an investigation. They used the PASCO sound sensor with the SPARKvue HD app on the iPad to test the sound of a kitchen timer as it traveled through solids, liquids, and gases. The sensor measured the sound and transmitted data wirelessly to the SPARKvue HD app on an iPad where it was recorded and graphed.

In order to test how sound travels through solids, the sensor was placed directly under a desk while the timer sat atop it. The sensor was sealed in a plastic bag and submerged into a tank of water to test the transmission of sound through liquids. Finally, the sensor was held next to the timer to test how sound travels through air.

Students also recorded each trial using iMovie to create a video highlighting their work. The movie was embedded in an e-book, which was shared and published through the Apple iBookstore.

Animating movement of plate tectonics

Submitted by	Holly Stabler, Donna Klein Jewish Academy, Boca Raton, FL
Grade level	5th-grade Science
Objectives	Research and demonstrate understanding of plate movements in different parts of the world.
Apps/tools	iMotion HD app
Materials needed	Play dough

The students studied five geographical areas of the Earth to learn about their distinctive plate movements. In the culminating activity, groups of students were assigned to one of the five areas of the world (Hawaii, Japan, California, Iceland, and the Himalayas).

They researched the geography of their areas, plate movement, and consequences of the movement in their areas. When their research was approved, the students were ready to create a storyboard for their animation. They drew a rough overview with six slides with details of how they wanted to present their animation. Students created objects out of different-colored play dough and placed them on a laminated background. The stop-motion animations were created with the iMotion HD app. The movements demonstrated were divergent and convergent boundaries, hot spots, and mountain building. Students took at least 100 photos, moving their play dough very slowly between each snapshot. The end product was a series of videos that were uploaded and shared online.

Additional Apps for Math and Science

The primary focus of this chapter is on processes that stress investigation, experimentation, and real-world application of scientific and mathematical principles. That isn't to say that there aren't many excellent apps that also provide important instruction, simulated experiences, opportunities for differentiated learning, and excellent game-based approaches to the learning of important principles.

The list of apps changes rapidly; you can refer to the updated recommended apps on `http://list.ly/people/SamGliksman` or at `http://iPadEducators.ning.com`. Here are a few to start with.

Frog Dissection

The ethics of animal dissection have been debated for quite some time. Calling itself the "greener alternative for teaching dissection in the classroom," the Frog Dissection app (see Figure 11-9) is geared toward middle-school students who are learning about organs and organ systems as part of their life-science curriculum.

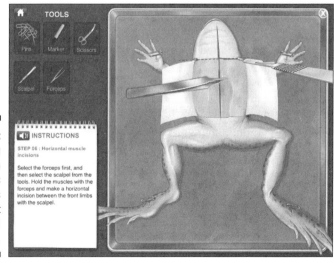

Figure 11-9: The Frog Dissection app enables students to dissect a virtual specimen.

Rather than dissect an actual animal, students dissect a virtual specimen with all the trappings that come with the real procedure. The app comes with all the dissection tools and detailed instructions to complete the procedure. When dissection is complete, the frog's organs are exposed for further study. With the aid of vivid 3D imagery, students are able to visualize the internal organs very effectively.

The Frog Dissection app is an excellent example of the educational promise offered by a rising tide of vivid, realistic simulations offering students experiences that may otherwise be unattainable.

DragonBox

With all due respect to the many excellent algebra teachers out there, many of us have had that teacher who droned on with endless explanations of formulas and solutions. DragonBox uses a game-based approach that has students solve puzzles by moving cards around onscreen. The principles required to solve the puzzles are based on . . . (keep this to yourself) fundamental algebraic concepts! Yes, you learn the principles of algebra by playing a fun game. That does seem to break all the rules, now, doesn't it? There are two versions of the game — one for ages 5 and up and a second for ages 12 and up.

Khan Academy

If you've been on a remote safari in the Panamanian jungle for the last few years and haven't heard of Khan Academy (see Figure 11-10), it contains more than 4,000 tutorial videos on a wide variety of topics in math and science. Granted, it isn't always Oscar-winning material, but when it's late at night and you really need help understanding Negative Exponent Intuition (seriously? I have no clue whatsoever . . .), you can just open the Khan Academy app and watch the video.

The nifty subtitles feature enables you to tap any line of dialogue listed and jump right to that point in the video.

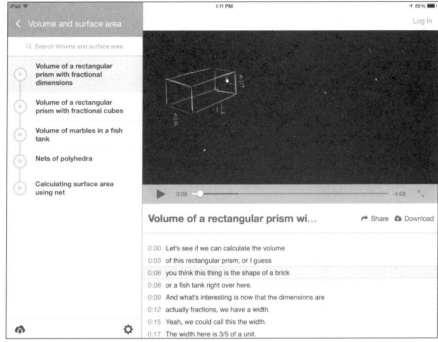

Figure 11-10:
The Khan Academy app contains more than 4,000 tutorials in math and science.

Monster Physics

With Monster Physics (see Figure 11-11), you can build your own virtual machines — from cars to rocket ships — using parts including wheels, wings, propellers, magnets, rockets, and claws. Kids learn physics by building and refining their inventions and completing missions.

Build virtual machines by combining different wheels, rockets, propellers, cannons, magnets, claws, wings, and more. Monster Physics renders your creation, and then you can actually operate it in real time. Drive your car, pilot your rocket into space, or try flying that thingamajig you built that doesn't look like it'll ever get off the ground! Learn physics by solving missions and building and refining your inventions. Monster Physics challenges you with 50 missions to solve, from simple to mind-bending. Many missions can be solved with a wide variety of solutions, enabling you to test all sorts of creative approaches.

If you believe, as I do, that having fun is a key element to learning, try building a contraption that solves some missions. You may learn a few key physics concepts along the way!

Figure 11-11:
Learn physics by building inventions and solving missions in Monster Physics.

Chapter 12

Using Assistive Technologies

Schools have traditionally adopted a "one size fits all" philosophy when it comes to mainstream education. Students are grouped by age and academic discipline and are then expected to use the same textbooks, sit in the same lectures, do the same homework, and submit the same (typically written) assignments. It's the easiest way to deal with large numbers of students, but it doesn't accommodate the sometimes vast differences in learning styles, preferences, and individual challenges faced by so many students in our schools. The past decade has seen a positive movement toward more differentiated learning, and many students now receive assistance and accommodations that enable them to learn more effectively and remain within standard school environments.

Apple has typically built features into its hardware to assist anyone who has difficulties with vision, hearing, communication, motor skills, and more. iPads are no exception, and the educational sector that has benefited most from iPad use is possibly special education. Built-in features for screen reading, support for playback of closed-captioned content, and other universal access features make it a natural for students with special needs. They simplify use for students with vision impairment or difficulty hearing, or those who have a physical disability. Further, as you discover throughout this book, there's a thriving market for every need, and there are certainly some standout apps that assist students with special learning needs.

In this chapter, I take a look at the assistive technology features built into the iPad. The four main categories of features are Vision, Hearing, Learning, and Physical & Motor. I also take a quick survey of some of the leading apps that are being used successfully by students with special education needs. One of the most satisfying benefits of these innovative new technologies is that you can leave that "one size fits all" model in your rear-view mirror and instead offer genuine assistance to students with learning challenges.

Accessibility Features on the iPad

The following steps show you how to find the iPad's accessibility features:

1. **Tap the Settings icon on your iPad Home screen.**

2. **Tap General in the menu on the left of the Settings screen.**

3. **Scroll down and tap Accessibility to access all the accessibility features (see Figure 12-1).**

   They are organized into Vision, Hearing, Learning, and Physical & Motor categories.

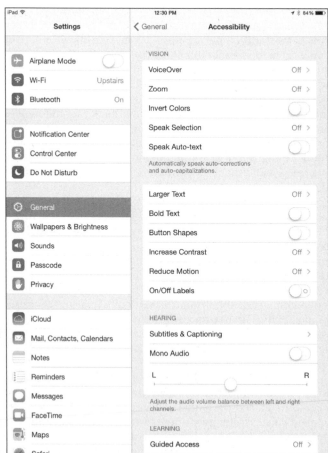

Figure 12-1:
The iPad's accessibility features are listed in the Settings page.

You can also activate VoiceOver using iTunes on your computer. Select your iPad in the Devices category and then click Configure Universal Access at the bottom of the Sync Options page.

A recent addition to the Accessibility options is Switch Control for the physically impaired. Switch Control allows you to use Bluetooth-enabled switch hardware to navigate onscreen items and perform tasks.

Vision

Featuring the VoiceOver screen reader, the iPad comes with many accessibility features that simplify the user interface for anyone with impaired vision.

VoiceOver

VoiceOver is a gesture-based screen reader that enables you to navigate and interact with the iPad even if you can't see the screen. For example:

- **Touch anything onscreen to hear a description of it.** Touch apps on the home page or elements in a web page or an app, and their text or functional description will be announced.

- **Double-tap to select.** A single tap selects an item and announces the description, and a double-tap activates the selected item.

- **Scroll with three fingers.** Scroll up and down or left and right by swiping with three fingers.

- **Drag your finger to hear about elements on any screen.** Drag your finger around the iPad Home screen, and as it passes over an app icon, VoiceOver announces the name of the app and reminds you to double-tap the icon to open it. The same applies to any web page or screen within an app. Place your finger in the top corner and drag it slowly around the page. VoiceOver helps you discover and understand the location and context of items on the screen.

- **Have notification alerts read aloud:** As you receive notifications onscreen, VoiceOver detects and announces them to you.

- **Receive system information:** VoiceOver also gives you information about your device. Tap the icon for battery level, network signal level, or time of day, and VoiceOver announces the data to you.

✔ **Adjust the speaking speed:** Have you ever had that friend who talks so quickly, you never understand a word that's being said? Even worse might be the person who drones along so slowly that it starts putting you to sleep. That'll never happen with VoiceOver: It allows you to set whatever speed best suits you. It also uses sound effects to announce events such as an app opening or when the iPad switches between landscape and portrait modes. Never to be outdone, VoiceOver lowers the sound level of any background noise or music when it needs to tell you something. Wow! I'd give anything to be able to do that with my kids!

✔ *Parlez-vous français?* VoiceOver can speak to you in 36 languages. Whether you choose Arabic, Chinese, Spanish, or Russian, your iPad will shoot the breeze with you in your preferred language.

Using VoiceOver gestures

VoiceOver uses a series of simple gestures to interact with the iPad. They include the following:

✔ **Tap once** to select an item onscreen and hear a description of it. Selected items appear with a black rectangle around them, called the VoiceOver cursor, as shown in Figure 12-2.

This item is selected.

Figure 12-2:
The VoiceOver cursor is a black rectangle around the currently selected item.

✔ **Double-tap** to activate it.

✔ **Drag your finger** to move between items onscreen. You hear a click as you move off one item and onto another, and VoiceOver begins reading the next item.

✔ **Flick left or right with one finger** to move between items. Can't find an app or a menu choice? You could search for it by dragging your finger around the screen, but you can also simply flick left and right to move the VoiceOver cursor to the next or previous available item. By flicking, you can make precise choices without having to physically find an object onscreen. For example, imagine you're trying to find a specific email in your email app. Keep flicking, and VoiceOver will read each email down the list until you find the one you want. Double-tap anywhere on the screen to open the email.

✔ **Use a two-finger double-tap** to play or pause (music, video, speaking).

✔ **Use a three-finger tap** on the Home screen to find out how many pages of apps there are and which page you're currently on.

✔ **Flick three fingers left or right** to move between your different Home screens.

✔ **Flick three fingers up or down** to scroll one page at a time.

✔ **Flick two fingers up** to read everything on the current screen, including menus and buttons.

✔ **Flick two fingers down** to read everything from the current position forward.

✔ **Use a three-finger double-tap** to toggle between VoiceOver speech off and speech on.

Triple-clicking the Home button

Triple-tapping the Home button can be set as a quick and easy Accessibility shortcut that toggles features on and off. Tap Settings, General, and Accessibility, and you find the option to turn on the Accessibility Shortcut at the bottom of the screen. Select to allow a triple-click on the Home button as a shortcut to activate VoiceOver, Invert Colors, Zoom, Switch Control, or AssistiveTouch (as shown in Figure 12-3).

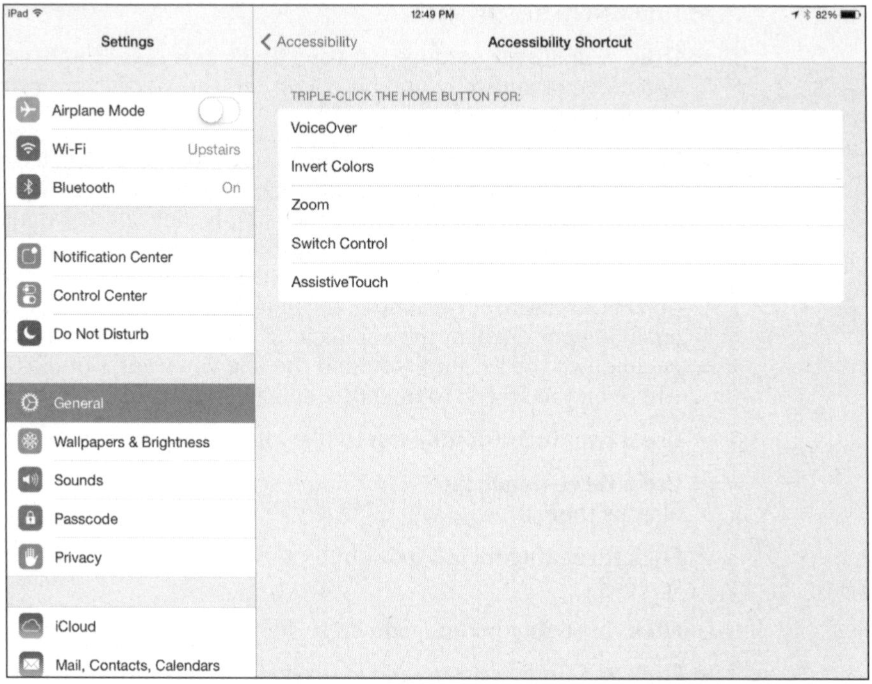

iPad 🔋	12:49 PM	⏻ 🔋 82%
Settings	‹ Accessibility	**Accessibility Shortcut**

TRIPLE-CLICK THE HOME BUTTON FOR:

➤ Airplane Mode ⬜

🛜 Wi-Fi   Upstairs

🔵 Bluetooth   On

🔲 Notification Center

🔲 Control Center

🌙 Do Not Disturb

⚙️ General

🌸 Wallpapers & Brightness

🔊 Sounds

🔒 Passcode

✋ Privacy

☁️ iCloud

✉️ Mail, Contacts, Calendars

VoiceOver

Invert Colors

Zoom

Switch Control

AssistiveTouch

Figure 12-3:
Triple-clicking the Home button can be set to quickly toggle core assistive features.

The triple-click feature can be extremely helpful if your iPad is shared between users who need a quick method for turning Accessibility features on and off. It's particularly helpful when VoiceOver is turned on and you have to work with it while trying to get to the Accessibility menu and turn it off.

You might think of VoiceOver as a function strictly for people with visual impairment. Everyone has way too much to do these days; there's never enough time to sit and read quietly. Many of us spend large chunks of our day on the move, going from place to place. Setting VoiceOver to be activated with a triple-click of the Home button enables you to easily call on a digital reading companion whenever you can't read yourself. Whether you're using your treadmill or sitting in traffic, opening an e-book or pulling up an article from the web, triple-click the Home button to activate VoiceOver, and let it read the content to you. When you're done, a simple triple-click turns VoiceOver off again.

Typing with VoiceOver

Tap Settings⇨General⇨Accessibility⇨VoiceOver, and one of the options you
see in the menu is Typing Feedback. Use that option to set the way VoiceOver
responds when you type. VoiceOver can speak each character, word, both, or
nothing, as shown in Figure 12-4. The default setting is set to have VoiceOver
speak each character as you type and then the whole word when you finish it
by entering a space or punctuation.

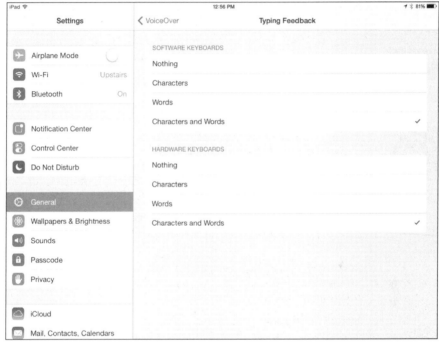

Figure 12-4:
When
you type,
VoiceOver
can speak
each char-
acter, word,
both, or
nothing.

When you're using the keyboard, VoiceOver speaks each character you touch
and repeats it again in a different voice to confirm that you just typed it. Use
one hand to select the keys, sliding your finger on the screen to the key you
want, and then tap the screen with any finger on your other hand to insert
the character in the text. It takes a little practice, but after you get the hang of
the slide-tap combination, it gets a lot easier. You can also move your cursor
left or right in the text by flicking up or down.

If you find typing difficult, consider trying dictation instead. Look for the microphone button on the bottom of the iPad's virtual keyboard. Just tap it and talk to dictate things such as emails or notes. Your words are converted to text, numbers, and symbols.

Using other VoiceOver features

VoiceOver offers quite a few options to keep it as customized as possible. Some of the options include the following:

- **The rotor:** The rotor is a virtual controller that you activate by rotating two fingers on the screen as though you were turning a dial. It changes the way VoiceOver moves through a document with an up or down single-finger flick. For example, you might be reading an email, and a single flick reads the email character by character. That makes it difficult to get through the text. Use the rotor and change the flick to read the email text word by word.

- **Spoken hints:** VoiceOver continually gives you spoken hints. That setting is on by default and can be useful when you're first learning how to use it. After a while, you'll probably be comfortable enough to turn these hints off. Tap Settings➪General➪Accessibility➪VoiceOver. The first item on that menu is SpeakHints, and you can tap to turn it off.

- **VoiceOver in iBooks:** VoiceOver works effectively within iBooks. With a single flick in any e-book, you can have your books read aloud. When you want to browse for new books, VoiceOver helps you access and look through selections in the online bookstore.

- **Audible notifications:** Activate audio alerts for events such as incoming and outgoing mail and calendar appointments by turning on the Speak Notifications option.

- **Braille support:** The iPad supports and connects to Bluetooth Braille displays. You can use the displays to read VoiceOver output, and input keys and other controls enable you to control the iPad when you have VoiceOver turned on.

Accessibility features in iBooks

iBooks has several features built in that customize the reading experience for all users, including those with vision impairment. You can switch between reading in portrait or landscape orientation, depending on your taste. You can change text fonts and modify the font size to be larger or smaller. You can also alter the page background color, and iBooks works with the Invert Colors text setting.

Zoom

Several apps on the iPad have a built-in zoom function, and it's as simple as a single pinch onscreen. The zoom function in Accessibility, however, lets you magnify the entire screen and helps you get a closer look at your iPad display at any time, whatever you happen to be doing. Zoom works on your Home screen, the Spotlight search screens, and in any app.

Using Zoom is simple:

1. **Tap the Setting icon.**

2. **Tap General in the left menu.**

3. **Select Accessibility.**

4. **Tap Zoom, and toggle the switch to On.**

   Double-tap with three fingers to instantly zoom in 200 percent. Double-tap with three fingers again, and the iPad returns to the normal 100-percent display. If you want more control, double-tap and drag three fingers.

   As you drag your fingers upward, the display increases the zoom up to 500 percent; drag them down to reduce the zoom level. After you set the level of magnification, you can move around the zoomed-in screen by dragging with three fingers in any direction. All your familiar iPad functions and gestures continue to work as normal.

Large Text

Use this feature to enlarge the font size in any apps that support dynamic sizing of text. You can go up all the way to 56-point text.

Invert Colors

Some people prefer their display in higher contrast. If you are one of those people, you may consider using the Invert Colors option (see Figure 12-5), which changes your iPad display to white on black. Like Zoom, this works across all apps, and it can also be used with Zoom and VoiceOver. Turn it on in the Accessibility menu in Settings.

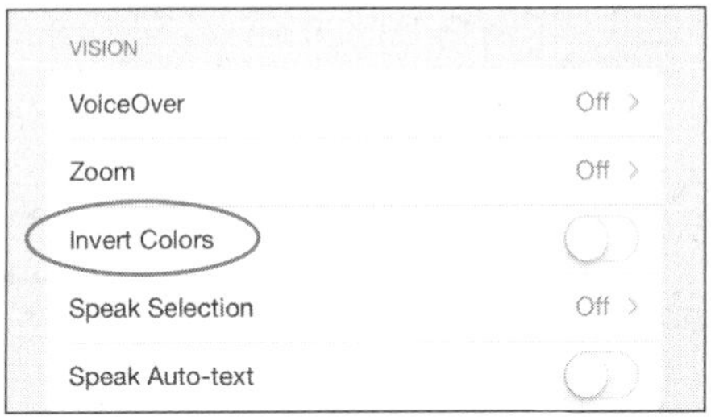

Figure 12-5:
The Invert Colors option applies a reverse video effect to your iPad display.

VISION	
VoiceOver	Off >
Zoom	Off >
Invert Colors	
Speak Selection	Off >
Speak Auto-text	

Asking Siri for assistance

You've probably heard of Siri, Apple's voice-activated personal assistant. Activate Siri in the General section of your Settings app and then she'll be available to help out with everyday tasks such as sending messages, making a phone call, scheduling a meeting, and even turning on or off features such as VoiceOver, Guided Access, and Invert Colors. Just press and hold the Home button to ask for Siri's help.

Feeling hungry? Try asking her where you can get pizza and she'll give you the location of all the nearby pizza restaurants.

Oh, and Siri has quite the sense of humor. Press and hold the Home button to talk to Siri, then ask "Do you like hockey?" and see how she responds.

Speak Selection

You may not require VoiceOver to be active when you use the iPad, but there may be times you'd like the iPad to read a certain few words to you. The Speak Selection option in Accessibility does just that when turned on. Select any text in a website, email, or anywhere else, and Speak Selection reads the highlighted text aloud. It also gives you formatting options, such as cut, copy, and paste.

Speak Auto-Text

If you have the Speak Auto-Text feature turned on, the iPad plays a sound effect and the suggested word is spoken automatically as you type. To accept the suggestion, tap the spacebar. To ignore it, keep typing.

Hearing

Education with iPads uses a variety of media and audio and is certainly an increasingly important method for communicating and expressing knowledge. The iPad offers features to help those with hearing difficulties:

✔ **Subtitles and captioning:** Turn this option on and media such as movies, TV shows, and podcasts display closed captioning and subtitles. You can even tailor their font and style to your own personal preferences.

✔ **Mono audio and channel balance:** This option combines the left and right stereo channels into a single mono audio signal output. Mono Audio enables users with hearing loss in one ear to hear both channels in the other ear. Tap Settings⇨General⇨Accessibility; Mono Audio is the Hearing category toward the bottom of the screen. Tap to turn it off.

You can also adjust the balance of the output between the left and right channels by using the slider directly under the Mono Audio option in the Hearing section, as shown in Figure 12-6.

Figure 12-6:
Set Mono
Audio or
adjust chan-
nel balance
for those
with hearing
impairments.

Drag to adjust channel balance

✔ **Headsets:** In addition to the standard speakers, the iPad comes with an audio jack you can use to plug in earphones, earbuds, noise-canceling headphones, and amplified speaker systems. It also works with Bluetooth wireless headsets.

✔ **FaceTime:** FaceTime is a great tool for people who want to communicate using sign language or by lip reading. Video chat enables users to see hand and finger gestures, as well as facial expressions.

Learning

Guided Access is a feature that helps students with learning difficulties remain on task. When Guided Access is enabled, a parent or teacher can limit use of the iPad to one app by disabling the Home button. It also allows you to restrict touch input on certain areas of the screen.

To start Guided Access, first turn it on in the Accessibility options of the Settings app and then triple-tap the Home button in the app you want to use.

Physical and motor skills

The iPad has a wonderfully designed interface with lots of intuitive multi-touch gestures that enable users to interact with it in simple yet powerful ways. Some users, however, such as the elderly and those with a physical disability, have difficulties with fine motor skills and multitouch gestures. Swiping, pinching, and other gestures can be challenging. Apple released an AssistiveTouch feature in iOS 5 specifically designed with those users in mind. The AssistiveTouch feature allows you to mimic most of the multitouch gestures and button clicks with a single tap onscreen. You can also create your own custom gestures.

Turn AssistiveTouch on in the Accessibility settings. Remember that you get there by tapping Settings➪General➪Accessibility at the bottom of the display. The Accessibility page has a category toward the bottom for Physical & Motor features, and that's where the AssistiveTouch feature is listed. Tap once to enter the AssistiveTouch page, and tap again on the button to turn it on.

The first thing you notice is that a large round dot appears in one of the corners of the display. Whenever you press the dot, it displays a menu, shown in Figure 12-7, of single-tap AssistiveTouch options for Siri, Device functions, Home, and any Favorites you may have defined as new gestures. Everything can be maneuvered with a single tap of the options onscreen.

Figure 12-7:
The Assistive-Touch menu allows users to control the iPad with single taps.

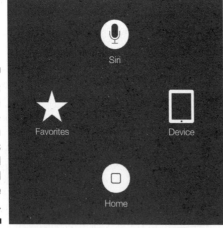

Assessing Accessibility Apps

Much of the power of the iPad lies in the fact that developers have created very innovative and helpful apps for specific purposes. That is certainly the case with accessibility apps, and the following sections describe just a few of the most popular options.

Proloquo2Go

It's estimated that around 2.5 million Americans are speech-disabled to the extent that they experience significant difficulty being understood by other people. This can be due to a variety of reasons but is often caused by amyotropic lateral sclerosis or, as it's more commonly known, Lou Gehrig's disease. Many people who suffer from this combination of vocal and motor skills weakness often purchase and use an Augmentative and Alternative Communication (AAC) device. These devices allow users to select combinations of symbols, words, and sounds, and convert them to synthesized speech. A typical AAC device can cost several thousand dollars.

Proloquo2Go is an AAC app that works on an iPad and provides similar functionality to these expensive AAC devices for a small fraction of the cost. That's because it uses the existing hardware features of the iPad. Proloquo2Go includes a library of more than 14,000 symbols, automatic conjugations, word prediction, multiuser support, and the capability to fully customize vocabularies for users along a broad continuum of abilities, from beginning symbolic communication to full literacy. Proloquo2Go provides a range of natural sounding text-to-speech voices, both male and female, adult and child, and with American or British accents.

You build phrases by tapping symbols (see Figure 12-8) with words and phrases under them. For example, the Home screen offers categories such as "I want," "I need help," "food," "drinks," and so on. Tapping one gives you underlying words and phrases. As you tap a symbol, the phrase is added to the top and spoken. The built-in logic takes you to connected phrases automatically to help complete the sentence. In addition, the interface is extremely flexible and customizable; you can add words and phrases to the app's vocabulary. It's a terrific communication aid for users with this type of disability.

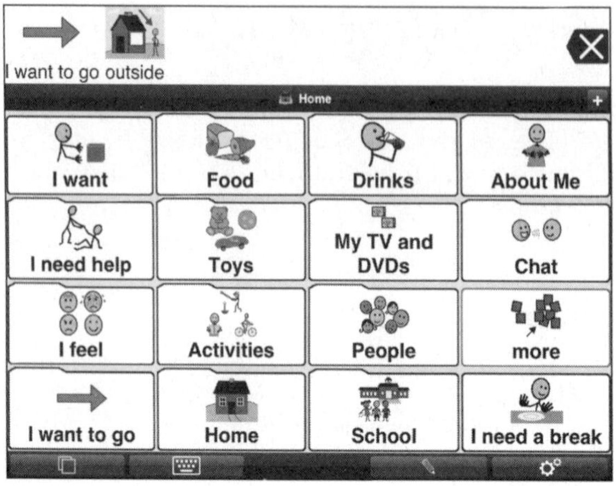

Figure 12-8:
Proloquo-2Go enables users to commu-nicate by tapping on symbols.

Notability

Notability is an excellent note-taking app for any user. One area in which it excels is in the ability to offer different note-taking tools that cater to specific preferences of users. Type your notes or write them by hand. Visual learners can use the Pen tool to add sketches on the page as they write their notes. Most importantly, tap the microphone to record audio that synchronizes with your notes. Not sure what the instructor meant when he was talking about evolution? Move to that portion of your notes and tap the Play button to hear what your teacher was saying. Refer to Chapter 9 for more information on using Notability.

Digit-Eyes

Digit-Eyes (see Figure 12-9) is a wonderfully creative iPhone app for those with serious visual impairment. Digit-Eyes enables people without vision to create and read bar code labels. Simply use your iPad (or iPhone) to scan product packaging for UPC/EAN codes, and Digit-Eyes automatically identi-fies the code and tells you the name of the product. Turn on your device's VoiceOver function — as described earlier in this chapter — and Digit-Eyes reads aloud for you. With the aid of Digit-Eyes, you can scan and hear the names of more than 7.5 million products, often including the full description, usage instructions, and ingredients — and in ten languages.

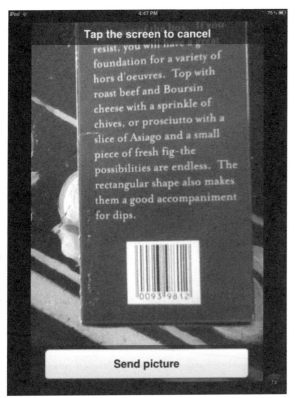

Figure 12-9:
Digit-Eyes
helps the
visually
impaired by
identifying
and reading
bar codes.

If that were all Digit-Eyes did, it would be a great product. However, it also enables you to print your own bar codes directly from the Digit-Eyes web-site (www.digit-eyes.com) on ordinary labels. You can then attach those labels to anything that you want to scan and identify.

Now I'll take that concept one step further. The Digit-Eyes bar codes you print may contain text that VoiceOver reads or can be used to record audio on your iPad that's played when the label is scanned. Why would you do that? Suppose that you bought a packet of fresh salmon from the supermarket. When the bar code is read, Digit-Eyes correctly tells you that the package contains salmon. Now assume that you get more salmon. Which is the older package? Print any standard label and use Digit-Eyes to record yourself saying "Salmon bought on Tuesday, March 17." Your problem is magically solved . . . well, unless your guests hate fish.

Here's a clever thought: Print and record audio for bar codes that you put on containers. You can rerecord the audio labels for those bar codes as often as you need. Every time you put something new in the container, use Digit-Eyes to record a new audio label, and you'll know what's in it. If you use plastic containers for perishable food items, simply add a bar code to the container and record the date of anything you put in it! Great idea, huh? I think I'll record some applause for the bar code I just printed.

Using the Reader in Safari

We all find it difficult to focus when reading text on a web page. Colors, advertisements, related articles . . . seems that the page is full of items that are screaming for your attention and distracting you from the task of reading the text. One simple tap and it's all gone. Really. Tap the Reader icon in the address bar of Safari (see Figure 12-10) and it presents the page in uncluttered, easy-to-read text.

Reader icon

Figure 12-10: Use Safari's Reader function to remove all the distracting page clutter.

Part V
Expressing Yourself with Media

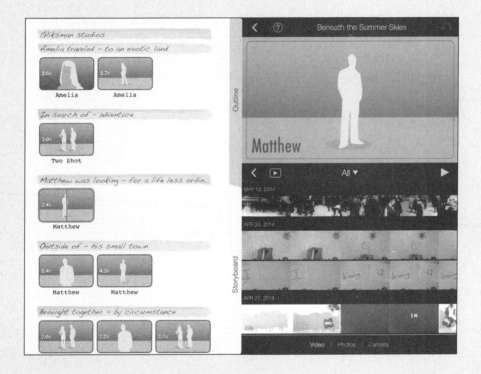

In this part . . .

- ✔ Construct digital stories with integrated media
- ✔ Create and edit video
- ✔ Produce educational animations
- ✔ Record and use audio
- ✔ Using screencasts to communicate understanding
- ✔ Create digital art

Chapter 13

Digital Storytelling in Education

In This Chapter

▶ Evaluating the importance of storytelling in education

▶ Assessing how technology has changed the nature of storytelling

▶ Turning learners into engaged digital storytellers

*W*e tell stories. We've always told stories throughout human history. They can be fictional or nonfictional. Stories can be the creation of imaginative fables, the recording of personal or historical experience, or an expression of knowledge. They always reflect the perspective of the story-teller and are subjective and personal by nature. Storytelling is an integral part of education that spans all ages and academic disciplines.

Storytelling is how we make sense of the world around us. It's how we pass knowledge, cultural traditions, narratives, and more from one generation to the next. It's what connects us to the generations that came before us and what binds us to the generations that will come after our time.

Digital storytelling is simply the ancient art of telling stories enriched through the use of multimedia technologies. The skills and literacies developed through digital storytelling are increasingly important as more of our com-munications rely on multimedia. As I discuss in this chapter, communications have become very rich and diverse. With its built-in microphone and cameras (iPad 2 and higher), the iPad offers a wide range of alternatives for students to express themselves with media. I cover some of the most popular options in the chapters that follow.

Understanding the Role of Technology in Storytelling

The digital aspect of storytelling raises the art to a new level of experience. The emergence of technology and digital media has resulted in some significant departures from the traditional role of storytelling in education:

Stories have become media-rich experiences. Billions of mobile devices are in the hands of people worldwide, and an ever-increasing percentage of those devices contain video cameras, still cameras, and microphones. Whenever anything of personal significance happens, it can be captured and chronicled in digital media (as shown in Figure 13-1) that we edit, process, and publish. Within minutes, that moment is available to friends and family around the world. Media has become the language of today.

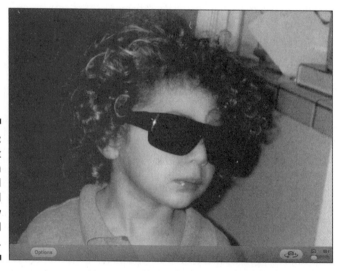

Figure 13-1: Any moment or event can be captured and shared instantly using digital media.

Don't get me wrong. Reading and writing remain crucial educational components. However, if you want to prepare students for life in 21st-century society, it's essential to help them develop and use a broad range of communication skills. Schools have begun to recognize the importance of multimedia use in education. Fortunately, with its built-in microphone, camera, and a host of multimedia apps, the iPad is an extraordinary tool for creating and integrating multimedia into education.

When you think of storytelling from a traditional perspective, you might conjure up any of these images:

- ✔ Danny Kaye telling a story to a group of children seated on the ground. (If you don't know who Danny Kaye is, look up the movie *Hans Christian Andersen.*)
- ✔ A kindergarten teacher reading a book to a group of young students.
- ✔ A parent reading a bedtime story to a child.

The common thread is the clarity of role definition: The adult tells the story, and the child listens; the teacher imparts knowledge, and the students listen and learn. (That's the theory, anyway.) All those images show a clear relationship between adult and child, expert and learner, craftsman and apprentice.

Then we reached the information age. Technology is expanding knowledge at accelerating rates. Passively absorbing information that is then regurgitated can't pass for learning any longer in the information age. Students must develop the skills necessary to constantly learn by searching for, interpreting, and analyzing information, and then applying what they've learned to real-world problems throughout life. Students are becoming producers of knowledge: digital storytellers who use technology to express themselves. And it's a role that's become an integral part of their lives outside school. Facebook, YouTube, Twitter, and more . . . technology has turned everyone into a story producer in one form or another.

Students traditionally produced a product for an audience of one: their teacher. Thanks to the Internet and the power of social networking, those digital stories can now be shared worldwide in an instant. Producers of a digital story today can communicate with people and communities anywhere around the globe through the power of a device — such as an iPad — that they hold in their hands.

Engaging Learners through Digital Storytelling

If you own an iPad (and I presume you do, since you are reading this book!), you have access to a host of apps and tools for creating digital stories. Use them for creative expression, communicating information, entertaining, expressing comprehension, tutoring purposes, and much more. Here are just a few ideas:

✔ Create a narrated slide-show story to demonstrate the understanding of new vocabulary.

✔ Use a video or *screencast* (a recording of interactions on a computer or iPad display) to explain a complex scientific concept.

✔ Create an audio or video interview of your grandparents for a family history project.

✔ Create a historical narrative of a pivotal event using images and audio.

✔ Create a first-person audio journal of a person who lived during a significant event in history.

✔ Explain a mathematical concept by creating a screencast tutorial.

✔ Use audio podcasting to practice reading and speaking in a foreign language.

✔ Demonstrate a portfolio of work with personal narrative describing each piece, its objectives, and development.

✔ Narrate a character story or a personal journal with a musical soundtrack.

Digital storytelling makes for engaging lessons that allow students to create and publish content rather than just passively consuming it. It empowers every student with the opportunity to develop his voice and personalize it through the use of media.

Throw away that lesson plan that calls for students to "read Chapter 5 and answer questions." You have a wide variety of options for applying digital storytelling to your curriculum. I discuss a few of them in the next few chapters.

Chapter 14

Lights, Camera, Learning

. . . .

In This Chapter

▶ Examining the different steps in a multimedia project

▶ Creating a movie storyboard with Popplet

▶ Producing short narrated movies with SonicPics

▶ Trimming video directly in your iPad's Camera Roll

▶ Creating multimedia productions with iMovie

▶ Exploring other creative options for video editing

. . . .

*O*pen your browser to a popular news page such as Yahoo!, and the lead story is often some scandal about an actor or actress. Movies have become mainstays of our culture, and there's no denying their popularity. We love watching and creating movies, and they definitely have their place in education. Although creating and editing video used to require special cameras and expensive desktop software, we're now able produce movies easily and inexpensively with a simple mobile device.

Creating a short movie can be a great way to narrate a story with new vocabulary words, practice a foreign language, "interview" a famous figure, create a school news broadcast, and so much more. Students love creating videos. Their enthusiasm for learning activities tends to skyrocket when they can express themselves with video. Frankly, between the two of us, I've conducted many teacher workshops with video activities, and I can tell you that adults aren't really any different.

Just as reading and writing occupied a special place in our learning, video has become an important component in the education of our children and students. It doesn't replace the role of reading and writing — in many respects they work together. Students will read and research background information for a movie project and write a script before performing in front of a camera. The use of media has a place in education, from the first-grade vocabulary project to the more complex productions of high-school students.

In this chapter, I demonstrate how you can integrate video into a variety of educational settings. I show you how to create and edit short narrated slide-show videos as well as more intricate video productions. This chapter also guides you toward many of the creative educational applications that these multimedia projects offer across grade levels and throughout the curriculum.

Planning Your Production

I've heard many people express the thought that multimedia projects aren't "serious" schoolwork. They're right from the perspective that a digital storytelling project shouldn't be the school equivalent of that 30-second pet cat video on YouTube. Student work often reflects the standards and expectations that the teacher has expressed.

Any educational project or activity benefits from careful forethought and planning; that's most certainly the case with a multimedia production. The objective isn't to stand in front of a camera spontaneously and start recording. It also doesn't mean dispensing with more traditional forms of story crafting, such as researching facts, interviewing people, writing the story, or scripting the dialogue.

Many important phases should precede the production of any significant multimedia project:

✔ **Collaborate.** Multimedia assignments make great team projects. They include multiple phases with opportunities for each student to gravitate toward his or her particular strengths, whether those are research and reading, organization, writing, visual design and editing, performing, or something else.

✔ **Research.** Any project worth its weight requires students to do some digging and massaging of information. Don't forget that effective research is more than grabbing some facts from the first link in a Google search. For example, suppose they had to prepare a narrated slide show on the life of a U.S. president. That's an opportune time to discuss the elements of effective research with students. You can pose questions to your students such as these: How do you decide where and what to search? What factors about the president are important to your project? You'll more than likely come up with boatloads of information. How are you filtering the search results? Is the information accurate, and how can it be verified?

✔ **Select and create supporting materials.** Collect and/or create materials such as images, music, and more. Discuss the impact of visuals. What images match the sentiment students are trying to express? How does music set the scene for a story? One teacher I know demonstrates this very effectively by showing short political election advertisements. It's very revealing to note the way images and music are selected to positively or negatively reflect upon candidates' positions.

✔ **Discuss copyright issues.** Consider discussing issues such as copyright, ownership, and usage rights.

✔ **Create a storyboard.** Plan and organize. One way to do this effectively is to create a storyboard that maps out the project visually step by step.

✔ **Write a script.** Just because you're advocating the use of multimedia doesn't mean that you abandon important traditional skills such as writing. Writing an accompanying script can be a vital part of the multimedia project, and you certainly should consider asking students to submit their scripts along with their final digital media.

Assessments should reflect the elements of a project you consider educationally important. That can extend beyond the final media piece to include elements such as the storyboard, the script, and even the research or collection of resources used in the project. Create and clarify your assessment rubric. It will communicate the project elements that you consider important and result in a more thorough final product.

An effective method for planning any media project is to create a storyboard that clearly lays out all the scenes and plot development. A storyboard is a form of flow chart that visually maps out how to progress from one step to the next in a project. Each step can also include the relevant details, images, links, and text.

One popular iPad app that lets you map your ideas visually is Popplet Lite, which also comes in a paid version called Popplet. It has a simple interface (see Figure 14-1) that enables you to create and place notes called Popples on a board. Add content to your notes and move them around so they connect to other Popples and form relationships. It's simple and cool, and it can serve a wide variety of functions. This list gives you the basics of getting started with Popplet:

✔ **Meet the Pinboard.** When you first open Popplet, it presents a blank area called the Pinboard. You create your visual map by placing Popples on the Pinboard.

✔ **Place some Popples.** Double-tap anywhere on the Pinboard to place a Popple, which is a digital note. Grab the corner to resize it, and tap the Popple itself to move it around on the Pinboard. Add content such as images, text, or a freehand drawing to it by tapping any of the icons on the bottom. You can even take a live photo with your camera!

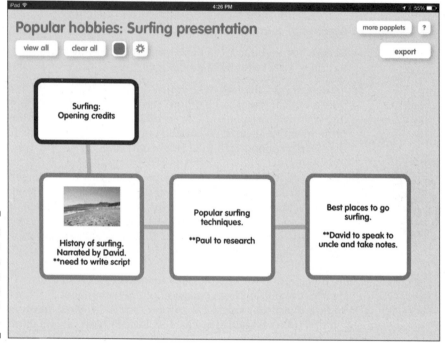

Figure 14-1:
Popplet Lite enables students to visually map the tasks in a project.

✔ **Connect the dots!** Tap to select a Popple and you get a little circle on each side of it. Tap and drag the circle to a new location to create a new, linked Popple with a line connecting the two of them. Pretty easy, wasn't it? You can also double-tap the Pinboard to create a new Popple and then pull out a line between it and another Popple to make a connection.

✔ **Keep going as far as you want.** If you're putting a lot of information into your Popples, you'll run out of room on your iPad screen pretty quickly. Just place your finger anywhere on the Pinboard and slide it out toward the edge to get additional space. The existing Popples slide out the side of the screen as you get more space for new ones. If you start to feel insecure and need to see all your Popples at once, tap the View All button on the top of the Pinboard. Have faith: They're all still there!

✔ **Share from Popplet Lite.** Tap the Export button in the top-right corner when you're done. If you're using the Lite version, you can email your work as a PDF document or a JPG image. If you purchased the full version, you have additional options to collaborate with other users, share Popplets online, and more.

We live in a visual world. Many things that can be written can also be mapped visually. Popplet is a great tool for creating storyboards (see Figure 14-2). It's also actually a great tool for a variety of other purposes, such as planning a section in a book's chapter. You can also use it to map out a period of history, graph a family tree, demonstrate the relationships between factors that contribute to a scientific outcome, list resources for a course, map themes in a novel, show steps in a cooking recipe, and more. The more options you can give learners for connecting with information, the more you can accommodate and differentiate between alternative learning preferences.

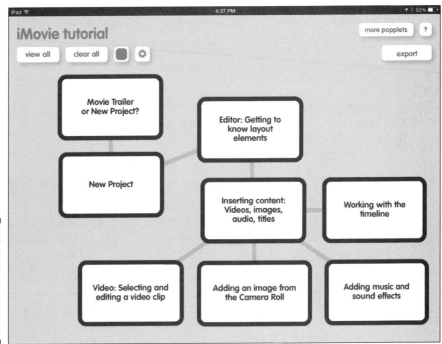

Figure 14-2:
Using
Popplet to
plan the
writing of a
section on
iMovie.

Designing Short, Simple Movies with SonicPics

An increasing number of us walk around with constant access to a smartphone with a built-in camera. Combine that with mobile Internet access, and you can take and distribute images and video anywhere on the planet instantly. And that's increasingly what our students are doing outside of school. Our families may have searched old shoeboxes for snapshots when we were kids, but today's students create complete digital libraries that they share on websites such as Facebook. They're very comfortable communicating with images and video.

In this section, I show you methods that can be used to create short movies. These methods can certainly be used with any age level, but they're so simple that they are especially suited for use with younger children.

All you have to do is select some images and start narrating as you flip through them. The end product is a magical little movie. Using the SonicPics app is really that simple. The video quality may not win you the Oscar you've always coveted, but it can be wonderfully effective as an educational tool.

Has anyone ever thrust a microphone or camera in front of your face and told you to say something clever? It's very difficult and more than a little intimidating. I don't recommend spontaneously recording yourself without any preparation. Take some time to map out your movie before you begin to create it. Think about the story you want to tell, and write the narration that will accompany the slides. Remember, it's all about the preparation.

Create your video story in SonicPics using the following steps:

1. **Start a new SonicPics project by tapping the plus (+) icon on the opening screen.**

   You're prompted to give your project a title and description. Enter them in the text fields and tap Create.

2. **Select a photo.**

   You should have your images all set to go and stored in your Camera Roll so that you can enter them in the photo-editing screen as shown in Figure 14-3. Tap the Camera icon in the bottom right of the opening panel to select your first photo from your Camera Roll. Tap in the Title or Description text areas under the photo to add your own text. If you need to change the image, just tap the Camera icon again and select a different image.

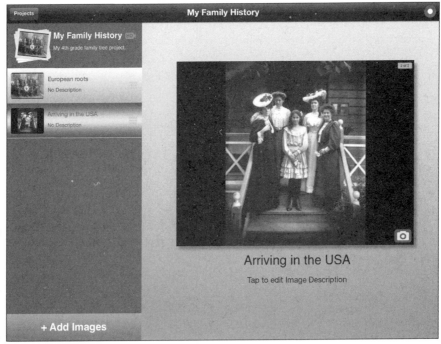

Figure 14-3:
Create a
SonicPics
video by first
selecting
images.

3. **Add and arrange images.**

   As you add photos, your images are displayed in order within the column on the left of the screen. Tap Add Images along the bottom of the left column to continue adding photos. If you need to change the order of the images, tap and hold the three-lined icon on the right of any image and drag it up or down to a new location in the sequence (see Figure 14-4).

4. **Record your narration.**

   I hope you've done your homework and have a script prepared because the next step is to record your narration. Tap the red Record button on the top right of your screen to enter the recording phase of your project (see Figure 14-5). Note the following when recording:

   - Tap the Pause button at any time to stop and collect your thoughts; then tap it again to resume.

   - Your narration is synchronized with the image on display. When you're done with that image, swipe to the left and move on to the next image. You can also tap the Photos icon to jump to a specific image in your sequence.

- Tap the curved arrow Share icon on the bottom right when you've finished all your recordings. You're prompted to save the project. SonicPics saves the video and returns you to your SonicPics Recordings library.

5. Watch and share your masterpiece.

Sit back, break out the popcorn, and prepare to enjoy your movie by tapping the large Play icon on your project to watch it. Tap the Share icon under your project in the Recordings library to send it to your Camera Roll (Save to Library), send it via email, and more.

6. Go back and edit the project.

It's OK, even Steven Spielberg occasionally wants to make some changes to his movies. Tap the Project button on the top toolbar to go back, tap the project you want to edit, and change the images or recordings. Trying to be perfect can be such a burden, can't it?

Tap, hold, and drag an image to change its location.

Figure 14-4:
Tap and drag the lined icon on any image to change its position in your movie.

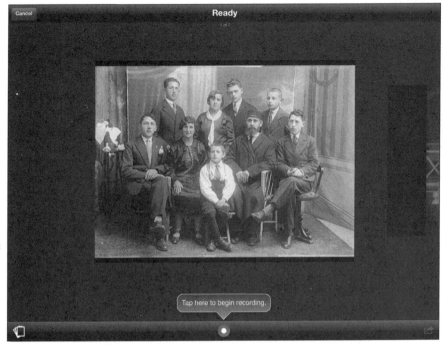

Figure 14-5:
Narrate your
SonicPics
video over
the images.

SonicPics is one of the simplest ways to create a digital movie on your iPad. I love the look on children's faces when they create their first video. It's such a simple process, and the results can be quite magical. Try it out for yourself and see.

Allocate adequate time for students to work on their narration and slides before recording, and make this a clear and essential priority. If they have to rush into the creation of the videos without adequate preparation time to research, plan, and script, you won't exploit the full educational potential of multimedia projects.

Creating and Editing Video

The fantastic capabilities of the many apps that use the iPad's camera tap into the creative potential that exists inside all of us. And if you're lucky enough to have a third-generation or higher iPad, you also benefit from features such as 1080p HD quality video and image stabilization. Chapter 2 delves into how to shoot video with your iPad. Now go ahead and put that video to good use.

Here are some tips for taking effective video on the iPad:

- ✔ The first and most obvious thing to keep in mind is to keep your educational objectives front and center. It's unlikely you'll be applying for any Academy Awards. (Yes, I deliberately said "unlikely" and not "impossible.") Students certainly can produce amazing results with video, but if you're after dramatic cinematic effects, you'll probably want to use a more robust video editor on the Mac.

- ✔ The best way to use and put together video on iPads is to keep your clips fairly short and entertaining. Long video clips often make it difficult to hold the viewer's attention.

- ✔ Make sure you have abundant light available and preferably not shining directly into the camera. Also, don't move from one lighting situation to another while shooting video. If you have to shoot under different lighting conditions, turn off the camera and start a new clip at the second location after giving the camera a few seconds to adjust to the new lighting conditions.

- ✔ You should normally shoot your video in landscape mode. Think of your TV or a movie screen. You want your video to have the same orientation.

- ✔ Don't combine clips taken in portrait mode with landscape photos.

- ✔ Video gets a little scary and blurred if you get too close to your subject. Stay a minimum of an arm's length away when shooting.

- ✔ Whether you have an iPad 2 or higher (which has an image stabilization feature), keep as still as possible when taking your video. Motion blur is disturbing; too much of it will make your viewers seasick. Consider using an iPad stand that holds the iPad firm and steady.

- ✔ Everyone knows where the lens is on a regular camera . . . but that isn't always true on an iPad. Know where the camera is located physically on your iPad, and then do yourself a favor by keeping your fingers clear of it — something I didn't do while snapping Figure 14-6. The greatest video on Earth will be ruined by the sudden appearance of a giant forefinger in the frame!

- ✔ Resist the urge to show off, waltzing around taking video while holding the iPad in one hand. Hold it steady in both hands with your elbows tucked in to your sides.

- ✔ Experiment and have fun with the video. Trim your clips creatively, and put them together with interesting transitions. Try adding an interesting soundtrack. Pan and zoom where appropriate.

Figure 14-6:
Know where
the iPad
camera is
located,
and keep
your fingers
clear!

Trimming video in the Camera Roll

Despite all my protests to the contrary, my family continually insists I'm no Steven Spielberg when it comes to shooting movies on my iPad. I guess there's no accounting for taste. Don't worry, we can all keep our moviemaking reputations intact and trim video right there in the Camera Roll before anyone else gets a look at it. It'll be our little secret. Here's how:

1. **Select a video by tapping in the Camera Roll.**

   It is displayed onscreen. The frame viewer and trim controls appear on top of the video in your display.

2. **Drag the slide control arrows at the start or end of the frame viewer at the top of the screen to trim the video (see Figure 14-7).**

3. **Tap the Play button under the video to preview the trimmed version; then tap Trim when you're satisfied.**

4. **Save the new version over the old copy or save it as a new video.**

Video files, especially high-definition video files or large and long movies, eat up your iPad's space faster than anything else. Review your Camera Roll frequently and trim or delete your videos. You can also move your files to your computer using iTunes or an app such as PhotoSync (refer to Chapter 19) and delete them from your iPad.

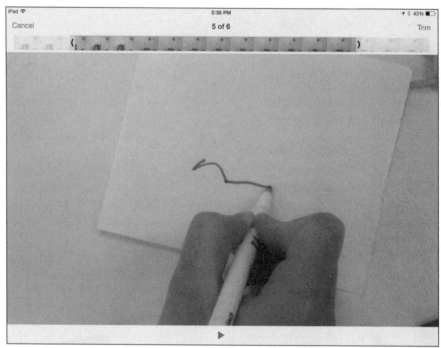

Figure 14-7:
Drag the
slide con-
trol over
the frame
viewer to
trim your
video.

Shooting video with your iPad versus pro equipment

I've been asked, "When should I use an iPad for creating and editing video and when should I get more professional equipment?" You may have used digital video cameras and editors such as iMovie for the Mac. The iPad video camera is always available, mobile, and simple to access and integrate into any learning process as needed. It's important, however, to retain a realistic perspective when using iPads for video projects. They're tremendous tools for smaller projects, but you won't be shooting the next *Godzilla* with your iPad. Don't get me wrong. Encourage your students to shoot for the moon: Just make sure to keep your own expectations firmly on the ground.

Using iMovie

You'll usually want to do more than just trim your movie clip. In those cases, it's well worth considering an app such as Apple's iMovie. iMovie has been on the Mac for quite some time and is part of the Mac's iLife suite of software products. The version of iMovie for the iPad has fewer features than the full Mac version, but it's a more-than-capable alternative for shorter, less-sophisticated movie projects. Although it isn't intended for heavy movie editing, it does offer enough options to enable casual filmmakers to shoot video, use some simple editing tools, and turn out a memorable movie in a few short minutes. It's a perfect tool for most video applications in education.

You begin your movie venture with a simple tap of the plus (+) icon on the top of iMovie's opening screen (see Figure 14-8). You see tabs along the top for Video, Projects, and Theater. With the Projects tab selected, you can start a new project or access and share existing projects. A pop-up menu prompts you to start a new project from scratch or choose a new trailer from iMovie's movie trailer themes. Let's take a stroll through both avenues.

Tap an existing project to edit or share it.　　　　Start a new project.

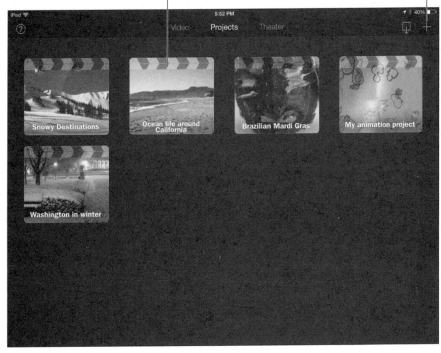

Figure 14-8: iMovie's screen is where you start new projects and access existing ones.

Start a new trailer

Movie trailers are theme templates that are already set up for your movie. Themes include elements such as a custom title screen design, transition effects, and theme music. All you need to do is customize the movie by inserting your content into the theme's prearranged slots.

Themes encompass popular movie categories such as Scary, Romance, Narrative, Retro, and Superhero (see Figure 14-9). For example, if you have footage of the kids at Halloween, you may select the Scary theme. It comes complete with a scary background track, titles, effects, and more. You could select the Expedition trailer for the video you took of last summer's holiday. And of course, the footage of you stumbling into first base in the staff softball game would be a perfect fit for the Swashbuckler theme.

Figure 14-9:
Select and customize an iMovie trailer theme for quick and simple movies.

To create a movie using a Trailer theme, follow these steps:

1. **From the iMovie Home screen, tap the plus (+) icon and select New Trailer from the pop-up menu.**

   Preview the themes by tapping the Play button. When you've decided on one, tap the Create Trailer button on the top menu bar to select the highlighted theme. Now you're ready to start customizing it with your content.

2. **Tap the Outline tab (see Figure 14-10), and tap in any text field to edit the Movie Name, Credits, and more.**

Titles   Outline tab

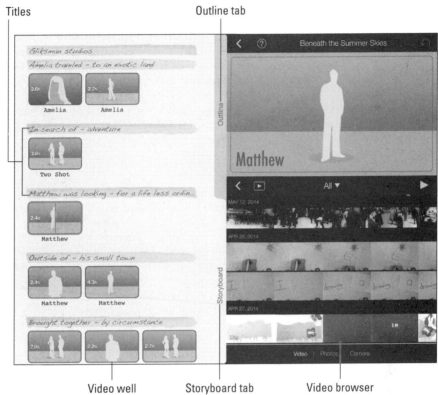

Figure 14-10: Tap an item in the Outline or Storyboard tab to add text and video.

Video well   Storyboard tab   Video browser

3. **Add content to the Storyboard tab and Video wells.**

The Storyboard tab is where you edit the various components of your trailer:

- Edit any title of a slide by tapping in the text field in the Storyboard and changing the text.

- The Storyboard also includes a number of Video wells to which you can add video. The placeholder image suggests what type of video to add (Action, Group, Closeup, and so forth). Tap any Video well to edit it.

- Your available videos display in the Video browser in the lower-right corner of your screen. Make sure to select Video from the options listed beneath the browser. Tap any section of a video clip to highlight it, and then tap the little arrow that pops up to add that video to the selected video well. Note that each video well has an allocated time displayed on it, and iMovie crops the corresponding amount of time from your video when it inserts it.

- You can tap any filled Video well to edit the video in it in the Video browser window. Turn on that video's audio by tapping the volume control at the bottom left of the browser window. You can select which portion of the video plays by tapping and dragging the video through the yellow selection outline in the browser window. Play your selected portion at any time by tapping the Play button.

Trailers are an easy way to create quick, simple movies — so easy that it may only take a few minutes to customize the Outline text, add some photos and movie clips into the Storyboard, and go order the popcorn. With butter, please.

Start a new project

You also have the option to start a new project when you tap the plus (+) icon on iMovie's opening screen. Choose this when you're creating and editing a movie from scratch by yourself.

Start by selecting a movie theme from the list and tap Create Movie. You're taken to the iMovie editing screen, which is divided into three sections (see Figure 14-11):

✔ The top-right section displays the available media on your iPad.

✔ The top-left section is your movie preview window.

✔ The bottom section is the movie timeline.

To create a movie from scratch, follow these steps:

1. **Tap the plus (+) icon to start a new movie project.**

2. **Select a theme and tap Create Movie.**

   The iMovie editing screen appears (refer to Figure 14-11). iMovie gives you a number of content options, and these steps show you the process of adding content. Note that if you've already added content, it appears in the timeline at the bottom of the screen. Any additional content is added to your movie at the current insertion point — the *playhead* (a red vertical line) — in your timeline.

   Make sure to position the playhead at the right point before inserting new content.

3. **Tap the Video button on the Media Browser toolbar in the top right of your display.**

   All your available video clips in the Media Browser are displayed. You can do the following:

- Preview any clip by dragging your finger along it in the browser or by tapping it and then tapping the Play button.

- Add an entire clip by tapping to select it and then tapping the insertion arrow that pops up immediately afterward. You can also tap the three-dot More icon and choose to only add the audio track or add the video as a window over existing content in the timeline instead of displaying it full screen.

- Trim the clip before adding it (when you tap and select any clip, yellow trim handles appear at either end of it) by dragging its trim handles so that they encompass just the part of the clip you want to use. When you're ready, tap the blue arrow to insert your clip.

Note that it's always good practice to shoot a couple of seconds before your action and a couple of seconds after it ends. Having those extra seconds gives you footage to trim so you can capture exactly what you need.

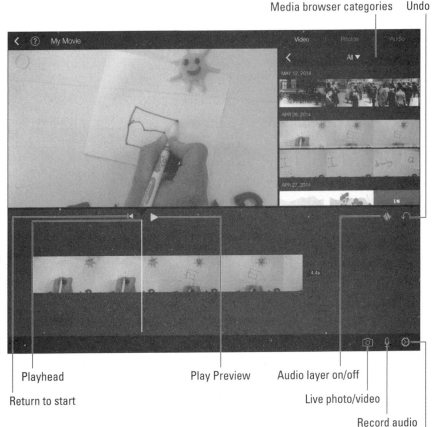

Figure 14-11:
The components of the iMovie editing screen.

As you insert videos into your project, iMovie adds an orange outline on the bottom of the clip in the Media Browser. Even though you can use videos as many times as you want in a project, that little orange line makes it easy for you to see which clips you've already used and which you haven't. They do think of everything, don't they?

4. Tap the Photos tab on top of the Media Browser to display the images in your Camera Roll.

5. Tap any image to insert it into your timeline.

If your playhead is in the middle of a video clip, the photo will be inserted at the start or end of the clip, whichever is closest.

Photos display for a few seconds and automatically get a *Ken Burns effect* (a panning and zooming effect named after the famous American documentary filmmaker) applied to them.

You can easily edit those photo timings and effects. I take a peek at how to do that in the next section.

iMovie enables you to take photos and video on the go as you create and edit your movie. See the little Camera icon on the bottom toolbar (refer to Figure 14-11)? Tap it to bring up your iPad camera, all ready for you to snap an image or take some video footage (see Figure 14-12). Just say "Cheese" and shoot whatever you like, and the image or video is automatically added to your movie. Easy peasy.

Figure 14-12:
Tap the
Camera icon
in iMovie
and start the
Camera app
to add live
footage.

Respect copyrights

Although iMovie allows you to access and use any iTunes song as the soundtrack for your video, you still have to respect the content owner's copyright. The doctrine of "fair use" allows limited use of copyrighted material within the context of classroom instruction. Using a small snippet of a Beatles song may sound great as the backdrop to part of your History project, but don't plan on including the entire White Album and posting the video on a public web forum!

6. **Tap the Audio tab on the Media Browser toolbar to add a soundtrack and effects.**

   You'll see a selection of menu choices:

   - *Theme Music* lists audio tracks that come included with iMovie, and a number of choices such as Playlist and Artists allow you to access and use music in your iTunes library.

   - The *Sound Effects* category even gives you a library of entertaining audio clips to use in your project. (What project would be complete without a rooster crowing?)

7. **Add narration to your movie by positioning the playhead in your timeline and tapping the microphone icon on the bottom toolbar.**

8. **Tap Record on the pop-up menu to start recording and tap Stop when you're done.**

9. **Tap the gear icon in the lower-right corner to access the Project Setting menu and choose a theme.**

   iMovie comes with a collection of themes. Each theme has a specific default style for the title screen, transitions, and theme music. You'll see themes ranging from Modern to CNN iReport, and each one gives your movie its own distinct flavor. You'll also see an option to turn the theme music on or off.

10. **Swipe, split, and edit in the timeline.**

    Here's just a short selection of some simple but powerful options to edit your movie project:

    - *Zoom in and out.* Unpinch your fingers in the timeline to zoom in and see a more detailed frame view of your movie. Zooming is helpful if you need to be more precise when splitting clips or adjusting background music.

- *Split a video clip.* Scroll the timeline so that the red playhead is positioned where you want to split the video clip. Select the clip in the timeline by tapping it. It's highlighted with an outline. Tap Split in the menu that appears on the bottom toolbar to split the clip at the playhead. Splitting a clip is useful for trimming parts and adding transitions, titles, and more.

- *Delete a clip or photo.* Tap the element in the timeline and you see a menu along the bottom toolbar. Tap the Trash icon to delete the clip or photo. You can also tap and drag an element out of the timeline to delete it.

- *Add titles.* You can add a title to any clip or image in the timeline. Tap any element in the timeline, and tap Title in the menus along the bottom toolbar. Select a title type such as Opening or Closing. iMovie adds a text box to that clip or image in the style of the movie theme that you selected. Tap the text box in the Preview window and add your own custom title text.

- *Edit transitions.* Every time you add an element in your project timeline, iMovie adds a default transition. The transitions are based upon the project theme that you selected, but you can change them easily.

  To change a transition, tap the icon for the transition you'd like to edit. A menu of options appears along the bottom toolbar. Tap to select Cross-Dissolve, Theme, or None to remove it altogether. You can also change the duration of the transition to the desired time by tapping the time displayed on the bottom toolbar and selecting a different time from the pop-up menu..

- *Add a fade-in and fade-out to the project.* Tap the Project Settings icon in the top right of the editor screen. Turn the options on for Fade in from Black and Fade out to Black.

11. **When you're done editing, tap the arrow icon on the left of the top toolbar to return to the project screen.**

12. **Tap the large name of your project on the top of the screen to edit and rename it.**

13. **Tap the Play icon to prepare and play back your movie . . . then enjoy the show.**

14. **Tap the Share icon to pop up a list of sharing options.**

    Options include preparing a final, compressed version of your video that's placed in your Camera Roll and uploaded to YouTube, Vimeo, and Facebook, as well as other video-sharing services. You can also send your iMovie file to your iTunes account, where it can be easily transferred and edited on another device.

Exploring other video apps

Although iMovie is the most popular option for creating and editing movies on the iPad, there are certainly many other apps that offer additional features . . . and many more are released all the time. Here's a quick rundown of a few of them to consider.

Avid Studio

Avid Studio has a very intuitive user interface and most of the same features for adding and editing content as iMovie. There's a handy selection of additional features for the adventurous among you who want to venture out and explore your creative options. Here are a few:

✔ Avid Studio allows you to add and edit up to three additional audio tracks in your movie. Use them to create complex sound effects, audio transitions, and more sophisticated background audio.

Transition effects between clips are enhanced with a far larger range of options, including high-quality dissolves and fades.

✔ Create picture-in-picture effects.

✔ Create professional titles with full control over fonts, sizes, colors, rotation, and more.

Reel Director

This is another popular video editing app for the iPad. Reel Director excels with impressive tools for adding titles and subtitles, and includes an impressive range of transition effects.

Silent Film Studio

This is actually an iPhone app but takes an extremely unique and creative slant on videos by turning them into old-fashioned silent movies. Add music, titles, and transition cards, and vary the playback speed of the video. If you update with the in-app purchase, you get additional functions, including the option to add retro music to your silent movie.

CollabraCam

You thought that just taking and editing video on a mobile device was a leap forward? CollabraCam (shown in Figure 14-13) enables you to simultaneously control, shoot, and edit live video from multiple cameras on other iPads, iPhones, or iPod touches. Each device needs to have CollabraCam installed on it and be on the same wireless network. One device acts as the "director," viewing, recording, and editing live video streams from up to four other devices. You can also silently communicate with your camera operators and pass along instructions. The final assembled video is exported to the Camera Roll on the director's device.

Figure 14-13: CollabraCam allows you to control and shoot live video from multiple cameras.

Chapter 15

Animating Your Lessons

Communication is the heart of learning, and we adopt different communicative techniques at the various stages of our lives. When you're a kid, you love to express yourself by using your imagination in all sorts of creative ways: You role-play, dress up, and make up stories with colorful characters. Playing in these ways — animating, if you will, the stories and ideas you imagine — is a vital part of growing and learning about the world around you. It's also an important part of the learning process in school, and many iPad apps seek to tap into the potential of learning by creating colorful stories. I discuss two such apps here: Sock Puppets (which enables you to create animated shows featuring those lovable critters) and Comic Life (which helps you create your own cartoon strip).

Staging a Sock-Puppets Show

We all played with puppets at some point in our childhood. My daughter's first joke was when she pulled a sock over her hand and pretended it could talk. Children will give the puppet a name and character, and use it to make up stories that exercise their imagination and express their feelings.

One digital equivalent is an iPad app called Sock Puppets (shown in Figure 15-1). It's an adorable app that lets you create sophisticated little sock-puppet shows . . . and it's impossible not to have fun using it. There's a free version and a paid version called Sock Puppets Complete that comes with additional content and longer recording time. Both are available in the App Store.

Note that there's a free version of Sock Puppets and a second, paid version called Sock Puppets Complete. The paid version offers longer recording times, additional characters, props, and scenes, as well as the ability to save your movie to the Camera Roll.

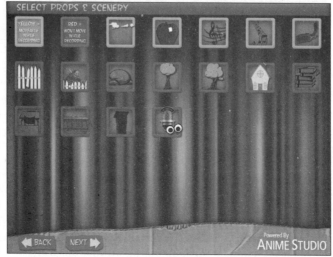

Figure 15-1:
Select puppets, props, and backgrounds for your Sock Puppet show.

Create puppet shows by selecting your puppets and positioning them on a stage with backgrounds and props. Tap the Record button and start talking. Tap one of the puppets, and it lip-syncs while also applying a cute little cartoonish effect to the audio of your voice. If you want to tap into your inner Spielberg, you can even develop your plot by switching backgrounds and moving your puppet extravaganza to different locations. When you're done, the show is converted to an entertaining little movie that you can watch and force on your friends . . . um, I mean share with your friends.

Always try to structure activities with your educational goals in mind. Integrate use of the Sock Puppets app into your lesson plans. Why settle for the same old stale vocabulary exercises every week when you can occasionally have children work together and use vocabulary lists in puppet shows? Be creative. Ask children to create and retell stories, review books, explain simple math or science concepts, act out appropriate behavior in social situations, and more. As always, remember to stress the importance of preparation before recording. Often, it's the preparation time where most of the learning takes place.

Yes, I know the Sock Puppets app is designed for kids, but let's be honest: We both know that you can't resist trying it out for yourself. So go ahead and put on your director's cap and create your very own puppet movie. Here's how:

1. **Tap the Sock Puppets icon on your iPad home page to start the app and then tap the New option on the opening-screen menu.**

   This starts a new story.

   You're presented with a row of puppet characters.

2. **Tap the puppets you'd like to cast in your movie (any number you'd like), and tap the Next arrow (at the bottom of the screen).**

   Note that you can purchase additional puppets, backgrounds, and props from the opening-menu screen.

   The next screen offers a selection of backgrounds to use as sets in your show. Remember that you can use more than one and switch between them during the show.

3. **Select and tap the backgrounds of your choice, and then tap the Next arrow.**

   Backgrounds sit behind your characters and cannot be moved.

   Now you're ready to decorate your puppet sets with props, such as podiums and microphones, and scenery. Props with a red frame are in a fixed position; you can move those that have a yellow frame wherever you'd like them.

4. **Tap the props and scenery of your choice to place them in your show; tap Next when you're done.**

   The app sets up your stage, and you're ready to start recording.

5. **Move your puppets and props into their positions.**

   If you selected more than one background, you see a strip with your background icons along the top-right corner of the screen (shown in Figure 15-2).

Share

Save | Options

Record/Stop Play | Home | Backgrounds

Figure 15-2:
Puppets
lip-sync to
the sound of
your voice
during the
recording.

6. **Tap any background to select it.**

7. **Tap the round Record button on the top of your screen to start (and it becomes a Stop button).**

   Keep the following in mind while you're recording:

   - *Talking puppet:* If you've selected more than one puppet, you see one of them has a little arrow over its head. That means it's the actively selected puppet, and as you start talking, it lip-syncs to the sound of your voice. Tap any other puppet when you want it to become the active puppet.

   - *Moving puppets, props, and backgrounds:* You can change the positions of puppets and props during your show by tapping and dragging them. Change the background and move your show to a new location by tapping any of the background icons on the strip at the top-right corner of your screen.

   - *Recording time:* When you record, you see a timer on the screen. It counts down from 30 seconds, which is the maximum length of the show. You can purchase an option for extended recording time as an in-app purchase from the Store on the app's main menu page or purchase the Sock Puppets Complete version, which comes with longer recording times and additional content.

8. **Tap the Stop button when you're finished.**

9. **Tap the Play button to view your show.**

    The first thing you'll notice is that you sound like you've inhaled a mouthful of helium. That's the cute little effect the app has applied to the voices in your movie. You can control the pitch of the effect in the Settings option on the Home screen.

    The puppet show plays back with all the sound and movement that you recorded.

10. **Save your project by tapping the Disk icon on the top row.**

11. **Share your show.**

    Tap the Share icon (the puppet with two waves above its head) to share your show as a movie. The free version of Sock Puppets offers the option to share shows on Facebook or YouTube.

One issue I have with Sock Puppets is that the free version only allows sharing of puppet show movies on YouTube and Facebook. Although you theoretically could create a private class account, such sites are blocked in many school districts. That makes the free version extremely difficult to use unless you buy the Save to Photo in-app option from the Store on the Sock Puppets home page. That option adds the capability to save video to the iPad Photo Library where you can email or distribute it as needed. The developers should have recognized the importance of that option to classroom use and included it in the basic version.

Many apps offer the choice of purchasing additional content and features from within the app itself. In the case of Sock Puppets, you can purchase items such as additional backgrounds and puppets. You can also purchase a feature that extends the recording of the app from 30 seconds to 90 seconds. Apps that offer in-app purchasing usually have a button that enables you to buy the additional options using your iTunes account. One important difference to note for educators is that apps can often be purchased through Apple's Volume Purchasing Program (VPP) at an average 50-percent discount in larger quantities. At the moment, there isn't any method for purchasing in-app options through the VPP at a discount; you pay the full fee per copy.

Puppet Pals 2

Another impressive app for creating puppet shows is Puppet Pals 2, which works in much the same way as Sock Puppets: You select and position puppets, backgrounds, and props. You build puppets by selecting and matching varying configurations of bodies and heads. A nice additional feature is that Puppet Pals allows you to create your own custom puppets — *actors,* as they are called in the app — by cropping existing photos and placing a head on top of one of the puppet body options. In that way, students can insert themselves or any other character into a puppet show. Puppet Pals 2 also has sophisticated built-in animations that allow you to move characters' arms and legs as they walk down a street, place them in vehicles that animate with engine sounds and turning wheels as they move, and scenes where characters can do things such as ride animals and swim underwater.

Select your puppet actors and scenes; then record your narration as you move them around the sets. You can export your final Puppet Pals productions as movies directly to your Camera Roll.

Feeling adventurous? Create and export several short Puppet Pals movies to your Camera Roll and then stitch them together in iMovie with titles, transitions, and even sound effects! I'm here to help — just take a leap over to Chapter 14 if you want some guidance using iMovie.

Living the Comic Life

I absolutely loved reading comics as a kid. Intrigue, superheroes, mysteries, or comedies — it didn't matter. The characters were imaginative, and the colors brought the stories to life vividly. The minute I finished one story, I'd want to start another.

Now with the assistance of digital tools, you can do more than read comics: You can create them! What's more, you don't have to be a master artist to create your own comics. The Comic Life app is the iPad version of a software program that has been popular for several years. Comic Life makes it easy to select a template; drop in balloons, captions, and images; and create comics that you can read on your iPad, print, or share via email or Facebook. The latest version also has an In Tray option, which enables you to share your comics with other iPads nearby.

If you think of comics as simply another method for creating stories that have a specific visual style, you'll recognize that they can have wide use in education:

✔ Research an important historic event such as Columbus's voyage to discover America or the Apollo mission to the moon and create a comic that retells the story in detail.

✔ Imagine reading an act in *Hamlet* and asking students to condense the essence of the plot into a comic rewritten in their own words and using modern-day characters.

✔ Create a comic that uses a story to teach important principles such as first aid or safety. Show students the start and end scenes, and have them write what happens in between.

✔ Practice the use of foreign-language skills by creating a comic in another language.

✔ Create a comic book detailing the life cycle of an insect or animal.

Making your comic

Creating your own comic is simple and requires just a few steps. You don't even have to run off to a phone booth and change into your Superman costume! Okay, if you're under 30, you probably don't even know what a phone booth is . . .

To make your own comic, open the Comic Life app by tapping its icon on your iPad's Home screen. Then follow these steps:

1. **Tap the + icon on the opening screen, and select Create Comic.**

   The screen switches to showing you templates. Swipe through the previews to see all the options; a blank template enables you to create your own style.

2. **Tap the template of your choice.**

   Now you can choose a title for your comic, plus captions, images, word bubbles, and more (see Figure 15-3).

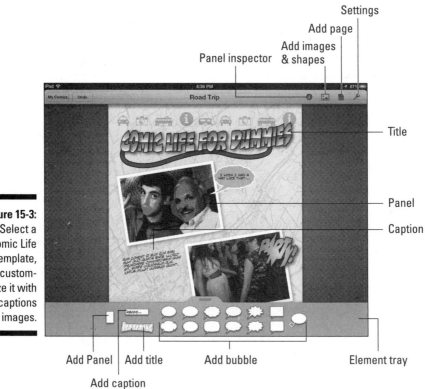

Figure 15-3:
Select a
Comic Life
template,
and custom-
ize it with
captions
and images.

3. **Customize your comic.**

   Although you have many options, customizing your comic is easy and quick:

- *Editing placeholder objects:* If you selected a pre-styled template, your page is arranged with customizable placeholders for the title, images, and text captions. Double-tap any object to edit it. In Figure 15-4, I'm ready to add a title. You can also tap and drag any object to move it to a different part of your page. The basic elements of your page include titles, text captions, panels for images, and text bubbles.

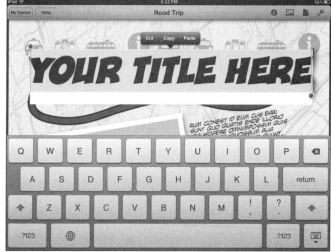

Figure 15-4: Double-tap an object to change its contents.

- *Adding panels:* Panels are the primary objects for adding and placing images in your comics. To add a panel, drag the Panel icon from the Element Tray at the bottom of the screen to any part of your page. See that little photo button in the center of your empty panel? Tap it to add an image from your Photo Library or take a picture with the built-in camera.

  Add titles, captions, and bubbles: The Element Tray at the bottom of the screen has additional objects that you can add to your page. Tap or drag one onto your page to add; then tap again to edit it.

- *Changing styles with the Panel Inspector:* Experiment and give your comic a personal touch by playing with styles and effects in the Panel Inspector. Tap any object on your page to select it and then tap the Panel Inspector icon on the top toolbar to change the look and feel of it. For example, change the color and shape of your panels, the style of your titles and captions, or select an image and apply an effect to it, as shown in Figure 15-5.

Figure 15-5:
Apply effects with the Panel Inspector.

- *Add, reorder, and remove pages:* Tap the Page icon in the top toolbar, and you see three tabs.

  The Comic tab shows you thumbnails of the different pages in your comic. Tap any page to make it the current editing page, and tap the empty page with the + icon to add a new page. Tap the selected page, and a pop-up menu gives you options to duplicate or delete it. Last, tap and drag any page to change the order of where it appears.

  The Template page enables you to browse the predefined pages included in the template you've chosen. Tap any thumbnail to add it to your comic after the current page.

  The Layout tab contains predefined pages with different arrangements of panel layouts. Tap one to add it to your comic.

Your comic is automatically saved.

4. **Tap the My Comics button to return to the screen with all your comics.**

Sharing your comic

Your comic deserves an audience.

Who would have saved the world from the Green Goblin if the creator of Spider-Man never shared his comics with the rest of the world? You can also distribute and share your comic — and you have a number of choices.

You can browse all your comics in the My Comics view. If you're editing your comic, just tap the My Comics button on the top left to go to My Comics.

Select any of your comics by tapping it. Tap the curved Export arrow in the row of icons under the preview and take a look at your options (shown in Figure 15-6):

✓ **Copy To:** Select this option to see a variety of options to copy your comic off your iPad. Your options include exporting to your iTunes library or to a Dropbox account or WebDAV server if you have either.

✓ **Share:** Tap the Share option on the menu, and you have options to share your comic on your Facebook or Twitter account (provided that you have either), send it via email, or save it to your Photo Library. You can also use the Open In option to save the comic as a PDF document and open it in another app on your iPad. That makes it easy to move the comic to a cloud storage account such as Google Drive or Dropbox.

✓ **Print:** Tap the Print option on the menu, and select your printer. For more information on setting up a printer, refer to Chapter 19.

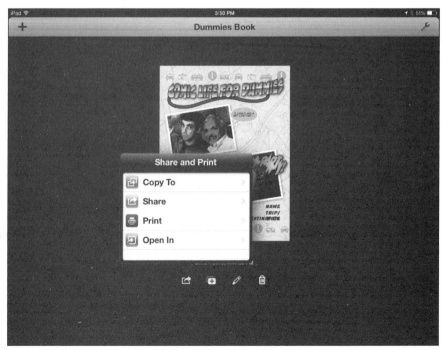

Figure 15-6:
Print and share your comic in the My Comics view.

You can also send your comics to other iPads using the In Tray feature. This feature is seriously cool. Each version of Comic Life can be set up with an In Tray to receive comics sent by other users. Follow these steps:

1. **Tap the Settings icon (wrench) in the top-right corner of the My Comics view screen, and select Open In Trays from the menu.**

   Any In Trays that are open for receiving comics on nearby iPads are displayed.

2. **Select a destination In Tray.**

   The In Tray slides down to the bottom of the screen, enabling you to choose comics from your collections.

3. **Tap and drag any of your comics down to the destination In Tray.**

   A progress meter appears as the comic is copied.

Creating Stop-Motion Animation

Mix an iPad camera, some art supplies, the Animate It! app, and a healthy dose of imagination, and you can create some amazing stop-motion animation videos. Aardman Animations Studios, the creator of the *Wallace and Gromit* series, has created Animate It!, a wonderful app that lets you create your own stop-motion animations.

Traditionally, creating stop-motion animation was a cumbersome and time-consuming process. You'd have to physically arrange objects, walk back behind a camera, and snap a photo; then move the objects and repeat the process. Of course, if your objects weren't moved in exactly the right alignment and spacing, you'd have to shoot the frames again.

Animate It! lets you snap a series of images on your own portable device. Take it anywhere, create a scene, and animate on the go. You can create your scene and objects out of anything that's available. Plasticine (you've probably heard of claymation) is great. Use LEGO pieces, paper, puppets . . . anything. You can even draw or write something on paper and take images of the message/illustration developing and moving. Considering the quality of the output you can produce, using the app is relatively simple. And I can guarantee it's a boatload of fun.

Animate It! (see Figure 15-7) includes features and tools that bring any subject to life, including a time-lapse feature, variable frame rates (to ensure that your animation is smooth and consistent), as well as copy, paste, reorder, and frame deletion functions. You can export your creation in several formats, including HD.

Figure 15-7:
Create
amazing
stop-motion
animation
videos with
Animate It!

Why use stop-motion animation? I'm so glad you asked:

✔ **It makes you break down, analyze, and re-create an event in small, bite-sized pieces.** Consider using it in a science class, for example, to have students demonstrate the evolution of a process. It could be the water cycle showing the stages of transpiration, precipitation, and so forth. Maybe it's the life cycle of a butterfly.

✔ **Re-create events.** Use it in a social science class to get students to re-create a famous scene from history, such as the Battle of Little Big Horn or the American soldiers raising the flag on Iwo Jima in World War II. One motivated group of students did a stop-motion movie of U.S. history from the Native Americans to the moon landing! Okay, I admit, it was an abridged version of American history, but it was wonderfully entertaining nonetheless. Imagine the planning, research, and teamwork that went into that project.

✔ **Have students create a short animation to illustrate an event or scene from the book they're reading in literature.** It's a great alternative to dioramas.

Students can use action figures, plastic figurines, LEGO pieces, K'NEX, paper cutouts, drawings, Plasticine, or Play-Doh to create scenes. Kids will have a blast creating movies. Your biggest problem might be dragging them out of their chairs at the end of the lesson.

To create a stop-motion project, follow these steps:

1. **Develop an idea, and build your scene complete with props and objects that move.**

   Be creative! Use a variety of props and materials. Paper, LEGOs, plants, Plasticine . . . whatever is available to set up your scene, like the one shown in Figure 15-8. Here are a few tips to get you rolling:

   - Plan how your objects will move, and make sure you've built your objects out of material that can move in the way you've intended.

   - If you need objects to move through the air, think of a way to move them with string or wire.

   - To add titles and comments, just take photos of colorful, handwritten pieces of paper. You can have titles appear a letter at a time by taking photos of the message as it develops.

   - Set your scene in a spot with even lighting. The camera has a hard time dealing with shadows and glare.

Figure 15-8:
Set up your scene in advance by using creative materials and props.

2. **Start a new project by tapping the + icon on the top-right corner of the opening screen.**

3. **Set up your camera and take a picture by tapping the Camera button (see Figure 15-9) on the right side of the toolbar.**

   Your picture appears as a frame on a filmstrip along the bottom of the screen.

Animate It! shows you a ghosted copy of your previous photo onscreen to help you adjust your objects for the next photo. This helpful feature gives you a precise idea of where your last frame is and guides you in placing your objects.

Figure 15-9:
Tap the Camera icon to snap an image and then move your objects.

Export   Undo   Copy   Play   Review   Take photo

4. **Continue moving your objects and taking lots of pictures that tell your story.**

   Most users underestimate the number of images needed. Remember, you're taking every frame as a photo. Even at a fairly slow rate, you display between 6 and 12 images per second. Move your objects in reasonably small increments to keep the animation relatively smooth.

5. **Review and edit your stop-motion movie:**

   • To delete and move frames, touch and hold a frame to move it to a different position, or move it out of the timeline to see it "vaporized."

   • Tap the Undo button to erase your last action.

   • Review the last five frames by tapping the Review button.

   • Adjust the camera's exposure, white balance, and focus settings, and switch between front and rear cameras if your device supports these features. Tap the Review button and then tap the editing screen. The menu buttons appear onscreen.

6. **Tap the Play button to see your animation.**

7. **Tap the Settings icon on the top-right corner of your screen and select Project Settings.**

8. **On the Project Settings menu, use the sliding bar to adjust your playback speed.**

Even at the slowest playback speeds, your animation may sometimes move too quickly. In the middle of the toolbar, you see a button with two frames and an arrow. Highlight any frame and tap that button to duplicate the frame. Creating copies of your frames is a simple way to slow down the animation in areas where it moves too quickly.

9. **Tap the Export button on the toolbar and select an export size.**

Animate It! creates the final video and places it in your Camera Roll. I usually opt for the smaller sizes. Remember that bigger sizes lead to larger files, which may make them more cumbersome to share later.

One of the features you won't find in Animate It! is the capability to add or record audio. That may seem like a drawback, but it forces you to focus on presenting your message convincingly with visual elements rather than simply speaking into a microphone. If you want to add sound afterward, save your animation to the Camera Roll and edit it in an app such as iMovie, where you can add narration, sound effects, or even a soundtrack.

Time-lapse photography is when you set up a camera to take a series of photos over a period of time and then turn them into a video. It effectively enables you to accelerate a slowly changing scene and watch it in a fraction of the time.

Animate It! includes a time-lapse feature that allows you to set the capture time (for example, every 30 seconds), the duration in minutes, and the number of frames that you want to capture. The time lapse automatically stops when the required number of frames has been captured. Time lapse can be a wonderful way of documenting a changing scene. (Think sunset.) You could set up the iPad and take photos of the actions of a turtle or lizard in your classroom overnight. You just need to set up your iPad in a safe spot to record the action taking place.

Chapter 16

Speaking Your Mind with Podcasts

*A*s the name suggests, the term *podcasting* derives from a mixture of the words *iPod* and *broadcasting*. What generally separates podcasts from live radio broadcasts is that podcasts are usually stored online and can be subscribed to and heard at any time.

Although it's true that the concept of sharing audio broadcasts was popularized with iPods, podcasts can now be created with almost any mobile device or computer and accessed in a variety of ways over the Internet. Also, podcasting is not restricted to audio any longer. Podcasts can include images, videos, and more. Traditionally, podcasts are also posted on a site or a service such as iTunes so that others can subscribe to them and be notified as new podcasts within their subscriptions become available. iTunes remains popular, and now the iTunes U section has been split into a separate app, which includes college and K-12 educational courses with podcasts. However, podcasts can be shared through many different web services and methods.

So when I talk about podcasting, it can mean many things. In this chapter, I focus primarily on audio podcasts. I discuss how to use, enhance, and share them using iPads.

If you want to get the most educational bang for your podcasting buck, podcasting should be integrated into larger lesson plans and objectives, require students to do some planning and possibly research, and may involve some post-production editing. In fact, you could break down the process of podcasting into several distinct stages:

- ✔ **Preparing:** Including both teacher and student preparation and encompassing technical and educational questions.

- ✔ **Recording:** Looking at the different iPad options for recording your podcasts.

- ✔ **Editing:** Did it come out as intended? Is it too long or too short? Do you want to add soundtracks or images, or edit it in any other way?

- ✔ **Publishing:** Will it be public or private? Where will it be uploaded and available?

I could get all technical about digital formats and discuss sampling rates, bit depths, compression formats, and more, but I'm even boring myself, and you'd be snoozing before you got halfway through the chapter. I keep the technical complexities to a minimum and instead focus my efforts on ways to keep your podcasting simple, fun, and, of course, educational. Read this chapter, practice a few times, and then you'll be ready to go on air.

Putting an Educational Perspective on Podcasting

You may have noticed an annoying habit I have of always asking "Why?" It's probably a hangover from the days I made my parents crazy asking them the same question. However, it's important to constantly question and evaluate what you do, especially before plunging into a time-consuming commitment like podcasting. If schools spent more time debating "why" rather than simply following the "what and how" of common educational practices, we might end up with a system that better serves the needs of our students. So . . . why podcast?

- ✔ **The quick and obvious response is partly that you can.** We've always known the importance of vocal presentation skills, but technology now allows us opportunities to have students easily record, submit, and share podcasts. It's an ideal way for students to develop their abilities to express themselves verbally. In an era where you can chat or video call anyone in the world for a few cents, cultivating verbal presentation skills has risen in importance.

✔ **Podcasts can be published and shared.** You can opt to share within your local school community or even a worldwide audience. Traditionally, work was given to a single teacher. It's amazing how much it motivates students to know that they are producing work for an audience.

✔ **Podcasting is an effective collaborative activity.** Different group members can focus on skills such as research, planning, media, presentation, and more. Podcasting can also be cross-curricular.

✔ **Technology offers you the opportunity to shatter that one-size-fits-all model of education.** Some students are better writers, and others are more effective speakers. Give them an opportunity to develop their talents by occasionally allowing them to create podcasts instead of the traditional written assignment. Remember that opportunity can still be scaffolded on to rigorous written components such as research and scripts.

✔ **You can podcast from anywhere.** The places are almost endless — from a school sporting event, an interview with someone in the community, a school or family trip . . . anywhere you can take your mobile device.

✔ **Most conversations in class are dominated by the same handful of students.** Podcasting, which can be kept private and within the class, is a simple way to allow all students to voice opinions and showcase their talents.

✔ **Podcasting is a process that involves preparation, recording, editing, publishing, and possibly responding to comments and reactions.** There's a tendency to think of podcasting as a brief activity where someone sits down with a recording device and randomly records a short audio snippet. But it encompasses a variety of skills and can be a compelling educational activity for any group of students.

✔ **Podcasting is fun.** Have some fun and distribute student work as a podcast every now and again. You can incorporate some of the content or skills required in a mini lesson before giving them their work.

✔ **Podcasting is a great tool for any language lesson.** Whether students are learning English or English speakers are learning a foreign language, having them practice speech is the most difficult part to incorporate in class. We're all naturally shy to speak in a language until we're comfortable using it. Creating simple audio recordings is an easy and effective way to have students practice their verbal skills, and it can incorporate the learning of new vocabulary, writing skills, and more.

Preparing for Your Podcast

Start by defining what you're preparing. You want students to research, plan, and script an audio broadcast that can be published in a location where it becomes available for others to hear at any time. You may allow others to subscribe to future podcasts in the series as appropriate. The teacher defines the private or public extent of the audience. Although I focus on audio-based podcasting, there's also the option to incorporate images and video.

Looking for opportunities

Start by looking for opportunities to augment familiar old written projects with podcasting. Consider broadcasting activities either within or outside your standard curriculum. The following list offers some ideas:

- **Archives:** Many colleges and schools are using video podcasts as a way of archiving lessons or snippets of lessons for future reference.

- **Oral histories:** Podcasting can be used for interviewing family members and creating oral histories.

- **Special projects:** Use podcasts for special projects such as "This Week in History." Incorporate research and mock interviews.

  Another idea for a special project is to have students create a modern version of the old broadcast radio dramas. Find some episodes of old dramas on the Internet and play them for students. Websites such as www.archive.org and www.radiolovers.com have libraries of old radio shows you can listen to for free. Discuss how they were produced. Afterward, your students can write, produce, and publish their own episodes.

- **Professional development:** Podcasting and its close cousin, screencasting, can be used for professional development. Have teachers record tutorials and examples of technology use and then share them.

- **Communication:** Use podcasts to communicate within the community and with parents. Students can manage and produce their own podcasts such as "What We Learned This Week," "Upcoming Events," "News around School," and so on.

Allowing a degree of creative license

Technology empowers students to be creative. Don't make the mistake of giving them the technology and then mandating how it's to be used ("Submit a three-minute recording listing the five main achievements of Abraham Lincoln").

Children can do amazing things with technology when you give them the trust and autonomy to be creative. California schools have a unit on the missions in California every year. Many students go on a field trip to a mission, read about their history, and submit a written assignment. One school that I've worked with allowed students to take their iPads on their trip to a mission. Students recorded the bells, conducted interviews, snapped pictures, shot video, and more. They were given the opportunity and incentive to actually listen to the sounds around the mission. They were encouraged to explore and analyze structures they would normally ignore. They searched for fine details that would make interesting photo opportunities. They actively sought out and interviewed people that lived at the mission. Giving students the freedom to use media creatively adds a very rich dimension to their experience and learning.

Clarifying the planning process

Podcasting isn't just about the actual recording. The most effective learning may come in the preparatory stages, during which students research, collaborate, script, interview, and contact outside experts. Podcasting encompasses valuable skills above and beyond the simple act of recording, and I guarantee students will be enthusiastic and immersed in planning a production.

Make sure that you clarify what you expect of them in these planning stages. If you are evaluating their work, the most important part of the evaluation may occur before the actual podcast. Create and share a rubric and any required deliverables.

Collaborating

Podcasts are generally done in groups, and you might think that all you need to do is throw students together and the ingredients will magically cook themselves into a great collaborative assignment. You know that isn't the case. There are always the students who dominate the discussions and others who remain quiet. Some do the tasks they enjoy but avoid more mundane duties. And, of course, there are those who leave the work to others, members of that latter group who get angry and resentful at having to complete most of the project themselves. Plan collaboration carefully. Some teachers have been successful defining roles for team members and then drawing numbers to decide which roles are assigned to each member. Others create groups that combine students with different skills.

Considering technical issues

Where and how will they record? How do you minimize background noise? What apps will be used for recording, editing, and publishing? Do you need external equipment such as microphones or stands? The Internet is a wonderful resource, and many educators have gone down this road. Reach out to other teachers in online educational communities or sites such as Twitter. There's a wealth of knowledge and experienced teachers willing to help you get started.

Publishing a podcast

The practice of podcasting has traditionally meant uploading a series of recordings to iTunes, where listeners can subscribe and listen to them at any time . . . and isn't it funny how anything that lasts even a few years in technology becomes "tradition"!

There are now a variety of sites and services to create and store recordings. Some even enable live online broadcasts in both audio and video format. The criteria for defining a podcast in this chapter are very simple: It should require some planning, recording, publishing to a private or public audience, and (obviously) have educational value. Technologies change way too rapidly for any of us to remain purists when it comes to defining practices.

Producing and Publishing Your Podcast

The planning is complete, and the students are ready to start recording on their iPads. As part of your planning process, you've probably looked at some options for recording. You may want to consider more than simple audio recording. Do you want the students to be able to produce a short musical theme for their podcast? Do you want to publish it with an image?

Just as important is how you will distribute the final product. Who will have access and how? If you plan on making podcasts a regular event, you want to consider allowing listeners to subscribe and be notified every time a new podcast is published.

In this section, I review some of the more popular alternatives on the iPad.

GarageBand

GarageBand (shown in Figure 16-1) has been around for a few years on the Mac and is known as a powerful tool for making music. However, it has a voice feature that can be used for adding vocals to music . . . or just as easily for recording your voice on a podcast. Even better, you can use the same tool for creating a musical opening or background soundtrack.

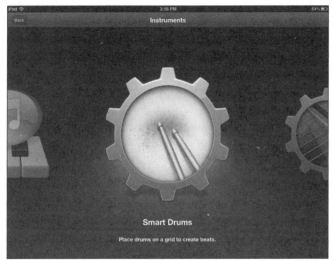

Figure 16-1: GarageBand has Smart Instruments that make it easy to produce theme music.

With the range of options offered for music and voice along with the capability to export and publish your final product, GarageBand has become the popular choice for many people producing simple podcasts on iPads.

Going into a full tutorial on using GarageBand to create music is outside the scope of this book. GarageBand tutorials exist in abundance on the Internet, and you can always take a look at the *Macs All-in-One For Dummies,* 4th Edition, by Joe Hutsko and Barbara Boyd (John Wiley & Sons, Inc.), for additional information. The following step list, however, gives you a quick-and-dirty introduction to using GarageBand for podcasting:

1. **Create a new song with a few simple tracks, as shown in Figure 16-2, to use as a themed intro.**

Figure 16-2:
A musi-
cal theme
can be as
little as a
few simple
instruments
tracks.

2. **Save your theme by tapping the My Songs button in the top left of the display.**

   Your file is saved and you're returned to the My Songs page.

   Of course, you may also consider adding some royalty-free music.

3. **Make a copy of your theme music by tapping and holding your Theme in the My Songs browser and then tapping the + copy icon.**

4. **Tap Done and then select your copy to use for your podcast.**

   You go back to TrackView, where you can tap the Instruments button on the top toolbar.

5. **Tap the Audio Recorder (shown in Figure 16-3) to begin recording the podcast.**

   You're taken to the audio recording screen. Look for the + icon in the top right. Tap it and you see that it shows you the Song Sections in your recording. Tap the Section and change your recording length to Automatic so you can speak for as long as needed.

6. **Tap the Record button, and speak clearly and directly into the iPad microphone.**

   The iPad mic is located in the top-left corner when the iPad is facing you (with the Home button at the bottom). You could also use an external microphone attached to the iPad. I discuss external mics a little later.

7. **Tap the Record button at any time to stop. Listen and rerecord as often as needed.**

Figure 16-3:
Select
the Audio
Recorder to
record the
spoken
portion
of your
podcast.

8. **Tap the 3-lined Tracks icon on the top toolbar to switch to Track View.**

   Recordings can be composed of multiple tracks that are mixed together creatively. Track View gives you access to all the tracks in your recording. Select and edit the audio track you just recorded, or insert additional tracks with background music and sound effects. Go ahead and experiment!

9. **Tap and hold the podcast in your My Songs view, and then tap the Share icon at the right of the top toolbar to select how you want to share it.**

   Your options include uploading to a SoundCloud account (which I discuss in the next section), saving it to your Facebook account, saving to YouTube, or using the Open In function to take it into another app such as iMovie if you want to add images or video. You can also share it via iTunes or email.

   You can publish your GarageBand podcast via iTunes. Tap iTunes from the Share menu, and save your podcast as an iTunes file or as a GarageBand file for editing on a different computer. To publish, select iTunes. Now start iTunes on your computer with your iPad connected wirelessly or by cable. Click your iPad in the source list and select your iPad's Apps pane on the top tabs. Scroll to the File Sharing options at the bottom of the window and select GarageBand. Your podcast should be listed, and you can drag it to your desktop or any folder. At that point you're ready to submit to iTunes.

Go to www.apple.com/itunes/podcasts/specs.html for all the details of podcast submission.

You can also publish your podcast by uploading to a blog-based website such as WordPress. Apple also provides Podcast Producer as part of its Mac OS X Server installations; you may want to look into it as an option for publishing your podcasts.

Keep things moving if you want to maintain interest. Try to keep topic segments around seven minutes or less. Using guests or recorded interviews is a great way to mix the conversation flow and tone. You should also consider incorporating musical backgrounds and little jingles as a way to transition between topics in a longer podcast.

SoundCloud

SoundCloud (`http://soundcloud.com`) describes itself as "a social sound platform" where registered users share original music, spoken word, comedy, radio shows, and any other audio recordings. Use SoundCloud directly over the web at the website or from the SoundCloud app on your device.

The recording process is simple. Just open an account, start recording (by tapping the Rec button, shown in Figure 16-4), and decide how you want to share the audio. You can upload it to your account and share it with the world, or keep it completely private.

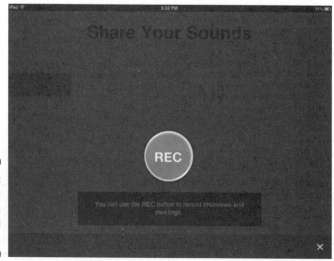

Figure 16-4:
Tap Rec
to start a
SoundCloud
recording.

Every account has a public page, but you can elect to keep recordings private and share them by specifying people that will have access or via a secret link.

Audioboo

As is the case with SoundCloud, Audioboo (see Figure 16-5) works both over the web at `http://audioboo.fm` or via a downloadable app on your device. Record your "boo" and then publish it to your account. The free account limits your recordings to ten minutes each, which should be more than enough. You can add titles, tags, geolocation info, and a photo to the recording before you upload it, and it's all saved with the recording.

Audioboo recordings are public, so you should probably check your school's policy before publishing student recordings. A simple way to manage recordings is to have everyone use one class account. In that way, you can log into the account on any browser or within the Audioboo app and have access to all student recordings.

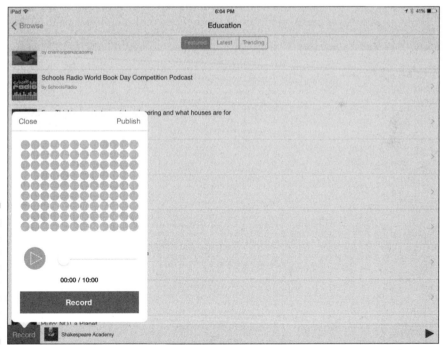

Figure 16-5: Use Audioboo for simple recordings of up to three minutes.

Using Microphones

The single most important accessory is a good-quality microphone. The microphone gives you higher-quality audio and minimizes background noise. Remember that you need only a few microphones because you won't have all students recording simultaneously. You can choose from expensive, high-end mics to more reasonably priced ones. Here are two microphone options to consider:

- ✔ **Apogee MiC 96K:** MiC is a professional-quality microphone that connects to an iPad, iPhone, or a Mac or Windows computer. MiC is about the size of an iPhone and can record vocals, voiceovers, instruments, interviews, and everything in between, and build a track right on GarageBand. The quality is great, and if you're recording music or producing more professional podcasts, it's a great choice. The bad news: It's fairly expensive at around $200.

- ✔ **Samson Meteor Mic:** The Meteor is a great little microphone recording voice or music and it's reasonably priced at about $60. The catch is that it requires a USB connection and, of course, the iPad doesn't have one. Now before you throw a lot more money at a microphone that's designed to plug directly into your iPad, consider this little workaround. You can buy a Camera Connection Kit to connect your USB mic to your iPad. They are freely available online and have a USB interface on one side, whereas the other end plugs neatly into the dock connector on your iPad. My pleasure!

Chapter 17

Directing Your Own Screencasts

· ·

In This Chapter

▶ Exploring the role of screencasting in education

▶ Creating simple screencasts with ScreenChomp

▶ Designing more elaborate screencasts with Explain Everything

▶ Recording your iPad screen by mirroring it

· ·

A *screencast* is basically a recording of the interactions you see on a computer screen. For example, you might create a software tutorial by recording menu selections and button clicks on your laptop as you narrate the process. You may want to critique a piece of art by displaying it onscreen and commenting as you zoom and point at sections of the painting. Screencasting is a simple process that has many educational applications, some of which I discuss in this chapter.

Screencasting on the iPad differs slightly from traditional screencasting on computers. If technical discussions bore you to tears, feel free to put your fingers in your ears and jump quickly to the next paragraph. Screencasting software runs in the background, recording everything you do on a computer; by contrast, apps can run in the foreground or in a background state on an iPad or iOS device. An app that runs in the foreground fills the screen, and you have access to all its features. Some apps are designed to offer functionality that runs in the background. For example, an alarm app may run in the background, checking the time until it arrives at a designated time to wake you while you hurl abuse at it. Apps have limited functionality when they run in the background. The operating system on iPads doesn't allow you to run two apps at the same time and have them share the full functionality of the iPad. For example, only one app can access the audio output at a time. Instead, most screencasting apps on the iPad use a single screencast app where you can dynamically add and change content and record interactions within the app itself. Getting dizzy yet?

Screencasting across the Curriculum

Screencasting on desktops and laptops has been around for a number of years. Screencast software records whatever is displayed on your screen and enables you to add a voiceover narration during the recording — or edit and add to it after the fact.

Most screencast apps on the iPad give you a blank whiteboard interface and a set of tools to use during your recording. You can use these programs to create imaginative tutorials for just about anything that you can illustrate visually and explain.

What are some of the ways you might use screencasts? You can certainly use them to create tutorials for students who require additional help. You can easily upload these movies to the Internet or a classroom website where students can access them at any time. Whether you're explaining an algebraic equation or illustrating a concept in science, a screencast is an effective way to get your point across.

Here's another thought . . . *"The best way to learn anything is to teach it to someone else."* Isn't that what you've always been told? It's also a great philosophy to apply in school. The iPad enables students of all ages to learn through creating their own tutorials. Here are some benefits from doing so:

✔ **Students can teach you.** Take math as an example. You can always have students work out a problem and return the answer to you. Instead, try having students record a tutorial explaining the concept behind the solution to a particular problem.

Imagine the following situation: Your students have become proficient in single-digit addition, and now you'd like to progress to double-digit addition. You could take the traditional route of demonstrating a rule in front of the class, writing examples on the board, showing the students your method for solving the problem, and then sending them off to solve reams of problems using the rule you just taught them. That's certainly the method most often used. Consider an alternative approach. Send students off in pairs with a double-digit problem and ask them to discuss it and record a screencast detailing any approach — right or wrong — of solving it. No instruction. Encourage them to learn math by thinking like mathematicians. This gives students an opportunity to develop logic by expanding on their existing knowledge of single-digit addition. Also, using a screencast rather than a paper-based response allows them to explain and verbalize their logic and thoughts.

✔ **Students can teach each other.** Students can create screencasts to help each other with homework or problems. Compile the best screencast tutorials that students build into a curated library that all students can access — now and into the future.

✔ **Students can actually teach anyone if given the opportunity.** Display student tutorials on a blog or website and make them publicly available over the Internet to anyone requiring assistance. If privacy is a concern, you can always leave out any personal information.

Outsmarting iOS by mirroring your iPad

iOS doesn't allow both a foreground and background app to run simultaneously or interact with each other with full functionality. As a result, you can't have one app that runs in the background and records the interactions occurring on the screen within a different app on the same iPad. Of course, as is often the case with technology, you can often find a way to work around limitations.

One thing that I love about technology is the way it both feeds off innovation and also encourages it. Every time you chisel out a technological rule in stone, it challenges someone to quickly come along and rewrite it. So here's the problem. You can't record the interactions on your iPad screen. You can, however, record screen interactions on a computer using software such as QuickTime. Now . . . if only there

was a way to display your iPad on your computer so that you could then record it. Aha!

One way to record a screencast of an iPad app is to *mirror* your iPad, which means to display the iPad screen on the monitor of a laptop or desktop computer. If you download and install software called AirServer from the AirServerApp website (`www.airserverapp.com`) or an app called Reflector (`www.airsquirrels.com/reflector`), you can turn your laptop or desktop into an AirPlay receiver for your iPad screen. Your iPad is now displayed on your computer. Both AirPlay and Reflector have functions that allow you to record the interactions on your iPad, or you can even use software such as QuickTime to record the iPad displayed on your laptop! Pretty smart, no?

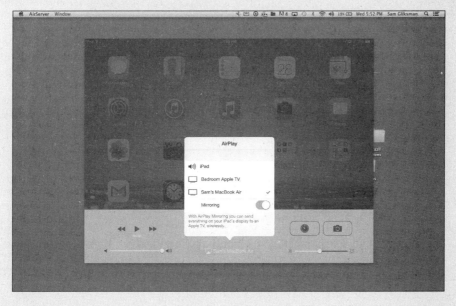

Creating Simple Screencasts with ScreenChomp

Creating screencasts with ScreenChomp couldn't be easier. Start the Screen-Chomp app by tapping its icon; then tap the large Draw and Record arrow in the top right of the opening menu screen to start a ScreenChomp. You'll be presented with a screen that looks very much like a whiteboard or, as the app publisher calls it, a *doodleboard,* as shown in Figure 17-1.

Figure 17-1: Screen-Chomp gives you a doodleboard with tools to record your screencast.

We tend to break down school into nice, neatly packaged academic courses. In reality, however, learning always tends to span varieties of skills and tra-ditional academic disciplines. You may be teaching mathematics, but any screencast or presentation is an opportunity to stress the importance of skills such as preparation, organization, rehearsal, and enunciation. Learning should never be one-dimensional.

Setting your stage

You can start recording your ScreenChomp with the default empty board, or you can prepare it ahead of your recording. Have you ever been to a stage play? The players could conceivably start with an empty stage, turn down the lights, and then bring out all the props while you sit there in your seat, but it would destroy the magic of the opening scene. There are also times when good teaching parallels theatrics, especially when you want to capture an audience's attention and draw them into your presentation.

If you want to create a tutorial on Impressionist art, for example, you could load images while recording, or you could preload a background image, such as the one shown in Figure 17-2, so that it's ready onscreen when you tap the button to start recording. I show you how to use all the tools to load images and more in the next section, but for now, just decide how you want your opening screen to look when you start the recording.

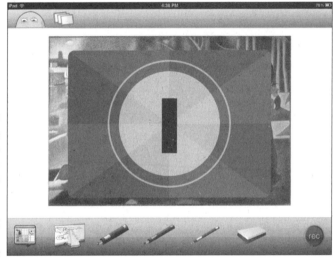

Figure 17-2:
Prepare your screen with objects you'll need when you start recording.

Using the ScreenChomp tools

The row under your ScreenChomp board includes a set of tools to use before and during your recording. I describe them here, starting from the left:

✓ **Background image:** Background images sit behind anything you draw onscreen. You can select your image from the library on your iPad or from a Dropbox account if you have one, or tap the button to take a photo with the iPad camera and have that inserted as your background. To clear your background image, tap the Background icon on the left of the bottom toolbar and select Remove Background.

✔ **Clear board:** Tap and hold this icon to erase everything on your board.

✔ **Markers:** There are three markers. Use the markers to draw on the board, whether you're writing numbers and working on a math problem, writing some text, highlighting a part of an image, or doodling a picture of your own. Tap and hold any of the marker icons to change their color and thickness.

✔ **Eraser:** Tap the eraser, and drag your finger over anything you've drawn on the board to erase it. Note that the eraser doesn't erase any part of your background image. You need to use the Remove Background option on the Background Image tool to do that.

And you're on air

After you've set the stage and prepared your narration, you're ready to go live. Follow these steps:

1. **Tap the Record button as shown in Figure 17-3.**

   ScreenChomp displays a short sequence of countdown numbers.

2. **Clear your throat and start recording when the count gets down to zero.**

   You don't have to record everything in one session.

3. **Use the Pause button to stop the recording at any point.**

   Take time to collect your thoughts, change or erase anything onscreen, and then tap to resume recording when you're ready.

4. **When you're done, tap the Stop button.**

5. **On the screen that appears, name your screencast and save it, or tap the large Trash icon to throw the screencast away and start over.**

6. **Upload and share your recording to the ScreenChomp website by tapping the ScreenChomp Share icon in the lower-right corner.**

   You don't need to create an account. When you share, your video is uploaded to ScreenChomp and you're returned to the main ScreenChomp screen. Tap the Files icon on the top toolbar and then select and tap any of your recordings. You'll be taken to the View screen where you can play and watch the video as shown in Figure 17-4. Tap the Share icon under the viewer and you can share your video in Twitter or via email, or you can tap Copy link to copy a link to your video that you can paste and share anywhere.

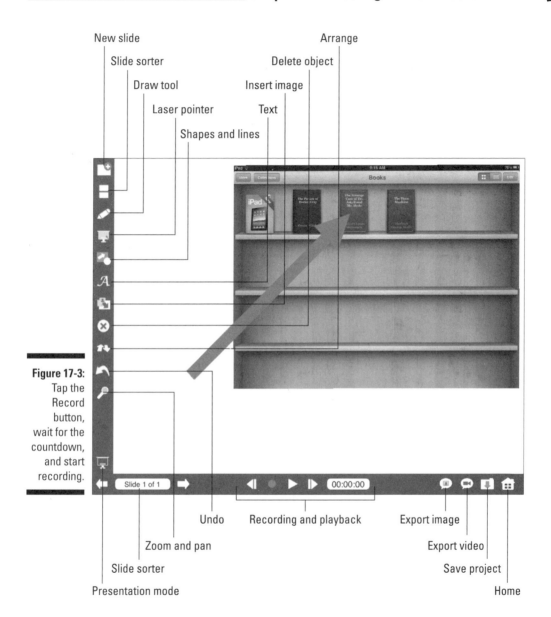

New slide

Slide sorter

Draw tool

Laser pointer

Shapes and lines

Arrange

Delete object

Insert image

Text

Figure 17-3:
Tap the
Record
button,
wait for the
countdown,
and start
recording.

Undo

Recording and playback

Export image

Zoom and pan

Export video

Slide sorter

Save project

Presentation mode

Home

Figure 17-4:
Share your Screen-Chomp video via email or Twitter, or you can copy and paste the link.

Creating Tutorials with Explain Everything

One of the most full-featured options for screencasting on the iPad is an app called Explain Everything. As the name indicates, it's a great app for creating all sorts of tutorials and recorded presentations. This app enables you to add images, videos, documents, and even web pages to your Explain Everything project. Explain Everything also does a wonderful job of linking to the cloud-based accounts you use, so you can import files and media from a variety of sources such as Google Drive, Dropbox, Evernote, and others. Arrange everything on screen and then record your screencast as you narrate and interact with content using tools for drawing, pointing, annotating, and more.

As shown in Figure 17-5, a column of tools appears on the left of the screen, and on the bottom of the screen are the slide selection arrows (on the left), the recording buttons (in the middle), and the Export and Save icons (on the right).

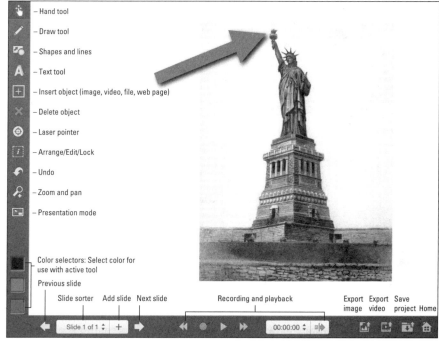

Figure 17-5:
Explain
Everything
has a variety
of tools for
creating
screencasts.

The Recording screen has a terrific assortment of tools for creating any project you might want. Use them before recording to design the slides for your screencast, or wow your audience as you use them during the screencast itself. In descending order from the top of the left column, your design tools include the following:

- ✔ **Hand:** Use it to tap and select an object. You can then move or resize it.

- ✔ **Draw:** Tap and hold the pen to change options such as pen tip and thickness. Use it for anything from scrawling some numbers to doodling a Picasso!

- ✔ **Shapes and Lines:** Tap to insert a shape; then tap and drag in your slide editor to draw it. Shapes include a circle, square, line, star, or arrow. Set the default shape by tapping and holding the Shape icon to open the menu options. Select your shape and settings for the shadow and border.

- ✔ **Text:** The Text tool is indispensable for people like me who couldn't write anything legible onscreen with my finger even if my life depended on it. Again, tap and hold to change text options such as size, font, and border.

- ✔ **Insert Object (image, video, document, and web page):** Add images or video from your iPad Photo Library or from any of your linked cloud accounts. You can also tap the From Camera option (iPad 2 and higher) to take a photo with the iPad camera and insert it directly. When you select an image to insert, you'll be presented with a screen with options to crop and rotate the image before insertion.

The Insert tool even has an option to insert a fully functioning web browser on your slide. Edit the top line of the browser to type the address of the website you want. Use the browser window to demonstrate and highlight content on any web page during your screencast. For example, if you want to create a tutorial about how to navigate the school website, you can insert a browser window into your Explain Everything project, type the web address of the school website, and demonstrate how to use it. Use the Pointer to highlight items and the Draw tool to mark up and annotate them.

✔ **Delete Object:** Tap the Delete icon and select any object by tapping it. The object is highlighted with a lined perimeter and a small x in the corner. Tap the x to remove it from your slide.

✔ **Laser Pointer:** Use the Laser Pointer during your screencast to highlight anything onscreen without marking it. Tap and hold it to choose the style of pointer.

✔ **Arrange/Edit/Lock:** Tap the I icon and select any object by tapping it. Pop-up menus are divided into Arrange, Edit, and Lock tabs. Use the Arrange menu to move the selected object behind or in front of other objects. The Edit menu offers object choices such as duplicate, copy, and set as background. Tap the Lock tab to lock object rotation, scale, and more.

✔ **Undo:** Don't you wish everything in life had an Undo tool? Well, Explain Everything does.

✔ **Zoom and Pan:** When you tap this icon, you can use the standard two-finger pinch and reverse-pinch gestures to zoom in and out of your slide.

✔ **Presentation Mode:** This tool hides most of the toolbar icons. Use it to present in full-screen mode, and tap it again to return to your normal screen with toolbars.

✔ **Color options:** Tap any of the three color squares on the bottom of the column for a quick color selection, or tap and hold to change color and opacity options for that color square.

Vocal feedback has been shown to be far more effective than the handwritten scribbles we normally give students in the margins of their work . . . and you can use Explain Everything to give students a more personalized narrative when commenting on their work. Use the Insert Object tool to insert a document from a cloud account, and then record your audio comments as you use the laser pointer and pen to annotate and highlight elements of the document. When you're done, save the project as a movie to their cloud folder.

Moving left along the bottom toolbar you'll find the following tools:

- ✔ **Previous Slide:** Tap the arrows to move one slide back or forward in your project.

- ✔ **Slide Sorter:** This tool displays thumbnails of all your slides. Tap and drag any one to a new location to change their order. Tap and hold if you want to delete a slide.

- ✔ **Add Slide:** Your screencast can have multiple slides. Add slides to your project by tapping the + icon. Adding slides is especially helpful if you want to arrange content on different slides and move between them while recording your screencast.

- ✔ **Record and Play:** Tap the round Record button when you're ready to start your recording and tap it again to stop. Use the Play button to play it back and if you tap and hold it for a second, a second Play button pops up that enables you to view the recording in full-screen mode without the toolbars.

Create your screencast in Explain Everything by following these steps:

1. **Tap the Explain Everything icon on the iPad to start the app.**

   The Explain Everything app opens and displays the home page, where you can select options to start a new project or edit an existing one.

2. **Tap the New Project button in the upper-left corner of your screen to get started.**

   Tap the + icon to start with a blank project and select a color scheme template from the pop-up menu.

3. **Tap the New Project from File icon (the + icon with page) to start a project by importing content from your Library or one of your linked cloud accounts.**

   You'll need to link to your cloud account first by tapping the Preferences button on the top right and linking your cloud services to Explain Everything.

   Explain Everything can import images, documents, and even presentations and spreadsheets. When imported, each document page, presentation slide, or photo is placed on a separate slide in Explain Everything.

   After you select one of the options for starting your project, Explain Everything displays the editing window, as shown in Figure 17-6. Time to roll up your sleeves and get to work!

Figure 17-6:
Editing an
Explain
Everything
screen-
cast that
includes a
fully func-
tioning web
browser.

4. Add a slide by tapping the Add Slide icon (refer to Figure 17-5).

5. Use the tools to add drawings, images, shapes, and text to the slide.

Draw, type, annotate, use the laser pointer, and more. The best screen-casts capture the viewer's attention by being entertaining and easy to understand. Make your screencast interesting and use the tools to help illustrate your points.

6. Repeat Steps 4 and 5 to add and edit more slides.

Remember that you can delete and arrange objects, sort slides, and undo anything you don't like (or did accidentally).

7. Prepare and rehearse your narration.

8. Tap the red Record button on the bottom of the screen, and start recording.

The timer indicates time elapsed as you record, and a Pause button appears. Tap the Pause button to stop while you adjust content, change the slides, or simply collect your thoughts. Tap Record to continue when you're ready.

9. **Edit your recording.**

   Tap the button with the recording time on the bottom toolbar and a timeline pops up with all the interactions in your recording, as shown in Figure 17-7. Tap and drag the timeline to "scrub" through it. Move back and forward to any point and rerecord from that point onward. Objects on the upper part of the timeline represent your actions. You can tap and hold any one of them, and a Delete option appears so that you can remove it if you want.

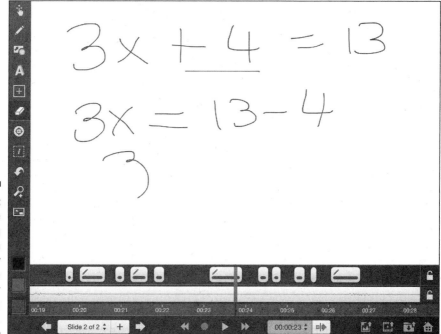

Figure 17-7: Tap the recording time button to display and move through your recording timeline.

 10. **Complete and save your screencast by tapping the folder icon with a downward arrow at the bottom-right corner of your screen (refer to Figure 17-5).**

  11. **Tap either the Export Image or Export Movie icon in the bottom-right corner of the display.**

   The Export dialog (shown in Figure 17-8) appears. You can choose to export your screencast as a movie, image, or even a PDF document; send it directly via email; or export it to the iPad's Photo Library, your YouTube account, Google Drive, Dropbox, and more.

Figure 17-8: Export your project as a movie to the Camera Roll, YouTube, or a cloud service.

Partnering with students

If you're teaching in an environment with lots of iPads, it's guaranteed that there will be times someone needs to explain how to use apps. Sure, you could spend your evenings and weekends trying to catch up and learn how to use the technology, but I can literally feel the level of tension rise as you think about it. Of course, you can ask your tech guy to help, but you know he's already running around helping 20 other people turn on projectors, fix their email, and get their documents to print. Let me remind you that you probably already have direct access to an amazing talent pool of technology experts who would be highly motivated if given the opportunity to help. Yes, your students!

Let your students create tutorials. Allow them to help other students who are having problems using technology. Need help using iMovie? Your iMovie expert is probably seated somewhere in your classroom and would love the opportunity to show what he or she can do: Just ask! Recognizing that you don't always have to be the expert and allowing students to become partners in the educational process will increase student motivation and result in a rich learning environment for everyone — including you. Try it!

Chapter 18

Releasing Your Inner Artist

*T*he iPad, and tablet computing in general, progressed rapidly from simple media consumption devices to devices that enable content creation and sharing. One of the areas where that's most evident is in the development of apps for producing different forms of art and media.

In this chapter, you're going to break out your virtual painting smocks and get your fingers dirty creating art. Also, don't assume that art is limited to that hour or two a week that kids go to their art lesson. Most traditional academic disciplines have artificial boundaries. They cross over and have relevance in other subject areas as well. Art can be used effectively in English literature, history, and most other subjects. Can you find or create music or art that represents the theme of a book? Some students who have difficulty expressing themselves verbally or with text would excel if given the opportunity to use their artistic abilities.

In recognition of the need to bolster STEM subjects (science, technology, engineering, and mathematics), educators often sacrifice the teaching and use of art in education. That is changing, however. Many now advocate for the teaching of STEAM: science, technology, engineering, art, and mathematics. The outside world is multifaceted. Apple, one of the world's most successful technology companies, would not be where it is today without Steve Jobs's strict emphasis on the art and design of Apple's products, packaging, and marketing. Our children are also not one-dimensional. They have different strengths and talents, and it's essential that we provide them ample opportunity to exercise all of them.

Fortunately, whether you're a professional artist or a kindergarten student, you have at your fingertips many iPad apps that you can use to tap into your creative potential and produce beautiful works. This chapter offers choices for smaller children who like to finger paint or create old-fashioned scenes out of felt. I show you how to make any educational topic more visual by grabbing images and annotating them. Finally, I look at one of the most popular drawing apps for those who want to unleash their inner van Gogh — and you'll never even have to clean a paintbrush!

Finger Painting with a Doodle Buddy

Every child is an artist by nature. I've never met any young children who didn't think they could draw or paint, and they always seem to derive such great pleasure out of taking tools and blending colors together into a personal work of art. It makes you wonder what happens to that innate creative urge as they grow older and school becomes more "serious" . . . but that's a topic better left for another day.

Digital painting is quick, convenient, and always available. No paint to buy and no mess to clean up. There are numerous apps that target users of all ages and levels — starting from simple finger paintings all the way through to detailed art and designs. Creating art is also fun and educational. Children can interpret stories through art, express their emotions, learn letters and vocabulary, and, most of all, have a wonderful time doing it.

The Doodle Buddy app is a great place for budding artists to start. The interface is simple and easy to navigate (see Figure 18-1). You select colors and paint with your fingers, with additional options for adding backgrounds and stamps. And if you don't like your drawing, just shake your iPad to clear the screen and start over again.

Open the app to see a canvas and set of tools. Select among the following list of options when creating a work of art in Doodle Buddy:

✓ **Draw:** Tap the Painting Tools icon. Select a tool. Your tool choices include Brush, Chalk, Glitter, Smudge, and Eraser. Tap to select your tool of choice and select a color. Use the slider along the bottom of the panel to set the width of your stroke. Tap the canvas and start doodling.

✓ **Stamp:** Add a stamp from the gallery of images. Tap to select your stamp and then tap in your canvas to stamp it into the drawing.

✓ **Stencil:** Select one of the stencils and tap in your drawing to insert it. Grab the handles to rotate or change the size of the stencil, and then paint over the stencil so that the color fills in the gaps. When you're done, tap the Painting Tools icon and the stencil disappears, leaving you with your perfectly stenciled drawing.

✔ **Text:** Select a font and type. Text appears in the currently active color, and you can grab the handles to rotate or resize it.

✔ **Background:** Tap the Background icon to add an image from the Doodle Buddy gallery or one from your iPad's Photo Library. Select the plain white background to remove any current background.

✔ **Undo or Clear:** Tap the icons on the bottom left of the image to undo your last action or clear the entire canvas. Note that Clear doesn't remove the background.

✔ **Save and Share:** Tap the Settings icon and save your image to the iPad Photo Library or share it via email.

Figure 18-1:
Doodle Buddy contains easy-to-use tools for children to create art.

Undo Clear   Painting Tools Stamp   Text Background   Settings

Stencil

The Doodle Buddy app is a free download but, as you know, there's no such thing as a free lunch. Banner ads are displayed every so often across the top of the screen as you use the app. Don't fret; it's easy to get rid of them. Tap the Settings icon in the lower-right corner and tap the Hide Ads option. It costs a small, in-app purchase fee, but you'll be rid of those annoying ads forever.

Creating Images Never Felt This Good

Did you ever play with felt boards when you were a kid? It's a simple concept. You get a large felt-covered board and then cut out large felt letters and images and place them on the board. Magically, friction holds it all together as you assemble your scene. You expected me to ask whether it "felt" good, didn't you? I'd never resort to using such corny puns.

With the aid of the right apps, the iPad is a device with a thousand faces. Use the Felt Board app and it does an amazing job of mimicking that big old felt board you used as a kid. Play with different backgrounds, dress up characters, and add props to assemble your felt masterpiece (see Figure 18-2). When you're done, save the image to your iPad Photo Library, where you can share it with others. Felt Board offers lots of opportunity for imaginative and visually creative play. It's a wonderful educational tool and a whole lot of fun.

Figure 18-2:
Select and position backgrounds, characters, and props to assemble your Felt Board.

I'm sure you can come up with a variety of creative ways to use Felt Board. Here's a short list to start you thinking:

✔ **Re-create stories:** Read a book with kids and have them re-create scenes from the story in Felt Board.

✔ **Participate in storytelling:** Ask them to make up and/or write a story, and then create the characters and scenes from the story in Felt Board. Try the opposite. Have them play with Felt Board to create a scene they like; then when they're done, ask them to tell a story about the scene. If you want to make it more fun, have them exchange the iPad with another student and create a story about someone else's Felt Board scene.

✔ **Narrate stories:** Create scenes in Felt Board and save them to the iPad Photo Library. Open up a screencasting app (see Chapter 17), insert the photos, and have the students record themselves narrating the parts of the story that go along with each scene.

✔ **Create an e-book:** Create scenes in Felt Board and save them to the iPad Photo Library. Open an e-book creation app such as Book Creator (see Chapter 10), insert the Felt Board scenes, and add the story. Typing can be difficult, so put on your thinking cap. Try handwriting the story, snapping a photo of it, and inserting an image of the handwritten text in the book. Maybe you can also use the recording features in Book Creator to tell the story with audio.

✔ **Visualize:** Have students place and arrange objects by color. Ask them to count and place different numbers of objects on their board. Use Felt Board to connect objects with a letter or to do simple arithmetic operations (see Figure 18-3).

Figure 18-3:
Use Felt Board for students to visualize arithmetical concepts, letters, colors, and more.

Of course. You were waiting for me to tell you how to use the app, right? Just follow these steps:

1. **Select a background.**

   Tap the chevron icon attached to the panel on the left of the Felt Board display. The panel slides out to show thumbnails of the different libraries of objects you can insert on your board. The very first icon represents backgrounds. Slide through the thumbnails and tap to select a background.

2. **Browse through the libraries of objects and tap to select items you want on your board.**

   Items drop right on to your board; you can move them around as needed. Expand or contract with two fingers to make items larger or smaller and twist an object with two fingers to rotate it.

3. **Insert characters and add elements such as hair, facial features, and clothing.**

   All the objects are scaled to fit exactly on your characters. Don't you wish it was that easy when you shopped for clothes? When you add elements to a character, they automatically attach and move with it. Tap the object once to unlock and reposition it.

4. **To delete items, tap the Recycle icon on the bottom right.**

   All the objects begin to wiggle, and you can tap on any object to delete it. When you're done deleting, tap the Recycle icon again.

5. **Tap the Camera icon to save your scene to the iPad Photo Library.**

   Once it's there, you can share it or use the image in other apps.

6. **Save to the Felt Board Gallery by tapping the Gallery icon on the right (it's the one that looks like four small photos).**

   The scene is saved to your Gallery for later use and editing. Tap the Gallery icon at any time to open a project from the Gallery, or start a new one by pressing the + icon in the Gallery.

Annotating Images with Skitch

Many times, you may want to mark up an existing photo or image with annotations, highlights, and notes. Skitch is an app that's great for those occasions.

Select an image from your iPad Photo Library or use your camera to capture a new one. Add arrows that point out details in an image (see Figure 18-4). Add text that informs and explains. Use the Pen tool to highlight, sketch, and write on the image. Add shapes, stamps, blur details, crop the image, and more. Use different colors and pen widths for emphasis. When you're done, save the annotated image to your iPad Photo Library and share it with others. There many practical reasons to mark up a photo, illustration, map, or any other image:

- ✔ **Explain:** Add detail to an image for a Science project. Take a photo of an object with specific dimensions or angles; then highlight and add notes for a project in Math.

- ✔ **Make suggestions:** Highlight parts of an illustration or text and use notes to offer suggestions on how to improve it.

- ✔ **Capture web pages:** Select Web from the menus on the bottom of the screen, and Skitch opens a web browser for you. Go to any website and tap Snap to take a screen shot of it. Add details highlighting the URL, elements on the page, and/or notes on how to use the site.

- ✔ **Sketch:** Select Draw from the menus on the bottom of the screen and use the Skitch tools to quickly sketch an image for someone. (Try saying "Sketch with Skitch" nine times quickly.)

- ✔ **Save and annotate maps:** Select Map from the menus on the bottom of the screen. Find the area you want on the map and tap Snap to take a screen shot of it. Mark up directions and any relevant details.

- ✔ **Blur details:** Use the Pixelate tool to blur private information in an image such as a license number or address.

- ✔ **Mark up a PDF:** Use the Open In feature in any app that uses PDF documents and select Skitch as the destination. Select the pages you want to mark up from the sidebar in Skitch. Highlight parts of the document and add notes in Skitch.

- ✔ **Share:** Tap the Share icon and share your image via email, Twitter, or Facebook. Skitch is owned by the same company that makes Evernote, and you can save images to an Evernote notebook or share them with others through a URL to the file in Evernote.

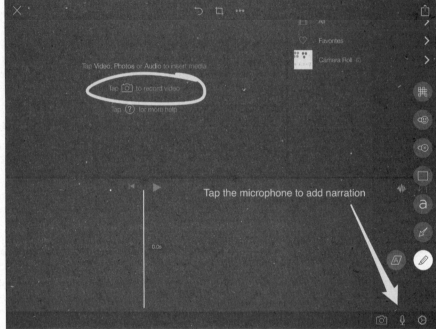

Figure 18-4:
Skitch has tools such as arrows, pens, and text that you can use to mark up images.

Painting a Masterpiece with Brushes 3

The brilliant thing about the Brushes 3 app (see Figure 18-5) is that it's used by artists all over the world, and yet it's still simple enough for beginners. It's a powerful tool for creating original artwork on the iPad, and paintings created with Brushes have been shown on the web and in galleries, and have illustrated the cover of *New Yorker* magazine. Even iconic pop artist David Hockney uses Brushes. The app features an advanced color picker, several realistic brushes, layers, and zooming to 32x — all in an uncomplicated but comprehensive interface. And your class of fourth-graders will love it just as much as David Hockney does.

Brushes has multiple layers that you can work on separately and that can be used with or without a stylus, which is a bonus in an educational setting. Another unique feature is that it has a Playback function that allows you to see any art redrawn onscreen. Its quick results certainly make it a hit with kids.

Figure 18-5:
The Brushes
iPad app
can be used
by begin-
ners and
professional
artists alike.

Copyright 2012, Debbie Azar

Getting started

The main steps in using the Brushes app are as follows:

1. **Tap the + button on the Gallery page to create a new blank painting.**

   Select the size and orientation of your canvas and tap Create.

2. **Choose your color, brush size, and shape, and begin painting with your finger or stylus.**

   Paint by moving your finger across the screen. It's as simple as that. If you want more detail, you can pinch to zoom up to 64x.

   Brushes creates a painting on multiple layers. Each layer is independent of the others, so you can work on a layer without disturbing the contents of the other layers.

3. **When you're finished, tap the Gallery button to return to Gallery.**

   Your painting is automatically saved. Brushes also enables you to share and export your paintings.

4. **Title your painting.**

   To name your masterpiece, tap the text under the image in the Gallery and replace it with your title.

The painting interface offers the following set of tools (along the bottom toolbar, as shown in Figure 18-6):

✔ **Color palette:** Tap the rectangle in the lower-left corner to bring up an RGB color wheel, as shown in Figure 18-7. Select a color from the boxes, or mix your own individualized palette by using the hue/saturation color wheel on the left. Note that you can also change the opacity by using the slider underneath the wheel.

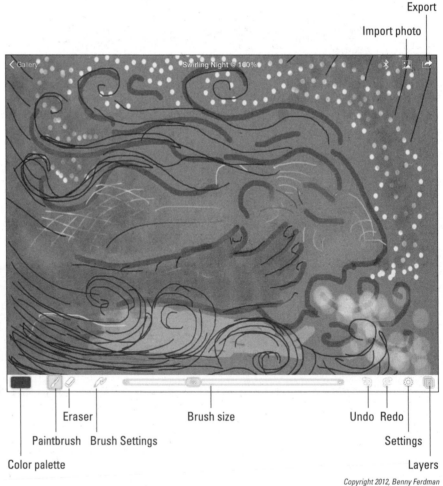

Export

Import photo

Figure 18-6:
The painting interface has a set of tools along the bottom toolbar.

Eraser   Brush size   Undo Redo

Paintbrush Brush Settings   Settings

Color palette   Layers

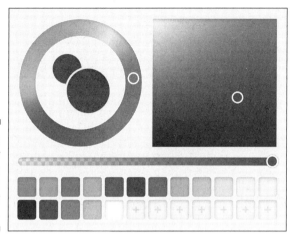

Figure 18-7:
Select your painting color from the color palette.

✔ Maybe I'm just a klutz, but my fingers weren't made for drawing on a touchscreen. If you're anything like me, invest in a stylus, and use it for writing and drawing. Also, I recommend paying a few extra dollars to get one that's responsive and accurate.

Sometimes you'll want to blend colors in your painting. Use the transparency slider to make any color more transparent and easier to blend.

✔ **Eyedropper:** Most paint programs have an Eyedropper tool that allows you to click or tap in an image to pick up a color. Brushes uses a simple shortcut. Tap and hold anywhere onscreen to activate the Eyedropper. It reads the color under your touch and makes it the active color. Note that after you use the Eyedropper, the active tool automatically reverts to the Paintbrush.

✔ **Paintbrush:** Select this tool to start painting.

✔ **Brush Settings:** Tap the Brush Settings to bring up the Settings menu, as shown in Figure 18-8. There's a sliding selection of brushes in a column, and each brush has its own unique shape and texture. Swipe through and tap to select a brush type. When you tap a brush, a small "edit" icon appears on it. If you edit the brush, you can change its density, spacing, angle, and more. Tap the + icon and you can even create your own brush type.

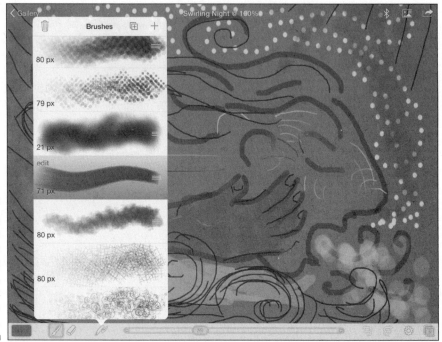

Figure 18-8:
Use the Brush Settings to select, edit, or even create a brush type.

Although the iPad is not pressure-sensitive, you can make lines with varying thickness that will give you the tapered look of a natural paintbrush stroke. Tap the Brush Settings icon and edit a brush to change Dynamic Weight, Dynamic Intensity, and Dynamic Angle. This enables you to create truly organic-looking lines.

✔ **Eraser:** This tool uses the same features as the Paintbrush except that it removes color instead of adding it. Use the Brush Settings to control the quality of the eraser. Just make sure you're on the right layer when you're using it.

✔ **Undo:** Use the Undo tool to step back through the actions you've taken. This feature is for all your "Ugh!" moments.

✔ **Redo:** It looked better before, didn't it? Press Redo to reverse your Undo.

✔ **Layers:** Layers is a cool feature that artists and designers use all the time in programs like Adobe Photoshop. Brushes allows you to create individual layers that can be separately manipulated and worked on. Work on any one layer without disturbing the contents of other layers. This feature gives you a lot more control over the final result, and layers can be rearranged, duplicated, locked, or discarded as needed. You can also adjust the opacity of each layer.

How would you use layers? You could have a colored layer as a background, do your drawing in a dark outline on the top layer, and color it in on the middle layer. You can change the background at any time without altering any other layer.

Tap the Layers icon to display the Layers menu, shown in Figure 18-9. Your layers appear as thumbnails with the base layer to the far left. Some things you can do with layers include the following:

- To add a new layer, tap the + icon on the top right.

- To delete a layer, select it by tapping; then tap the Trash icon.

- Use the slider on the bottom to change the opacity/transparency of a selected layer.

- Tap any layer to make it the active layer. The selected layer has a blue highlight around it.

- Change the order of your layers by tapping and dragging the lined icon to the right and dropping it in a new position.

Figure 18-9:
Work on any one layer without disturbing the contents of other layers.

Layers has many other cool features, and I encourage you to experiment with them. Half the fun is playing with all the different features and seeing how they affect your image.

Paint a little blob of your favorite colors on a separate layer of your painting. That way, using the Eyedropper tool, you can quickly select colors from your palette by tapping and holding the blobs.

Painting over a photograph

An important feature of Brushes is the capability to use photos as the basis for your artwork. In fact, this is the method used for creating the *New Yorker* magazine illustrations. Here are the steps:

1. **Tap the Import icon on the top navigation bar, and pick a photo from your Camera Roll.**

2. **Drag and pinch to position your photo, and tap Accept (or Cancel).**

3. **Add a layer for painting by tapping the Layer icon and then tapping +.**

4. **Select a paintbrush, sample a color from your photo by tapping and holding on it to bring up the Eyedropper tool (or pick an entirely different color), set your brush settings, and paint.**

Note: It's particularly effective to play with the opacity when painting over a photograph if you want to keep some original detail. Do you want to create an Impressionist painting? Sample the colors of the photo with your Eyedropper tool, and choose a large brush to trace the lines and colors of the scene. By getting rid of the detail and just highlighting colors and shapes, you can create an Impressionistic effect. Make sure to work on separate layers so that you can always undo or erase your steps while leaving the photo intact.

Those annoying telephone wires? Just paint them out. You can get different effects by playing with the blending modes in the Layers menu to have your layers interact in different ways. The best way to learn is by experimenting.

Watching a masterpiece evolve

Brushes records all the actions taken in a painting. You can then watch a "video" of your painting as it took place, revealing all the steps you took in creating your art. It's kind of magical — like those time-lapse movies of flowers blooming that you used to love as a kid. Just tap the Play button when you open a project from the Gallery to watch an exact replay of your painting process.

Part VI
The iPad Classroom

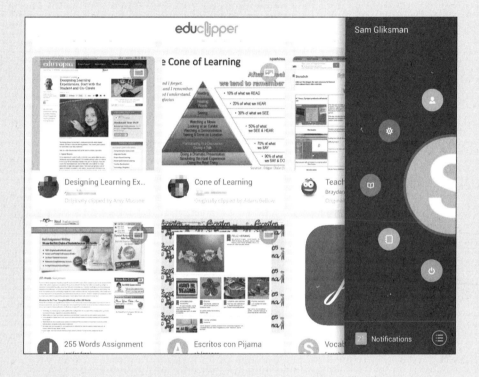

Visit www.dummies.com/extras/ipadineducation to read an article about tools and apps for collaborative learning with iPads.

In this part . . .

- ✔ Explore tools that facilitate simple and efficient classroom workflows
- ✔ Create presentations on your iPad
- ✔ Construct and present student portfolios of work
- ✔ Use quizzes and polls for greater feedback and interaction
- ✔ Examine tools and apps for collaborative learning with iPads

Chapter 19

Creating Effective Classroom Workflows

*i*Pads are the shining light in the latest wave of high-technology mobile devices. However, I constantly walk into classrooms where students have iPads only to see a teacher handing out photocopies or assignments being submitted on paper. It's more than ironic that schools are spending large budgets on innovative technologies, yet many schools are still mired in paper-based classroom workflows. Honestly, you can't blame them. There's no disk drive or USB port on an iPad, and it doesn't easily connect to the school network where students can drop work for a teacher. Exchanging information is a vital part of education, and most of the processes we've become comfortable using with computers simply don't work with iPads. What's a teacher supposed to do?

Don't stress. Help is on the way. There's a range of simple, viable resolutions to most of your classroom workflow needs. All you need are some easy-to-use tools and a little guidance. So just sit back, relax, and take your time browsing through the rest of this chapter as I describe some solutions.

Classroom Workflow Options

When you think of managing iPads in schools, the focus is generally on how to set up and use the device itself. What we forget is that school is essentially about communication and the exchange of information. Enabling simple and effective exchange of information is critical to the process of education. That nature of information exchange is typically called a workflow.

However, when you go to an architect, you don't just ask him to design a house. You begin by discussing needs and desires. What sort of house do you want? The same logic applies to the design of information workflows. In this section, I define some workflows for a 21st-century classroom, and later I'll dive into some of the solutions.

Consider the following workflow requirements:

✔ **Delivering information:** Content delivery was the staple of education in the 20th century, and even though we strive for a more student-centered approach to learning, there are still times when teachers need to deliver content. This is best served by a web-based service where teachers can "drop" the information in a folder and students can easily pick it up.

✔ **Submitting information:** Students need to be able to easily submit work to teachers. One important distinction today is that information is multifaceted. It's no longer just text. Information may be images, videos, or links to the web, and a workflow often has to deal with files that can be quite large.

✔ **Learning anywhere, anytime:** Key elements of 21st-century learning are access and communication. Students need to be able to work in class and have access to edit and share that work outside of class. Using secure cloud storage can enable that anywhere, anytime access.

✔ **Annotating, marking up, and returning documents:** Receiving constructive feedback is critical to learning. Many teachers require workflows that enable them to mark up and annotate documents, create a digital copy, and then return that copy to students in a secure location.

✔ **Enabling continuous student narrative:** A blog is an ongoing narrative owned and edited by a single student. What distinguishes it from a regular journal is that it can be shared privately with a single person such as a teacher, shared within a group, or shared with the general public.

✔ **Enabling collaborative work:** Students often need a secure location to share information and work together on projects securely.

Now let's move on and see some ways to structure solutions for these workflows.

Personal Cloud Storage and Sharing

It wasn't too long ago that everyone was buying increasingly large hard drives to store and back up their files. Although some people still take that route, many now opt for web-based or "cloud" storage services that have become extremely popular over the past few years. A cloud storage service such as Dropbox or Google Drive enables you to store and back up your files online, access them from any device, and easily share them with others. There are several excellent cloud services you can use on your iPad, and many offer free accounts with several gigabytes of storage space.

Dropbox is one of the many cloud-based solutions for file storage and sharing. It's popular because of its features, price, and the fact that it works across devices, platforms, and over the web.

Open a free account at www.dropbox.com. You can easily store files in a Dropbox folder from any device and set sharing permissions for the folder. Depending on the intended usage, you can keep the folder private, share it with individual Dropbox users, or make it available to anyone with the link. Some of the ways Dropbox can be used include the following:

- ✔ **Accessing your account on any device:** Access your Dropbox account over the web or download the Dropbox app on your iPad for even simpler access (see Figure 19-1). Open the app and sign into your account. Your Dropbox files will be available and you'll be able to add content from other apps on your iPad.

- ✔ **Saving to your Dropbox account:** Most iPad apps have a Share option that enables you to open the content in another app. Tap the Share icon in any app and use the Open In function, selecting Dropbox as the destination app. The Dropbox app opens and the content is filed in your Dropbox account.

- ✔ **Distributing information:** Pushing information out to students is a piece of cake. Select the folder or file you want to share, tap the Share icon, and select Copy Link. Distribute the link to students or anyone else to whom you'd like to grant access. The other person doesn't even need a Dropbox account.

- ✔ **Submitting work:** There are definitely more efficient ways to collect work from students. However, if you're in a pinch, students can submit their work without having an account as long as they have access to email. What's the secret? Check out http://sendtodropbox.com. Sign up and it creates an email address for your Dropbox account. Anyone can email content to that email address, and it's automatically filed in your Dropbox.

Figure 19-1:
Sharing and
access-
ing files
from any
device is
simple with
a Dropbox
account.

Dropbox is designed to be a wonderful solution for personal file storage and access. You can also use the sharing option as a simple and effective method for pushing out information to students. However, Dropbox doesn't have any administrative options for setting up and maintaining different accounts and folders for students. I wouldn't recommend creating and using a single classroom Dropbox account on every student iPad, as that gives each student the ability to accidentally move and delete anyone's folders and files. Yes, I said "accidentally."

If you're in the United States and want your students to sign up and use any web account or service, the Children's Online Privacy Protection Act (COPPA) requires that they either need to be at least 13 years old or that they have permission from a parent or guardian. I strongly recommend that you have a Responsible Use Policy signed by the children and their parents and that you include a section that explicitly grants permission to sign up for web accounts that are intended strictly for educational purposes.

Sharing and Collaborating with Google Apps

Google Drive lets you store and access your files anywhere on any device. As a personal cloud storage service, it's certainly comparable in features to Dropbox. Where Drive really excels is in its powerful options for sharing and collaborating on your work anytime and with anyone.

Google Drive and Docs are part of the GAFE suite, which contains a wide range of extremely valuable tools for any school or organization. Educational institutions can sign up for a free customized GAFE domain. You have the choice of creating Google Apps accounts for all staff and students or any subset of either. The GAFE suite contains several of the well-known apps you associate with Google. Apps include Gmail, Google Calendar, Drive, Docs, Sheets, Slides, Sites, and more. You can activate all of them or select only the ones that fit the current needs of your school. Most of the apps work across devices and provide powerful features for sharing and collaboration.

Google Drive is the hosting account for your content. If your school has signed up for a free GAFE domain, accounts can be set up and administered for all staff and/or students in your organization. Each student with a school Google/GAFE account will most likely have access to Google Drive, where they can store, share, and collaborate on their content. Content can be created in companion apps such as Google Docs and Google Sheets. Describing everything you can do with GAFE would likely take an entire book, but here's a quick rundown of some of the main features and options:

- ✔ **Using Drive:** Access Google Drive on the web by going to `http://drive.google.com` or by downloading the Drive app on your iPad.

- ✔ **Moving content into Drive:** Remember that you can use the Share/Open In function in most apps to move your content from that app into Drive. Tap the Share icon and select Drive as the destination app.

- ✔ **Creating content:** The Drive app on your iPad is used for access and sharing of your content. Create documents in the Google Docs app and save it back to a folder in Drive.

- ✔ **Sharing permissions:** Content saved in Drive can be shared. You can give others rights to view or edit any content in your Drive account. (See Figure 19-2.)

- ✔ **Distributing content:** Create a folder in Drive and give your students permissions to view it. From that point forward, anything you place in that folder will automatically be available to all students. Because you only gave them viewing rights, they will be able to open and create a copy of the document, but they won't be able to edit the original.

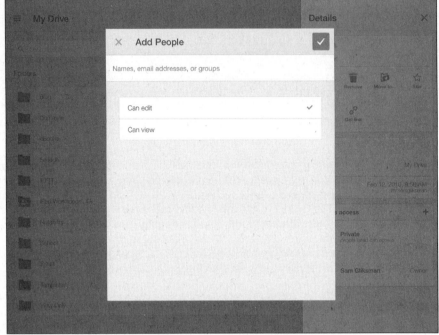

✔ **Sharing folders with students:** Create a folder for each student and give them editing permissions. You'll be able to open, review, and edit any document the student saves in that folder.

✔ **Unplugging the printer:** Create shared folders where students can drop off their work. You'll never need an ink cartridge again.

✔ **Commenting and feedback:** A critical part of every teacher's role is to offer constructive feedback to students. Too often, however, that feedback comes at the end of the process, when students have completed work and submitted it. Wouldn't it be great if you could "pop in" and give some advice as the students are working on their projects? When you're sharing a folder with a student, you have access to the files in it at any time. Open a document in Docs and use the Comment function to highlight parts of the document and give them meaningful feedback while they're still working on it. (See Figure 19-3.) Your comments may help improve the quality of the final work they submit.

✔ **Providing peer feedback:** Use the sharing features to allow students to edit and offer feedback on the work of other students.

✔ **Enabling group collaboration:** Students working in groups can share and collaborate on the same content. Two or more students can be working on the same document — even at the very same time. You can use the Revisions feature to track contributions made by each student. Create a shared folder and they can share and collaborate on documents and resources.

✔ **Department sharing:** Create a shared folder among teachers for lesson plans and resources used across your department or grade.

✔ **Going global:** Sharing doesn't have to stop at your classroom walls. Consider projects with classes and people in other parts of the world, and create shared folders to work collaboratively on content.

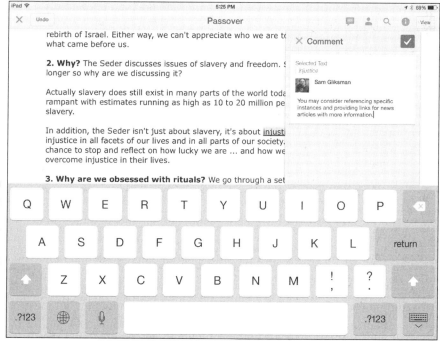

Figure 19-3: Sharing a Drive folder with each student enables you to open files and offer feedback.

Hapara makes you the master of your domain

Even if your organization is fortunate enough to have an IT department, it's often difficult to get overworked IT staff to provide the prompt assistance required to keep classes running smoothly. When it comes to organizing and administering the Google Drive content for your class, consider getting a tool that empowers you to take control. Hapara (`http://hapara.com`) just might be the tool you need.

Hapara gives teachers and administrators an overview of each student's most recent work in Google Drive. It organizes content by class and student, automatically creating a Drive folder for each student in your class and granting you shared access. The Teacher Dashboard simplifies the process of administration. Use the Smart Copy feature to quickly share files with the whole class or any group of students. Automatically create subject or assignment folders for all class members. Track student activity and hover over any student file to view its contents. Share student work with their parents. There are many options . . . all implemented with a few simple clicks.

Hapara is stacked with features that help make you the master of your (Google Apps) domain. And just for good measure, it also gives you administrative control of all your Google Sites, Blogger, and Picasa class accounts.

Paperless Assignments with Showbie

Showbie is an app that makes it relatively simple to assign, collect, and provide feedback on student work with iPads. And just between the two of us, it's free. OK, wise guy, yes, that does mean you can't get your money back if you don't like it, but I'm betting that you will.

Here's how you get started:

1. **Create an account.**

   Sign up for a teacher account online at `www.showbie.com`, or download the Showbie app and create a teacher account when you start the app.

2. **Create a class.**

   Tap the + icon on the bottom menus to create a new class. (See Figure 19-4.) Each class is given a unique code for identification. Distribute the class code to your students.

3. **Students join the class.**

   Students also need to have the Showbie app. If students don't already have an account, they're prompted to create one with a name and password when they first start the app. When prompted for a class to join, they enter your class code (see Figure 19-5). Note that each class has a unique code. To join additional classes, students tap the Settings icon on the top menus, tap the Join a Class option, and enter the unique code for that class.

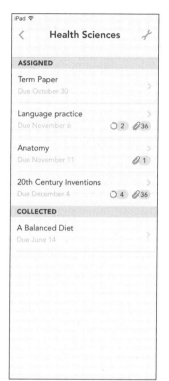

Figure 19-4:
Showbie
shows
your list
of classes
(left) and the
assignments
for each one
(right).

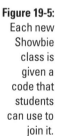
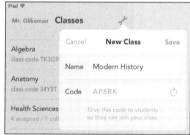

Figure 19-5:
Each new
Showbie
class is
given a
code that
students
can use to
join it.

Showbie is a great iPad app, but it also works with any Internet browser. That means you can use any computer or device to sign in to your account at www.showbie.com, and you get the exact same functionality that you have in the iPad app. It's a great solution for a multidevice environment or in situations where students have use of an iPad at school but need to continue their work on a different device at home.

Creating a Showbie assignment

Roll up your sleeves because now you're set up and ready to start creating assignments for your class. Tap any of the class names in the left column and follow me:

- ✔ **Create a new assignment.** Tap the Settings icon in the top menus to create a new assignment. Give your assignment a name and a due date. You can also lock your assignment while you prepare it, and it remains hidden to students until you return and unlock it.

- ✔ **Distribute instructions in the Shared Folder.** The assignment you just created is listed in the left column. Tap it to create and distribute information about the assignment. The left column contains the list of students that have joined your class and a Shared Folder on the top of the list. Tap the Shared Folder to create and distribute information about the assignment. Your options include the following:

  - *Add files.* When students open the assignment, they have access to all the information you leave in the Shared Folder. Tap the + icon on the top right of the display to add files for students. (See Figure 19-6.)

  - *Take a photo.* Tap the Camera icon to activate the camera and take a photo. Snap a photo of anything students might need for the assignment.

  - *Add media.* Tap the Photo Library icon to add any images or video from your iPad's Camera Roll.

  - *Comment*: Type instructions for students in a short text note that's dropped into the folder.

  - *Voice Note*: Clear your throat and use the iPad's microphone to record audio instructions for your students.

  - *Another App*: To save work from another iPad app into Showbie, open that app and use the Open In option. Select Showbie as the destination.

Submitting work for a Showbie assignment

Your assignment is automatically available to students when they log into the Showbie app. When they tap it, they're presented with the Shared Folder and any files that you've left for them. The proverbial ball is in their court. Let's take a look at how they submit their work to you.

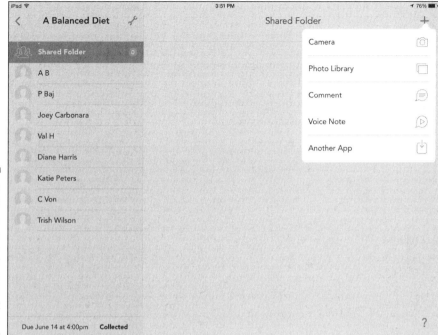

Figure 19-6:
Add
documents,
notes,
images,
video, or
audio to
the shared
assignment
folder.

Using an iPad in class opens all sorts of avenues for utilizing different media for custom expressions of knowledge. Students have access to a camera, microphone, and a host of creative apps. They can certainly submit a typed document for an assignment, but why not also utilize the wide and very rich range of options for submissions? When submitting work for an assignment, students have the very same file options you had when you added files to the Shared Folder. They can submit documents, access photos and video in the Photo Library, and even submit recorded audio. Here are a few ideas to get your creative juices flowing:

✔ Ask students to take or find images, maybe geometric shapes, illustrations of plants, anatomical diagrams, or historical maps. Then they can edit and add information to the images using Skitch (see Chapter 18), save the edited image to the Photo Library, and then submit it to a Showbie assignment.

✔ You're thinking of having them create an engaging video or animation, but you're scratching your head wondering how you'll access all those movies. No problem. Students open the assignment in Showbie, tap to add a file from the Photo Library, and select the video for submission.

✔ Wondering how their reading skills are progressing? Want to give them opportunities to practice their new Spanish-speaking skills? Create an assignment that asks them to use the Voice Note and they can record themselves reading or speaking.

You can submit almost any content to a Showbie assignment using the iPad's Share option. Most apps have a Share or Open In option. (See Figure 19-7.) Simply tap the Share icon within the app that was used to create the content. Select Showbie as the destination app, and Showbie prompts you with a list of open assignments for submission. Easy. Oh, and you never used a single sheet of paper!

Select Showbie as the destination

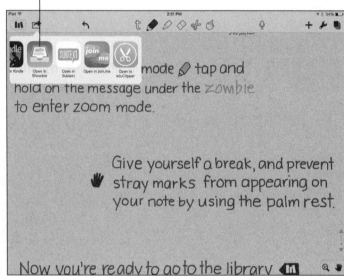

Figure 19-7:
Use the
Open In
function
in other
iPad apps
to submit
content to
a Showbie
assignment.

Reviewing the assignment and giving feedback

After students start submitting their assignments, you'll notice a small tag on the right of the assignment name indicating the number of submissions that have been received. Review the work with a few simple steps:

1. **Tap the assignment name to open it.**

   Students who have submitted work have small attachment icons next to their names.

2. **Tap any student's name to open that student's folder.**

   The submission is listed in the right side of the display, and you can simply tap it to open and review it. Note that if you upgrade to the paid version of Showbie, it includes tools for you to annotate the content.

Using a Learning Management System

Showbie is a wonderful app with the very specific focus of enabling the distribution, collection, and review of classroom assignments. As a teacher in the 21st century, you probably have a broader view of the nature of educational interactions that are required in your classes. If you have the appetite for something more substantive, you may want to consider using a Learning Management System (LMS) that's equipped with a wide range of tools you can access to build a more complete online learning environment. Most LMSes allow you to design and build a complete website for your class that's not only informative but also filled with a spectrum of video and assorted media, content libraries, resource links, interactive forms and polls, discussion forums, and much more. They offer teachers comprehensive administrative tools for maintaining class rosters, taking attendance, updating class calendars, distributing and grading assignments, maintaining

and publishing student grades, creating online assessments, and communicating with students and parents.

When selecting an LMS, you want to be very careful to select a system that works well on iPads as well as other computers and devices. You may find it simpler to use the LMS administrative tools on a desktop or laptop, while your students will be interacting with it on their iPads at school. It's very possible that they'll be accessing it with a different device at home.

Used effectively, an LMS becomes a focal point for class activities and creates an online environment that enhances and complements the learning that takes place in a brick-and-mortar classroom. Some of the more popular options that work effectively on iPads include Schoology (www.schoology.com), Edmodo (www.edmodo.com), and Haiku Learning (www.haikulearning.com).

3. **When you're done reviewing the work, return to the student's assignment folder and press the + icon on the top toolbar to leave your feedback.**

    Once again, you can leave an assortment of file types, from a Text Note to a recorded Voice Note.

As you respond to the submissions, a second tag appears next to the assignment name in the left column to indicate your responses.

Simple Workflows for Sharing Media

Your students created a wonderful puppet animation and exported it as a stunning video that you need to collect, assess, and share, but you're not exactly sure how that can be done. Sound like a familiar scenario? Simple workflow headaches such as this one can create serious speed bumps in your iPad program. Let's take a look at a few potential solutions for workflows with media.

Kicking it old school: Email

Yes, things are evolving so rapidly that email is now considered to be the "old" way of transferring files . . . but older can sometimes mean easier. As long as you saved the media to your Camera Roll, open the Photos app and select the images or videos. Tap the Share button and select the Email option.

✔ **Advantages:** It's simple and works on all versions of iOS without the need for any additional apps.

✔ **Disadvantages:** It requires an email setup on the iPad, which isn't always available in schools, especially in lower grades. Also, there's a limitation on the size of email file attachments, and many videos may simply be too large for email.

Using AirDrop

One of the nicest additions that came with iOS 7 is the ability to "AirDrop" images and videos from one iPad to any other device that is AirDrop-compatible. AirDrop requires an iPhone 5 or iPad fourth generation or later, and you need to be using iOS 7 or higher. Assuming you have the right device, AirDrop lets you share photos, videos, contacts, and other content from apps using the Share button. Here's how:

1. **Open your device at the Home screen and swipe up from the bottom of the screen to open the Control Center.**

2. **Tap the AirDrop option and set it to Everyone as shown on the left of the iPhone screen capture in Figure 19-8.**

3. **Open your Photos app and select the photos and videos you want to share.**

4. **Tap the Share button.**

   Anyone with an AirDrop-enabled device automatically appears in the AirDrop section, as shown in Figure 19-8 on the right.

5. **Tap the recipient's icon to send the files to them.**

Here's the good and the bad about AirDrop.

✔ **Advantages:** It's fast and doesn't need email, and there isn't a limitation on the file size.

✔ **Disadvantages:** AirDrop requires both sender and recipient to have an iPhone 5 or iPad fourth generation or later running iOS 7 or higher.

Select the AirDrop recipient

Figure 19-8: AirDrop can be used to send media from one iOS device to another.

Set AirDrop to Everyone

Moving media wirelessly with PhotoSync

Schools don't always have the latest devices in every classroom. The video you need may be on the student's iPad — yes, the iPad 2 that you've had in the classroom for the last two years. Swipe all you want, but AirDrop won't be available. The truth is also that you often need to collect work from many students and may not want to receive all the files using AirDrop because they arrive one by one, which requires you to tap and accept each one, and then they collect in your Camera Roll, where you may still need to sort and organize them. Enter PhotoSync.

PhotoSync is a file-transfer app specifically for moving images and video wirelessly (see Figure 19-9). Moreover, it can move them to any device, transfer them directly to any laptop or desktop computer, or even transfer them to many photo-sharing and cloud services such as Flickr, Picasa, Dropbox, and Google Drive.

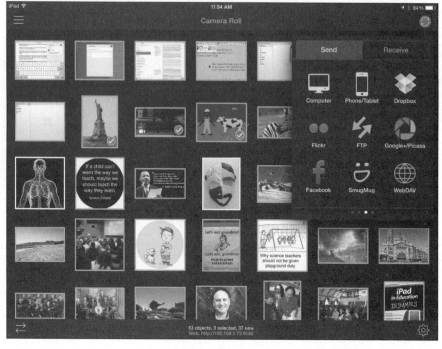

Figure 19-9:
Use
PhotoSync
to transfer
media
between
iOS devices,
computers,
and web
services.

Follow these steps:

1. **Download the PhotoSync app on each iPad (or iPhone).**

2. **If you plan on moving the files to a computer, install the PhotoSync software on your computer.**

   Download it free at www.photosync-app.com.

3. **Open PhotoSync on your device.**

4. **Tap and select the images and videos you want to transfer.**

5. **Tap the red icon with the circular arrows in the top-right corner of the screen to select your transfer destination.**

6. **Tap and select whether you want to send all images or just the selected images.**

7. **Select your destination.**

   Select Computer, iPhone/iPod/iPad, or any of the cloud service options listed. If you're transferring to your computer, ensure that you have the PhotoSync software downloaded and open on your computer. If you select a cloud service such as Dropbox, you're required to log into it when selecting it for the first time.

If you've selected Computer or an iOS device, a list pops up with all the available devices.

8. **Select your destination.**

   Off the files go . . . the transfer works in the background while you continue with your work. (OK, I know some of you are playing Angry Birds.)

One nifty additional feature is that you can also reverse the process, sending a set of images from your computer to the Camera Roll on your device.

AirPlay Mirroring iPads in Class

Using a mobile device such as the iPad gives you the ability to be, well, mobile! There's no reason to be the teacher that's anchored to the front of the room presenting a lecture on a whiteboard. You can move about the room and wirelessly project your iPad screen for everyone to see. It's called *AirPlay mirroring.* Try it, and I guarantee that you'll be the fairest of them all.

With the help of a relatively inexpensive Apple TV (around $100 and the size of a hockey puck), you can waltz around the class and wirelessly project your iPad screen at the front of the room. Here's how you do it:

1. **Connect the Apple TV to your projector.**

   Apple TV uses an HDMI cable, so you may need to purchase an inexpensive VGA-to-HDMI converter if your projector doesn't have an HDMI interface.

2. **Set up the Apple TV to the same Wi-Fi network as your iPad.**

3. **Swipe up from the bottom of your iPad screen to access the iPad Control Center.**

4. **Tap the AirPlay option to see a list of AirPlay devices.**

5. **Select the Apple TV in your room (see Figure 19-10).**

   Your iPad will be projected, and anything you display on your screen will be viewed by everyone in the room!

Consult the Apple website for more information about Apple TV: `www.apple.com/appletv`.

The 21st-century classroom is moving away from a place of frontal lecturing toward a learning environment that stresses discussion and collaboration. Technology can and should support that vision. The coolest part about iPad mirroring is that you can have students project their own iPads to the Apple TV as well. It's a wonderful way for students to share and a real bonus for collaborative activities when you want students to display their work for the rest of the class.

Figure 19-10:
Mirror your
iPad screen
to an Apple
TV to project
it wirelessly.

No Apple TV? No problem.

You may not be able to get that Apple TV in your classroom right away, but I have a couple of great alternatives for you to consider. You may have a laptop or desktop computer connected to your projector. We can turn that computer into an AirPlay receiver that acts the same as an Apple TV. And just between the two of us, it's a fraction of the cost.

If you have a computer that you can project, it would make sense that you could also project your iPad by displaying it on your computer screen, right? Well, run right away to www. airserverapp.com and download the AirServer software on your computer. Wait, don't go until I tell you what to do with it!

Make sure your computer is on the same network as your iPad. With AirServer running on

it, it acts as an AirPlay receiver — just as if it was an Apple TV. After you install the software, it should prompt you for a name and be running every time you boot up your computer. Swipe from the bottom of your iPad screen to reveal the Control Panel and tap AirPlay. You should see your computer listed as one of the AirPlay destinations. Select it and voilá — you see your iPad displayed on the computer monitor. Turn on the projector and pat yourself on the back.

Reflector is another excellent option for mirroring to a computer. Download it from www. airsquirrels.com/reflector. Note that both AirServer and Reflector have separate downloads that work on either Mac or Windows computers.

Printing from Your iPad

I've spent the majority of this chapter outlining options for digital workflows that don't require the use of paper. Until now. Whether you want to hang work on a wall or present a child's work to a parent, there are still those times when you need to print content from an iPad. So with all due respect to the ideal of a "paperless classroom," here are some ways you can print when it's absolutely necessary. Just do it after class when nobody is looking if it makes you feel better.

Printing with AirPrint

Good news: You can print from your iPad without the help of that expensive IT guy. AirPrint is a wireless technology that creates a connection between AirPrint-enabled applications on your iOS device and any printer that supports AirPrint technology. So, in short, you can print from your iPad . . . but only from iPad apps that include AirPrint support and only to printers that are AirPrint-enabled. Sounds complicated, but I break it down for you in this section.

 To check whether a printer is AirPrint-enabled, go to the Apple support website (`http://support.apple.com/kb/HT4356`), where a list is constantly being updated.

Apple apps such as Pages, Keynote, Mail, Photos, and Safari all support AirPrint. There are also many third-party apps from the App Store that support AirPrint. If you have an AirPrint-enabled printer, the process is easy: You simply tap Print from within your app, select from the list of AirPrint-enabled printers, and print. Follow these steps:

1. **Tap the Share icon in the app that contains your content.**

2. **Tap Print.**

   You see a list where (ideally) you can select your printer. If you can't find any printers listed, there are several possible reasons:

   - Your printer isn't turned on, has an error such as an empty paper tray, or needs a firmware update.

   - Your printer isn't connected to the same Wi-Fi network as your iPad. AirPrint works only if the two are on the same Wi-Fi network.

   - Your printer doesn't support AirPrint printing.

3. **If your printer is listed, configure the printer options and tap Print.**

At this point, you're either elated to see your print job coming out of the printer or cursing and reminiscing about the good old days when everything was handwritten. Relax — there are plenty of options for those with and without AirPrint-enabled printers.

Connecting to any printer

So your printer didn't show up as an option on the AirPrint list when you went to print? Join the club. The list of AirPrint-enabled printers is growing, but many of us still don't have one. Several app developers jumped in to fill that void and, in doing so, offer features way above and beyond simple printing from your iPad. Options include enabling you to print to any physical printer, as well as creating *virtual printers* that use the iPad print function to send content from iPad apps to a folder on any computer on your network.

Using Printopia

Download and install Printopia on your Mac computer. With the aid of Printopia, any printer that's available to your computer can be shared with iOS devices on the same wireless network. They'll just show up as an AirPrint-enabled print option for iPads whether they support AirPrint or not.

Printopia turns your computer into an AirPrint server, enabling you to share any or all of the shared or networked printers on your network. Whether you have an inkjet printer, a laser printer plugged into your router, or a network printer — whatever type of printer you have — if your Mac can print to it, Printopia shares it with your iOS devices.

Download the Printopia software on your Mac laptop or desktop, not your iPad. (Printopia only works on Mac computers, but I look at a comparable solution for Windows users in the next section.)

When Printopia is installed on your computer, go to any iOS app that supports printing and tap the Print button, and all of a sudden, all the printers connected to your computer show up as options — whether they support AirPrint or not!

To get started, follow these steps:

1. **Visit the ecamm website on your Mac computer.**

   Printopia must be downloaded on your computer. Open the browser on your Mac and go to the publisher's website at www.ecamm.com/mac/printopia.

2. **Download and set up Printopia.**

   Select whether you want the free trial or paid version of Printopia and download it. Follow the installation instructions. After installation, the Printopia dialog (see Figure 19-11) displays the list of printers connected to your computer. All of your available printers and the Printopia virtual printers are automatically enabled for sharing via AirPrint. (I explain how to use the virtual printers in the next section.)

Figure 19-11: Select printers to share, and Printopia makes them available to iOS devices.

3. **Select the ones you want to make available for sharing by clicking the check box to the left of the printer name.**

4. **Close the dialog when you're done.**

   Checked printers appear as available printing options for iPads on the network.

5. **Select the Print option in an app on your iPad.**

   The printers you shared in Printopia appear as print options. Easy.

Admit it. You got a little chill when you read that anyone on your wireless network could send content to the physical and virtual printers you set up in Printopia. You want to share but . . . "anyone"? That kid in Room 310 is definitely going to mess with you. Don't worry. Every physical and virtual printer you share in Printopia can be configured with password security. Even if someone has access to your wireless network and can therefore see your shared printers, he or she can't print or save files to your Mac without knowing and using the password. Click the Settings icon in Printopia and select the Setup Password option. Create a password and only give it to students as needed. Make sure you change it frequently. And I'd advise you to avoid that kid in Room 310.

Using virtual printers

Physical printing isn't the only function Printopia offers. Its *virtual printers* (which send your iPad content directly to any designated folder on a Mac) are great solutions for digital workflows as well. Click the + button at the bottom of your printer list in Printopia on your Mac for additional options. You'll see the following options:

✔ **Save to a folder on your Mac.** Designate a folder on your Mac as a virtual printer. When any iPad user on the same wireless network goes to print, they see that folder listed in their directory of printers. When they select it, a PDF copy of a document, or a JPG or PNG version of an image, is sent to that folder on your Mac.

Add unlimited virtual printers in the same manner. This enables iPad users to deliver content directly to your Mac. Let's say that you want to collect some Pages documents from student iPads. Create a folder on your Mac — let's call it Class Project. Click the + symbol under the printers in your Printopia dialog on your Mac and select the virtual printer Save to Folder on Mac. Select the Class Project folder you just created. Now students can send their documents right on to your Mac in a folder ready for your review. Printing from Pages is shown in Figure 19-12.

Keep your files organized by configuring multiple virtual printers with different save destinations. For example, set up one folder as a virtual printer on your Mac to collect the history project students are submitting. Set up another folder and virtual printer for the science assignment, and so on. In that way, student submissions will be neatly organized in separate folders on your Mac.

✔ **Save to folder in Dropbox.** If you recall, I mentioned Dropbox at the beginning of the chapter as a great service for personal cloud storage. You were paying attention, weren't you? Printopia allows you to create and designate any folder in your Dropbox account as a virtual printer.

Do you need to save expense receipts? Take a quick picture and send it to an Expenses folder you created on Dropbox. Having a special day at your child's soccer game? Create a folder and send the photos directly to it for easy organization and archiving.

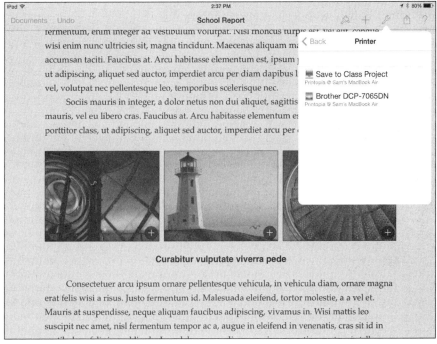

Figure 19-12:
The Send to Mac virtual printer sends files to any folder on your computer.

> ✔ **Send to an application on your Mac.** A feature in Printopia sends a copy of any content file on your iPad to your Mac and then opens it within a designated application.
>
> For example, I'm constantly taking screen shots and pictures on my iPad. Given my less-than-stellar photographic skills, I always end up needing to touch them up in a photo editor. Using Printopia, I can create a virtual printer that sends a file directly into Adobe Photoshop on my Mac.
>
> Tap the + sign under the printer list in the Printopia dialog, and select Send to Application. Select Adobe Photoshop as the application, and that's it. You now have a virtual printer that will send an image to your Mac and open it automatically in Photoshop! Figure 19-13 shows you the process. It's so incredibly convenient!

Printopia has done a wonderful job of satisfying users who still require some amount of paper printing, while also offering a host of virtual printer options for organizing and working with digital content. It's one of my indispensable tools.

Figure 19-13: Send to Application sends iPad content directly to an application on your Mac.

Using Windows printing solutions

If only everything in life could be perfect . . . but it isn't. There are two potential problems for some users looking to purchase Printopia: It doesn't work in Windows, and it shares printers with users on the same wireless network. Collobos Software offers a product called Presto that's close in functionality to Printopia and works on Windows PCs. Setup and use are remarkably similar, and you can download the software from www.collobos.com. Remember that just as with Printopia, the software is installed on your computer, not your iPad. It will then share your physical and virtual printers so that they can be accessed from the Print function on any iOS device.

Network printing

Printopia and Presto enable iPad users to print through a specific computer, but they need to be installed and running on different individual computers throughout the school. If there are students throughout the school that need to print from iPads, it may be worth considering a single solution that works throughout your school network. You can purchase Printopia Pro or the enterprise version of Presto and set up a single print server for all the iPads at your school. Another hardware-based alternative is xPrintServer from Lantronix (www.lantronix.com). Plug xPrintServer into your network and configure it with printers and permissions as needed.

Chapter 20

Presenting with Impact

. . . .

In This Chapter

▶ Using Keynote to create and present a presentation

▶ Using your PowerPoint presentation on an iPad

▶ Designing Haiku Deck presentations with visual impact

▶ Creating interactive lessons with Nearpod

. . . .

As I discuss in Chapter 1, I'm not an advocate for frontal lecturing in school. The use of technology should focus on empowering students to research, explore, discover, and create. Having said that, it doesn't mean that there's never any need for teachers to lecture and demonstrate on occasion. Teachers still need to teach core skills, present important information, facilitate class-room discussions, and more. And don't forget that students can use presenta-tion tools to express their understanding as well.

In this chapter, I look at a few ways to deliver presentations on an iPad:

✔ Creating and delivering presentations with Keynote on an iPad

✔ Designing image-based presentations with Haiku Deck

✔ Creating and delivering interactive lessons with Nearpod

✔ Creating presentations on a computer and then displaying them on an iPad

Check out your options and select the avenue that works for you. I also give you a walk-through of a new presentation and interactive lesson platform — Nearpod — that allows you to author and deliver presentations on iPads complete with interactive components that check and report on student comprehension.

Creating a Keynote Presentation

The iPad version of Keynote does an admirable job of encapsulating many of the basic functions of its more full-featured version for Macs. You can easily integrate media on your iPad and present it on your iPad. Here is a quick look at some of the many features you can use to build a stunning presentation:

1. **Tap the Keynote icon on your Home screen to open the app, and then tap the + icon to start a new presentation.**

   The screen that first appears when you open Keynote is the Document Manager.

2. **Tap the Create Presentation option.**

   You get a selection of design templates. Each theme comes with a selection of predesigned slide formats that contain placeholders for titles, text, images, and more.

3. **Select the theme of your choice.**

   You enter the presentation editor.

4. **Add slides by tapping the Add Slide icon at the bottom of the column to add a new slide.**

   When you add a slide, you are presented with a range of slide layouts that are included with the theme.

5. **Select a layout by tapping it.**

6. **Organize and edit your slides.**

   The Navigator (see Figure 20-1) displays your slides in the column on the left of the editor. From there, organize slides:

   - Tap any slide to select it.

   - Move a slide by simply tapping it in the Navigator and dragging it to a new location in your presentation.

   - Move multiple slides by tapping and holding one and then tapping additional slides with another finger.

Slide navigator

Return to document manager

Undo last change

Insert object

Tools   Play

Share

Format object

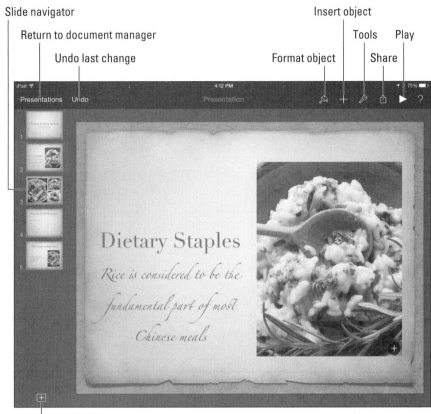

Figure 20-1:
Organize
and edit
your slide in
the Keynote
editor.

Add slide

7. **Add and edit text and objects such as images, charts, shapes, and tables.**

You can manipulate text and objects in these ways:

- *Edit text.* Double-tap text to edit and replace it with your own. Select any text and tap the Format icon on the top toolbar to change the font and style of the text.

- *Edit objects.* Tap and edit any object in your slides. When you select an object, handles appear around the selection. Drag a corner to resize the object or twist and rotate it. Drag the object to move it to a new location. Guidelines automatically appear to make it easy to align the object with other objects in your slide.

- *Add text and objects.* Tap the + Insert button on the top toolbar to add text, charts, tables, shapes, or media from your Photo galleries.

- *Change object styles.* Select an object in your slide and tap the Format paintbrush button on the top toolbar; a menu pops up (see Figure 20-2) that enables you to change the appearance of your object. Change colors, font, and styles of text. Add shadows, reflections, and frames to images and shapes. Play with the design of your objects to add maximum visual impact to your slides.

Figure 20-2: Use styles to add shadows, reflections, and frames to images.

- *Use charts to present data visually.* Tap any chart that you added, and select the Edit Data option on the pop-up menus to add your data to a spreadsheet. The chart updates to reflect your data.

- *Add object animations.* You can make objects appear dynamically on your slide by adding animation effects. Tap an object and select Animate from the pop-up menu. Experiment with the Build In options to alter how the object first appears on your slide. Build Out animations add a transition effect to the way the object disappears. Keynote demonstrates the animation for you when you apply it. Click the Done button to exit.

8. **Add slide transition effects**.

   Slide transitions are effects applied to the way one slide leads into the next during your presentation. Tap a slide in the Navigator to select it and then tap it a second time to pop up a menu of options (see Figure 20-3). Select Transition and experiment with the different transition effects. Tap Play and Keynote demonstrates the selected transition. Tap the Done button on the top right of your screen when you're finished.

Figure 20-3:
Add transi-
tion effects
between
the slides
in your
presentation.

9. **Tap the Play button on the right of your top toolbar.**

   The presentation plays in full screen from the current slide. Tap once or swipe left to move to the next slide, and slide right to go backward. Tap and hold on the slide to reveal the tray of highlighting tools. Select a highlighter and mark up the slide, pressing Done when you're finished. When you're done with the presentation, pinch with two fingers anywhere on your slide to go back into editing mode.

10. **Tap the Share button on the top toolbar to share your presentation.**

   You can send a copy of the presentation via email or to iTunes and then access it on your computer in Keynote, PDF, or PowerPoint format. If you have an iCloud account, you can have it backed up and synced to your other devices automatically. If you're saving your Keynote presentation to iCloud, the Share options enable you to share a link for others to access the presentation stored in your iCloud account.

Saving is the easiest part because your presentation is automatically saved for you — in the Document Manager — as you work.

11. **In the editor, tap the Presentations button in the top-left corner to return to the Document Manager to rename your presentation.**

12. **To rename a file, tap its name and replace it with a new name.**

13. **(Optional) Drag one presentation over another to organize them into folders.**

You can create your Keynote on a Mac or on your iPad. As much as I love Keynote for the iPad, if you're more comfortable on your laptop or desktop, it may be easier to create your presentation there. Be aware, however, that the versions of Keynote for Mac and Keynote for iPad are not the same, and you need to be careful to avoid potential pitfalls (such as your formatting getting all messed up) when displaying your Mac Keynote on an iPad.

Winning presentations aren't the result of dazzling slide transitions and animations. It helps to keep some simple rules in mind when creating your presentation:

- ✓ **Less is more.** Keep your slide text to a minimum. Your audience will become bored very quickly if you just read text from your slides.

- ✓ **Use imaginative visuals.** Choose images that capture people's attention and represent a point you're trying to make.

- ✓ **Challenge your audience to think.** Pose questions and encourage participation.

- ✓ **Prepare and rehearse.** The most convincing presentations occur when the speaker is well prepared and rehearsed.

Showing PowerPoint Presentations on an iPad

My more Mac-centric friends — and there are a lot of them in the education community — may get upset when I say that Keynote is a great program, but it's traditionally been regarded as the little cousin of PowerPoint. Most of us who have been giving presentations for years have been using PowerPoint and looking for ways to migrate those presentations over to Macs and iPads. Luckily, if you're in that same position, you have a potential solution.

It has taken a while, but Microsoft finally released long-awaited versions of the Microsoft Office suite of apps for the iPad in March 2014. The Office suite includes Microsoft Word, PowerPoint, Excel, Outlook, One Note, and more. Download the free PowerPoint app from the App Store and you can view and show your presentations (see Figure 20-4). If you want to create and edit presentations on your iPad, you need a subscription to Microsoft's Office 365 service. Subscriptions give you access to the full Office suite of apps on up to five PCs or Macs in addition to five mobile devices. Contact Microsoft for details if you're interested in Office 365 for your educational institution (`http://office.microsoft.com/en-us/academic/`).

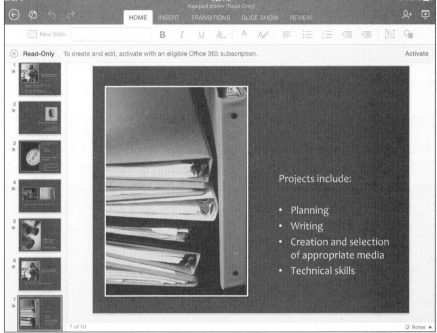

Figure 20-4: View and show PowerPoint presentations with Microsoft PowerPoint for iPad.

Designing Presentations with Visual Impact

How often have you sat through presentations where the presenter read text off projected slides? Call it a hunch, but I bet you were a little less than riveted by the presentation. Successful presentations are memorable because they're engaging and capture the attention of the audience — whether it's a famous speaker addressing a packed auditorium or a student presenting a project in class. And if we're talking about student presentations, let's not forget that the art of presenting isn't just about content mastery. It develops and exercises vital communication skills that are necessary throughout life.

I just called it "the art" of presenting. The recipe for a compelling presentation isn't composed of lists of bullet points, animations, or fancy transitions. Those long lists of bullet points could actually be the perfect cure for insomnia. In fact, comedian Don McMillan says, "The term 'bullet point' comes from people firing at annoying presenters." Effective presentations combine a unique and personal blend of ingredients:

✔ Confidence and poise that results from mastering your content and rehearsing your presentation.

✔ Well-developed communication skills that include voice projection, pitch and cadence, well-timed pauses, humor, and eye contact. We focus very heavily on written communication skills in school but rarely spend much time developing these key oral communication abilities.

✔ Memorable, eye-catching slides. Slides with large, striking images can deliver a message far more effectively than long lines of text.

And on that last point, Haiku Deck is the perfect app to help teachers or students develop engaging, image-based presentations.

Creating a Haiku Deck Presentation

1. **Open Haiku Deck.**

   Tap to open the Haiku Deck app.

2. **Create a new presentation.**

   Tap the + icon on the bottom toolbar to start a new presentation. You're prompted to type a title.

3. **Select a theme.**

   The presentation editor opens and the top row presents you with a collection of themes. Each one uses a different font and color scheme. Tap to select your choice of theme; then tap the slide editor in the middle of the display to start creating the presentation.

4. **Add slides, text, and images.**

   The Haiku Deck editor is simple. You won't find fancy animations, transitions, or wild text effects. What you find are simple tools for text, layout, and inserting images (see Figure 20-5). What really distinguishes Haiku

Deck from other presentation apps is the ability to search its libraries for high-quality images that become the focus of your presentation. Features include:

- *Edit text.* Tap the default title or subtitle fields to insert your own text.

- *Search for images.* This is the trademark feature of Haiku Deck. Tap the Insert image icon in the left column. Type a search term and Haiku Deck displays a grid of matching images along with a list of similar tags if you need to alter your search. (See Figure 20-6.) Note that some images have a small dollar sign icon. Those are images that require a fee for use. There's a huge range of free images, and if you only want those displayed, you can turn off the Show Premium Images option in Settings on the opening app display.

Slide layout

Insert image

Text format Notes   Play presentation

Figure 20-5: Haiku Deck is an ideal tool for creating striking, image-based presentations.

Slide manager Sign in   Add slide

Figure 20-6:
Search
Haiku Deck's
extensive
libraries of
high-quality
images you
can insert in
your slides.

- *Import images.* Tap the Insert Images icon and then tap Import to insert images from your iPad's Photo Library or from your account on services such as Dropbox, Flickr, Picasa, and Google Drive.

- *Change slide layout.* If you find that the text is covering part of a background image, tap the Tt icon in the left column and select an alternative layout from the options displayed.

- *Add notes.* Just because Haiku Deck gives you the tools and images to create stunning visual presentations doesn't mean you can't include additional details as text. Tap the Notes icon next to any slide to add details and links to other resources. Consider the scenario where you have students submit their Haiku Deck to you as an assignment. The Notes feature is a great vehicle for adding academic rigor. Notice also that Notes can be private or public — something to keep in mind if you decide to publish your Haiku Deck, as outlined later in the description of the Share option.

- *Add and organize slides.* Tap the + icon in the bottom-right corner to add a new slide. If you want to move a slide, tap and hold it in the slide manager as you drag it to a new position. Tap it once and a Settings icon appears with options to copy or delete the slide.

- *Play.* This one is simple. Get your popcorn and then tap the Play icon to watch your presentation full screen. Swipe to move between slides. Tap the Pencil icon in the upper corner when you're ready to return to edit mode. And don't make a mess with that popcorn.

- *Share your Haiku Deck.* Your Haiku Deck is saved on the iPad, but you need to create an account if you want to share or publish it. Tap the Share icon in the left column and create your account or sign into an existing account. You can also elect to create a single class account that you share with students. After you've signed in, you can tap Share to get the list of available options (see Figure 20-7). Note the Change Privacy option. Presentations can be set to Private, Restricted, or Public. Restricted and public files are uploaded to your account on the Haiku Deck website and given a unique URL that can be shared or e-mailed. Restricted presentations can only be viewed if you have the URL, whereas public files are also listed in the public Haiku Deck Gallery. In the case of private presentations, you may want to use the PPT/Keynote option, which converts the file and sends it via email.

Figure 20-7: Privacy settings for your Haiku Deck presentation can be public, restricted, or private.

Creating Interactive Classroom Lessons with Nearpod

There certainly are academic content and skills that require instruction; however, it's terribly difficult to keep the attention of students when you're plowing through a projected presentation. Nearpod is a presentation platform that seeks to inject elements of interaction into classroom presentations in an attempt to better engage students and provide feedback to teachers.

The teacher delivers the presentation as a "live session" that is assigned a unique PIN. Students then enter the PIN in the Nearpod app on their iPads. The presentation appears on screen while the teacher controls the progression of slides and the built-in interactions with students. Let's get you started so you can try it out.

Sign up for a Nearpod account

Download the Nearpod app or access Nearpod via the web at http://nearpod.com. You can create a free Nearpod account by using your Google login or creating a new login with Nearpod. Note that the account is for the person creating and hosting presentation sessions. Students won't need an account to access your lessons.

Creating a Nearpod presentation

Create your Nearpod presentation in your desktop browser by using the following steps:

1. **Log in on the web.**

   Open your web browser and go to http://nearpod.com. Log in to your Nearpod account.

2. **Create a new presentation.**

   Select My Library or Create from the menu. Click the New Presentation button on the upper toolbar. Start your presentation from scratch or import existing files by dragging and dropping them on to the page. Nearpod accepts common file formats such as PowerPoint or PDF documents and images in JPG or PNG format. After they're imported, your files are converted in Nearpod for editing and presentation.

3. Add content.

Add custom slides with media from your computer or the web (see Figure 20-8):

- Add images, video, and audio from your computer or from sites such as YouTube, Dropbox, and Google Drive.

- Compose slides with text, images, and audio.

- Add a website to your slide that students will be able to browse.

Figure 20-8:
Add content such as video, slide shows, and websites to your Nearpod presentation.

4. Add activities.

Add interactive slides with activities that include open-ended questions, polls, quizzes, and drawing tools. You can see each student response as you give the presentation. Some activity ideas include

- Asking an exploratory question to gauge students' opinions on a topic.

- Inserting a poll to see what they think or know.

- Presenting a lesson and then giving students a quiz to see what they understood.

- Using the drawing tools to have students sketch a geometric shape, answer a math problem, identify parts of a plant, and more.

5. **Arrange the slides.**

   Drag and drop your slides into the desired sequence.

6. **Save the presentation.**

   Use Settings to title your presentation and tap Done.

7. **Publish your presentation when prompted so that you can deliver it to your students at the appropriate time.**

Delivering your interactive presentation

You've put it all together and now you're ready to deliver your captivating presentation to your students. Here's how:

1. **Login to the Nearpod app or website and select My Library to access your presentations.**

2. **Open your presentation and select the Live Session option.**

   Nearpod gives you a PIN for your session. Share it with your students verbally or via email.

3. **Have students join the session.**

   Students open the Nearpod app on their iPads and enter the PIN number. The presentation downloads and displays your opening slide. (See Figure 20-9.) You control the flow of the presentation; the students remain on that slide until you move to the next one.

4. **Swipe to the next slide.**

   Students will be asked to enter their name.

   On your end you see a counter with the number of students that have joined the session. Tap or click it and you can see their names.

5. **Swipe to the next slide on your device to advance the presentations on each student's iPad.**

   Give students time to respond as you reach slides with interactive elements such as open-ended questions, quizzes, or slides with drawing tools. (See Figure 20-10.) For example, you can

   - View answers to questions and get immediate feedback on each student's progress.

   - Get quiz scores for each student. See which questions were answered correctly and which might require further explanation and corrective action.

   - Browse thumbnails of student responses to open-ended questions. You can select thumbnails to share with the class, and Nearpod pushes it out to every iPad screen. (See Figure 20-11.)

Figure 20-9:
The presentation is downloaded and displays the opening slide.

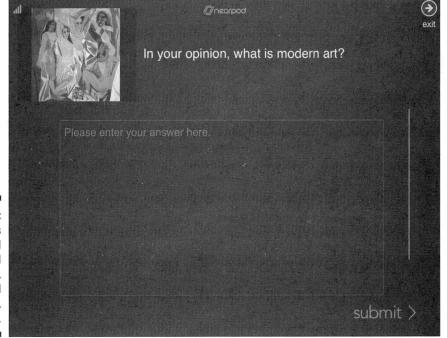

Figure 20-10:
Students can respond to Nearpod quizzes, open-ended questions, and more.

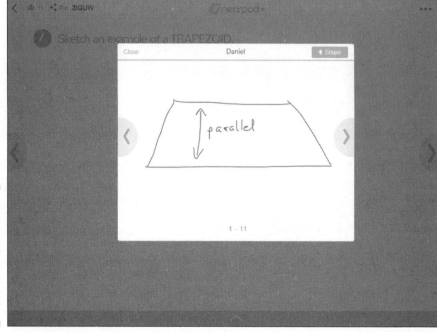

Figure 20-11:
Share
one and
Nearpod
displays
it on
everyone's
screen.

6. **Tap or click the Nearpod logo during your session and select Reports.**

   Nearpod generates a report with data on each student's responses and sends it to your registered email address.

Chapter 21

Developing Digital Portfolios

- -

In This Chapter

▶ Defining the requirements of an effective e-portfolio system

▶ Exploring components that constitute an individual e-portfolio

▶ Examining different tools for archiving and sharing student work

- -

*E*mployers are placing increasingly greater importance on seeing evidence of what job applicants have accomplished, and traditional resumes are slowly giving way to "e-portfolios" as the primary factor in determining an applicant's merit. Given the amount of work that is now stored in digital format, maintaining and presenting an impressive e-portfolio has never been easier.

An e-portfolio is both a storage system for digital files and a presentation platform for your best work — whether that be written pieces, photography, videos, presentations, performances, or anything else. There's no better place than school to start creating e-portfolios that demonstrate individual development and growth. E-portfolios can be a vehicle for showcasing talents and achievements, a tool for important self-reflection and deeper learning, or even a viable alternative to more traditional forms of assessment. Students can also be given ownership of their academic portfolios and eventually develop them into professional, career portfolios.

Setting Up an E-portfolio System

If it's not already, creating a system that enables students to edit and share digital portfolios should be high on your priority list. Many software systems have a "portfolio feature," but you need to carefully consider your goals before jumping into the water. Here are a few factors to ponder when selecting and setting up your portfolio system:

✔ **Storage:** What are you storing and where will you keep it? I still walk into far too many schools that use large internal network servers for file storage. Storing student portfolios on an internal server requires substantial amounts of network disk space — especially as portfolios should include a variety of different media and not just text. Yes, your IT person may warn that it's safer to keep content in-house, but when push comes to shove, would you rather rely on a company such as Google to secure your content (free of charge!) or that (very expensive) internal system of backup servers, drives, software, and backup power sources in the IT room that you never step into?

✔ **Access:** Who will be able to see it? Internal storage also denies access to anyone that's not logged into your network. The whole point of a portfolio is to create a vehicle for sharing and presenting work. As a result, I'd lean heavily toward using a web-based service for storing portfolios.

✔ **Portability:** Can students easily take the portfolio with them when they leave the school? Will they be able to continue developing and sharing it? You may already use a "walled garden," a service that limits sharing and access within the school itself. One example would be a learning management system that requires verification before gaining access. That's fine as long as it provides a function for the student to allow external access to their portfolio when required and/or a mechanism for the student to take the portfolio with them when they leave the school. Make sure to check.

✔ **Permissions:** Who will be able to edit it? Will it be a place for teachers to select and place student work or will the students have ownership and editing rights? It's clear that you'd want to allow selective viewing permissions for others to browse the work in a portfolio, but you should also consider how to allocate permissions for people to edit the content in the portfolio. Giving students editing permissions grants them a pride of ownership that empowers them with the desire to create content worthy of display. Most systems enable you to share editing rights with individual students.

✔ **Platform:** Will it work on all computers and devices? Ideally you'd use a system that is cross-platform. It needs to be a web-based system that works equally well on Windows computers, Mac computers, and mobile devices. If you're using iPads effectively, students will be creating media that needs to be moved into their portfolios easily on their iPads.

✔ **Tools:** What system will you use to manage it? Select a system that has the following characteristics:

- Simple workflow for moving content into portfolios

- Convenient interface for organizing and moving content

- Easy function for setting and sharing viewing rights

- Nice, clean interface for displaying the content, both in terms of seeing what's in the portfolio as well as the ability to open files and view them

Constructing an Effective E-portfolio

When you have a system in place, consider how to build individual e-portfolios. Filing digital files in a portfolio folder is a simple first step, but effective e-portfolios need to be organized, well presented, and reflective of the personality and passion of individual students. Here's a list of factors you may want to consider.

✔ **Documentation:** When a file is saved as a digital file, it's relatively easy to move and archive, but don't limit portfolios to those files. Students may be doing great work on paper, or they may have creative artifacts they have built or designed in science or art. Move it to a spot with good lighting, tap into your inner photo-journalist, and snap some images. Take screen shots of work on the iPad. Make documentation of student work a part of your everyday classroom procedure, whether or not it ends up in a portfolio.

✔ **Organization:** Store files in a shared folder and develop clear guidelines for classification and organization of the work. Use a spreadsheet and keep a matrix of categories for organizing and presenting work. Classifying by grade and subject is obvious, but consider also categorizing work by goals and standards as a way to demonstrate student achievements.

✔ **Ownership:** Remember that the ultimate goal of a portfolio is not for schools or teachers to share what they do in their classes; it's for students to showcase their individual work. You can always make suggestions, but give students the last word when deciding what to include in their portfolios.

✔ **Reflection:** Developing self-assessment skills is an important part of individual growth, and having students comment and reflect upon their work is an effective way to develop them. It's also a wonderful way to add personal voice to the presentation of a portfolio.

✔ **Signature:** Portfolios aren't just about work. They're about people. Add a biography section that allows students to tell viewers about their interests and activities.

✔ **Presentation and personality:** Whether it's an essay for English, a painting in art class, or a group project in science, the work done by students is an expression of everything that makes them unique individuals. Don't fall into the trap of using a standard template to present their work. It may make your life easier, but if you wanted a job that was easy, you would have taken that job as an ice cream taster, wouldn't you? By all means, set some guidelines, but give students the freedom and flexibility to design portfolio presentations in their own styles and to add their personal touch wherever and however appropriate.

You want to make it easy for people to browse the work in an e-portfolio. If you're including files that need to be opened, make sure to convert them into formats that are easily read on the web. Export documents as PDF files and convert images to JPG format.

Using Google Apps for E-portfolios

Chapter 19 describes how Google Apps can play a valuable role in managing digital workflows. With a variety of web-based applications for creating, storing, and sharing content, Google Apps can also be the perfect system for managing student e-portfolios. Here's a laundry list of ways you can use Google Apps for portfolio organization, management, and presentation:

✔ **Create a shared folder.** Create a shared e-portfolio folder for each student (see Figure 21-1). Make sure both student and teacher have editing permissions so that you both have rights to add and edit content in the folder. Depending on the age of the student and the way in which you decide to manage the workflow, you may decide to give viewing or editing permissions to other teachers as well. Also remember that you may need to review folder permissions annually as students move grade levels and teachers.

✔ **Add and organize content.** As students create content — on their iPads or elsewhere — they can add it to their e-portfolio folder. Most iPad apps have a Share function that enables users to copy content to other apps such as Google Drive (see Figure 21-2, left). Media created on the iPad can be saved to the Camera Roll, and Google Drive has an Upload function that moves any files from the Camera Roll to a folder on Google Drive (see Figure 21-2, right). It's all smooth sailing!

Shared ePortfolio folder

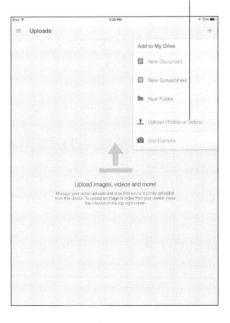

Figure 21-1:
Create
and share
a Google
Drive folder
with each
student for
his or her
portfolio.

Copy content from iPad apps to Drive

Upload media from the iPad's Camera Roll

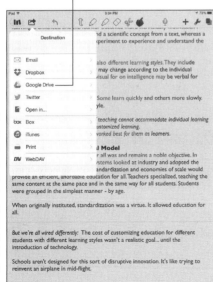

Figure 21-2:
Copy con-
tent to Drive
from iPad
apps (left) or
use Drive's
upload
function
(right) to add
media to the
portfolio.

Although you can upload videos to a folder in Google Drive, it may be easier to manage videos if you store them at a media-sharing site such as YouTube or Vimeo. I know what you're thinking . . . but that doesn't mean the videos have to be public. You can easily set up school or class accounts so that videos can only be accessed via a unique link. That makes it easy for students to embed them in a blog or website without having to move and upload large video files.

✔ **Present the portfolio.** The content should be organized and easily accessible in a Drive folder. Now, all that hard work deserves to be shared and seen. You have several options:

- *Google Sites:* Google Apps users can create their own websites using Google Sites. Give students guidance on design and organization while also allowing them the freedom to add their own personal touches. Students can create pages for different parts of the portfolios and add files from their portfolio folders.

- *Blog:* Give each student a personal blog and have them write blog posts that showcase the various components of their portfolio. You can use Google Blogger or any other blog service such as WordPress (http://wordpress.org) or Edublogs (http://edublogs.org).

✔ **Reflect and personalize.** Have students review the work in their portfolios and add their reflections. How did it meet the goals and standards? What stands out as something they take pride in and where might the work be improved? What did they learn and take away from the project? The reflections can be included as comments on the student website or blog post.

Encourage students to personalize their portfolios by adding a biography and customizing the site design where possible.

✔ **Comment.** Decide whether you want to allow teachers and peers to add comments to student portfolios. With proper guidance and instruction, providing constructive feedback can be a valuable educational exercise for both parties.

Building E-portfolios with eduClipper

eduClipper is far more than an app for maintaining portfolios. It's a learning community where users "clip" content and save it to their accounts — whether it's content they have created themselves or content they find on the web. (See Figure 21-3.) Clips are organized in boards that can be used for personal archiving and reference or shared with other users such as teachers, peers, learning groups, and more. Think of it as a super-charged scrapbook where you add all forms of digital content that you share with anyone you please. And it works as both an iPad app as well as through the `https://educlipper.net` website on any device with a web browser.

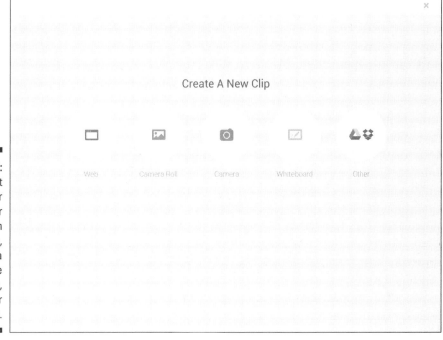

Figure 21-3: Clip content to your eduClipper board from the web, Camera Roll, Google Drive, and other sources.

eduClipper accounts come with a default portfolio board that is specifically designed for collecting and sharing clips. It's a simple, well-designed feature that makes it easy to collect, organize, and share portfolios of work. Just use the following steps:

1. **Create an account at `https://educlipper.net` or through the edu-Clipper iPad app.**

   Accounts are categorized by teacher and student.

2. **Sign into the app and tap the logo in the top-right corner of the screen to reveal the graphical menu of options (as shown in Figure 21-4).**

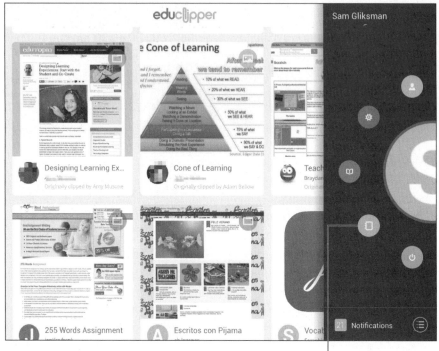

Figure 21-4:
Tap the
Portfolio
icon to
create,
edit, and
share your
eduClipper
portfolio
boards.

3. **Tap the Portfolio icon.**

4. **Tap the Add Portfolio button and create as many portfolio boards as necessary.**

   Enter a title and description for each. Think of them as storage folders. As mentioned earlier, make sure to weigh how you want to classify and organize your content before creating your boards.

5. **Select a background theme and layout template for your board.**

   You can easily edit and change themes and templates later if required.

6. **Start adding clips on the Add Content screen.**

   Use the Add a New Clip option to create a new clip from your Camera Roll, a whiteboard recording, files from your Google Drive or Dropbox account, or content you clip from a website. You can also choose to add any of the clips you may have already created. You'll find them listed on the bottom of the screen. When you're done, tap the Add to Portfolio option and the app returns you to the Portfolio screen.

Tap the Pencil icon on the Portfolio screen to edit the board and add clips, as shown in Figure 21-5. Tap any clip to edit the contents or add comments to it.

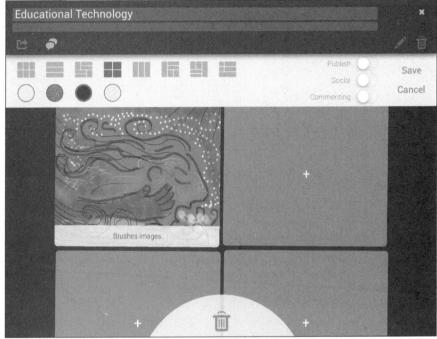

Figure 21-5:
Tap the Pencil icon to change your Portfolio design or add and edit its contents.

7. **Share your portfolio by tapping to select it and then tapping the curved Share icon on the top left.**

What use is it collecting and organizing all those clips if you don't share them with anyone? Share your Portfolio with other users via an emailed link or through social networking platforms (see Figure 21-6). You can also grab the embed code to add it to a blog or website.

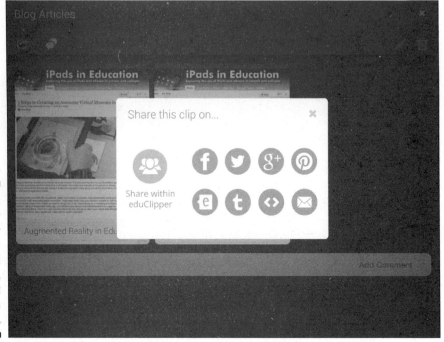

Figure 21-6:
Share your
eduClipper
portfolio via
email, social
networking,
or an embed
code on a
website.

Chapter 22

Quizzing Students with Socrative

In This Chapter

▶ Using quizzes for spontaneous feedback

▶ Gathering and using data from students

▶ Preparing and sharing quizzes

*Y*ou know the feeling. You invested hours preparing those wonderful new examples that would crystallize an important new concept for your students only to spend the last half hour demonstrating them to a classroom full of glazed eyes and blank faces. Was it too simple? Did they just not get it? Should I have taken my father's advice and taken up farming instead?

It can be difficult to know what's really going on in your students' heads. Unfortunately, you're all coming back tomorrow, and your plan was to move on to the next topic. You could always pause and ask, "Which one of you didn't understand what I was saying?" When you were a student, did you ever raise your hand when teachers asked that question? Think what a difference it might make to your teaching if you could flip a switch and discover when students aren't understanding something in class. If you have iPads or any other devices with a web browser in your class, you can.

Generating Quizzes

Socrative is a simple student response system that works on iPads and any other device with a web browser. When teachers sign up for a Socrative account, they get a virtual "room" where they can engage students in different educational exercises and games. It only takes a few seconds to start a Socrative quiz, which makes it a great tool for those spur-of-the-moment occasions when you need impromptu feedback about student opinion or understanding.

You can use Socrative by downloading the app or by going to the website at `www.socrative.com`. The images and examples used in the book are taken from the new version.

Use the following steps to get feedback from your students:

1. **Sign up for a free Socrative account.**

   Download the Socrative Teacher app or open your web browser and visit the Socrative website to sign up for a free teacher account.

2. **Have students join your room.**

   You get a unique room number when you sign up. Ask your students to use the Socrative Student app and join your room by entering the room number. Note that the number of students that have joined is displayed in your Teacher Dashboard. Students are notified that Socrative is waiting for the teacher to start an activity when they enter the room.

3. **Assign an activity.**

   When you sign in, you see the Teacher Dashboard, as shown in Figure 22-1. Now you're ready to roll. Just use the following steps:

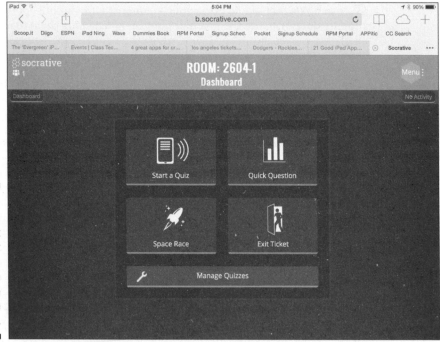

Figure 22-1: Teachers start planned or impromptu activities in Socrative from the Dashboard.

A. **Start an activity.**

   Start a quiz that you have prepared in advance or just start an impromptu activity by selecting the Quick Question option.

B. Select question type.

Select Quick Question and set your question type by choosing between Multiple Choice, True/False, and Short Answer.

C. Ask the question.

Give students the question orally or type it into the question field in Socrative. After you start the activity, students are prompted to answer on their iPads. Note that the short answer type has additional options you can set to allow multiple responses and ask for a student name. The default response is anonymous. More on that later.

D. Review student answers.

As students submit their answers, the responses are automatically displayed in the Teacher Dashboard as shown in Figure 22-2. You can obviously elect whether to project them for students to see or keep them private. If you've selected Short Answer, you have the option of showing the responses to students and asking them to vote on the most popular response. You can also remove any responses you don't want displayed.

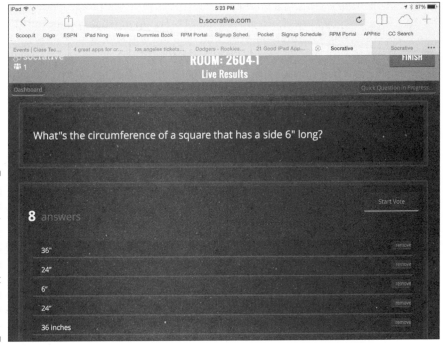

Figure 22-2:
Socrative's Teacher Dashboard automatically reveals student answers as they are submitted.

E. Request a report.

Select Finish when you're done and the activity will be closed to further responses. If you've used the Short Answer type, you can elect to have a report e-mailed or downloaded.

Appreciating the Value of Anonymity

Most students endure a long sequence of high-stakes testing throughout their years at school. It can be very stressful, and I'd be untruthful if I didn't admit to questioning the value of much of what passes for testing. Recording names and scores isn't always necessary, and short, anonymous tests can have great value under the right circumstances. Here are some reasons to keep Socrative questions anonymous:

✔ A core objective of assessment should be to provide feedback to the student. A short anonymous series of questions is a relatively stress-free method of satisfying that objective.

✔ Impromptu exit quizzes are a great way to determine whether students understood a lesson, and entry quizzes can be used to assess whether they're ready to move on and build upon what you assume they know. A quick anonymous quiz can be a fun and simple way to paint the big picture that helps you steer the right course.

✔ The same set of students usually dominate classroom discussions, and there are several students that rarely speak up. Anonymous short answer questions allow all students to voice an opinion without intimidation.

✔ There are situations, in which we're all a little reluctant to reveal how we really feel, especially when it has to be expressed in a room full of people. Allowing them the opportunity to speak anonymously may allow students to express opinions or reveal information they may otherwise be reluctant to share.

Collecting and Using Data from Students

Quizzing isn't just a way to find out whether students have the right answer to a question. Think of it as a way to gather data from students. Looking at it from that perspective, there are a variety of ways you can gather data that can be collectively analyzed and used constructively. Consider the following examples:

✔ **Word clouds:** Read a chapter from a book with your students. Using the Short Answer question in Socrative, ask them to submit at least three adjectives that describe one of the characters. Select and copy the responses in Socrative and then go to the www.wordle.net website to generate a word cloud, as shown in Figure 22-3. Word clouds are a great way to visually depict anything that can be described in text. You may even print and hang the word cloud on the wall and try the same exercise later in the book to see if students have changed their opinions about the character.

Figure 22-3: Copy student responses in Socrative and use Wordle to turn them into a word cloud.

✔ **Statistical measures:** Bring a small jar of jellybeans into class. Ask the students to guess the number of jellybeans in the jar. Create a Short Answer question in Socrative and ask students to submit their guesses. Select and copy the responses and then paste them into a spreadsheet where they can be easily sorted and analyzed. Use the data to demonstrate statistical concepts such as range, median, mode, and average.

✔ **Geographical data:** Google Maps is a terrific tool for visualizing data that has a geographical context. Suppose you're doing a family history project and you want to see where everyone's families lived two generations ago. Use the Short Answer question and ask students for the name of a grandparent and the city and country in which they lived. A typical response might be something like "Joseph Smith, London, England." Copy and paste the responses into any text editor and quickly separate the three fields on each line with a tab. Humor me and try it. Every line now has a name, city, and country — each field separated by a tab. Patience, we have just one more step. Go to the top and add an extra line with "headers" for each of the fields, separated by tabs. In the example case, you'd have "Name {tab} City {tab} Country."

Now copy all the data and go to the www.batchgeo.com website. BatchGeo generates detailed Google maps out of your data. Paste your data into BatchGeo and click the button to create a map. Within seconds you're presented with a wonderful Google map that has flags and detailed information over the location of each city you submitted.

Using Other Quiz Features

Socrative enables you to create quizzes that you can save and share with others. Prepared quizzes can include as many questions as you want. Some of the features include

- **Reports:** Indicate the correct answers to multiple choice and true/false questions, and Socrative generates a report with scores for each student.

- **Start a quiz:** Select the Start a Quiz option from the Teacher Dashboard when you're ready to open the quiz for students. As you deliver the quiz, you can set quiz options:

   - Allow students to work through the quiz at their own pace or control the flow and timing of each question.

   - Decide whether to display immediate feedback and explanations as students answer each question.

   - Randomize question and/or answer orders.

   - Disable the default prompt for student name.

- **Share quizzes:** Each quiz is given a unique SOC number. Give that number to any other teacher, and he can import your quiz to his account.

- **Space Race:** Split the class into groups and select Space Race from the Teacher Dashboard. Each group is assigned a colored rocket. (See Figure 22-4.) Select one of your quizzes, and group teams compete to answer the questions quickly and correctly as they advance their rockets across the screen.

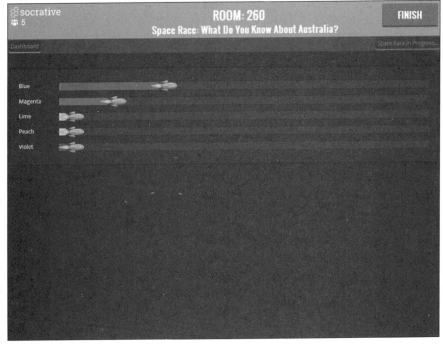

Figure 22-4:
Split students into groups that compete to answer quizzes in a Space Race.

One last word on Socrative. Students love responding to quizzes but they also enjoy creating them. One of the best ways to master a concept is by being able to analyze it and ask good questions. Consider allowing your students to create quizzes once in a while.

Alternative quiz systems

There are some other quiz systems worth considering. One of the easiest ways to create Math quizzes is by using the website www. thatquiz.org. There are loads of questions already prepared by topic and level of difficulty. Teachers can create a class and assign quizzes to students. Students can also generate quizzes as a quick way to test their own knowledge. ThatQuiz can also be used for quizzes in Vocabulary, Geography, and Science.

Another popular choice is Quizlet. It can be accessed over the web at www.quizlet. com or by downloading the Quizlet app. Quizlet is a free service that allows you to create and access flashcard sets for students. It contains more than 30 million study sets, and all of the material is generated by Quizlet users. Flashcards can also include audio.

Part VII

The Part of Tens

Read "10 Valuable iPad Accessories for Educational Use" at www.dummies.com/extras/ipadineducation.

In this part . . .

✔ Examine ten apps that make you a more productive
  educator

✔ Understand ten essential elements of a successful iPad
  deployment

Chapter 23

Ten Essential Apps for the Educator

*W*hat's necessary — or essential — for someone living in the Arctic is different from what's needed by someone living on the beach in Tahiti. Okay, they're both likely to eat a lot of fish, but that's about as similar as it gets. The same principle applies when selecting a list of "essential" apps. Not the fish — the fact that a high-school algebra teacher is likely to have very different academic needs than a second-grade teacher. So before you shoot off that "Why on Earth would I need that app?" email, let me explain that I'm listing apps that have widespread general usage and enable you to accomplish tasks that might otherwise be more difficult. These are apps for you — the educator. It's my short list of apps that are designed to make you more productive, informed, and connected.

In this chapter I list and summarize helpful apps according to their category of usage: productivity, reference, professional development, utilities, content management, and news. The list isn't exhaustive by any means, and of course, everyone has his own individual preferences. It will, however, provide a good starting point for anyone wanting to expand his use of the iPad. Some of the apps are mentioned elsewhere in the book. If that's the case, I'll point you to the chapters that contain more detailed information.

More essential apps

The following is a list of additional apps that are mentioned elsewhere in the book, with the chapter where you can find more about each:

- ✔ **Diigo:** Diigo is a social bookmarking tool that gives you the tools to collect content, highlight and annotate it, archive . . . and share it. See Chapter 6.

- ✔ **Evernote:** The dominant filing resource for anything and everything digital, Evernote lets you take notes, capture photos, create to-do lists, and record voice reminders. See Chapter 6.

- ✔ **Flipboard:** Offering a unique and beautifully designed alternative to browsing the web for news, Flipboard aggregates news into a personalized magazine based on publications you're interested in reading. See Chapter 6.

- ✔ **GoodReader:** GoodReader for iPad links to your Dropbox account, your Google Docs, Box.net, SkyDrive, SugarSync, a FTP server,

and a WebDAV server, and can even pull up all the attachments in your email accounts! See Chapter 8.

- ✔ **iMovie:** Widely regarded as the premiere video-editing tool for the iPad, the version on your iPad 2 or higher isn't quite as full-featured as the Mac version, but it's a very capable movie editor. See Chapter 14.

- ✔ **Notability:** A note-taking app for the iPad, Notability gives you the power to integrate handwritten notes, drawings, typing, audio, pictures, and PDF annotation all into one document. See Chapter 9.

- ✔ **Pages:** If you're even thinking of creating any document that rises above a simple text file, Pages is the app to purchase. See Chapter 9.

- ✔ **Printopia:** Install Printopia on any laptop or desktop computer, and your iPad will print anywhere it can. See Chapter 19.

Keep in mind also that apps frequently come and go. Today's essential app becomes outdated very quickly, and the indispensable utilities one year from now may not even have been conceived yet. To that end, you'll find an updated list on my website — http://iPadEducators.ning.com — where new and essential items will constantly be added to the list of apps you might want to consider (whether you live in the Arctic or Tahiti).

Wunderlist

We're all inundated with so much data and so many tasks, meetings, and responsibilities that life can seem a little overwhelming at times. If you're anything like me, your head feels so crammed full of things you have to do that sometimes it becomes too difficult to actually get any of them done. If you're in need of digital assistance, I have a "wunderful" app to suggest.

Wunderlist is a simple-to-use task manager that helps you get organized and on track (see Figure 23-1). Enter all your to-do items in Wunderlist and it takes away the burden of having to remember everything. Track anything, from items in your shopping list to project deadlines at work. Tap to open it and simply enter your item. Create tasks and subtasks, add reminders and due dates, add notes, and attach files. Organize your tasks into separate lists and share them with others.

A good assistant is always there to help when needed, and Wunderlist works on any device you have available. It syncs your lists across all your computers and mobile devices so that when you enter a task on your computer, you get a reminder on your phone when it needs to get done.

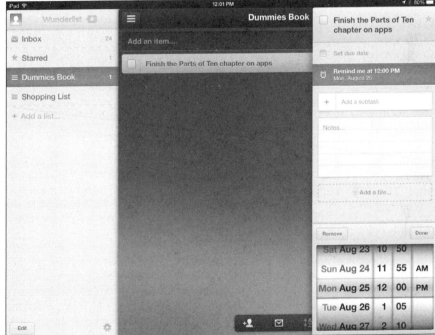

Figure 23-1: Wunderlist is a simple task manager that syncs across all your computers and mobile devices.

Pocket

There's so much information to read on the Internet that it's a full-time job just trying to keep up. You constantly run across pages and articles that you may need at some later time. Wouldn't it be great if you had an easy way to file and sort them? Pocket could be your solution (see Figure 23-2). It's extremely well designed and easy to use.

Figure 23-2:
Pocket presents your archived content in an easy-to-navigate visual grid.

Add a button to your browser toolbar, and whenever you find something on the web that you want to view later, tap the button, tag the content, and put it in Pocket. Pocket automatically syncs content to all your devices and computers so you can view it any time — and you can even read it without an Internet connection.

Access your Pocket account directly over the web or through the various apps it offers for different mobile devices. The iPad app presents your content archive in a beautifully designed and easy-to-navigate visual grid. Tag, share, and archive articles, videos, web pages, and more. Pocket also integrates with other apps so that you can easily pocket items referenced in apps such as Twitter and Flipboard. Check out Chapter 6 for more information on using the Pocket app.

Google Search

Google is the web tool that has become so ingrained in our daily life experience that it's actually become part of our language. We no longer search for information on a topic — we google it.

The Google Search app is a reference app that gives you that same easy access to the information on the web. In addition, the iPad Google Search app, shown in Figure 23-3, enables you to see search results and websites side by side to quickly browse pages and results. Swipe left and right to easily switch between the two. You can search by voice as well as typing, compare search results as web page snapshots in Instant Previews mode, use the Visual Search History to see past search results, and more.

Google Search is an app I reference several times a day. It's placed right in the middle of my iPad dock so that's it's never more than a tap away.

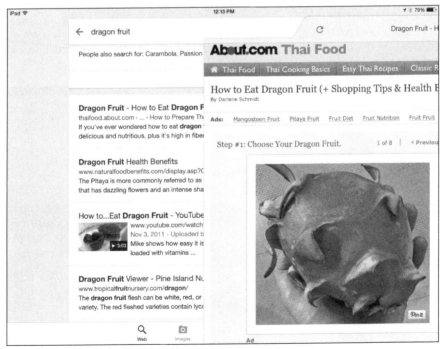

Figure 23-3: Swipe between side-by-side Google Search results and websites.

Google isn't your only source of quick information. If you're fortunate enough to have a third-generation iPad or higher, you can also use Siri to help you get information quickly. Activate Siri by holding down the Home button. Try saying, "How do you spell Mississippi?" Need help with Math? Ask Siri "What's 8 to the power of 6?" I have to admit that Siri's not only pretty smart at spelling and math, but she can recommend some pretty good restaurants for dinner as well! Go ahead, ask her.

Twitter

Many people view Twitter as the site where celebrities make outrageous statements or friends announce what they're eating. While there's certainly no shortage of that sort of information on Twitter, it's also a tremendous place to get the latest information on your particular area of interest.

Use Twitter in any web browser or download the app on your mobile device (see Figure 23-4). Open an account and start connecting with other educators. Discover and learn from the information they share. Follow hashtags to see what people are discussing in your area of interest. And get started by reading Chapter 7, where you'll learn exactly how you can use Twitter.

Figure 23-4:
Follow people on Twitter and use hashtags to find resources for learning.

Dropbox

There are many cloud storage services, and Apple has now entered the market with iCloud. Dropbox (see Figure 23-5) is the market leader and a great service for syncing documents and content across multiple devices. Just save or drop files into your Dropbox folder on a PC, Mac, or any other device. Take your iPad to class or a business meeting, or pull up a chair in the backyard, and open the Dropbox app. All your documents are synced across all devices and can be opened with a simple tap. Add any content to your Favorites list, and it downloads for offline reading when you aren't connected.

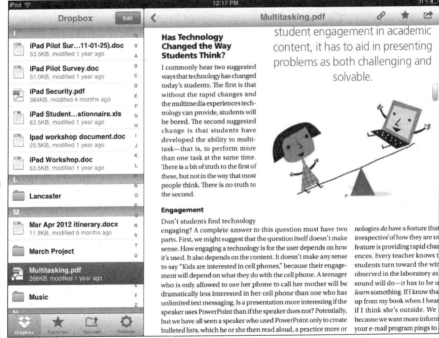

Figure 23-5: Use Dropbox to store and synchronize content among all your devices.

Dropbox is available as a share or export option in many popular apps and can be used to upload your photos, video, and other content. You can also share any of your Dropbox folders, making Dropbox an ideal tool for collaboration and communication. Use Dropbox folders to share work resources, project files, and photo albums with friends, coworkers, and family. Oh, and those little USB thumb drives you used for storing and moving files? They make great little building blocks when playing with the kids.

PhotoSync

We've all struggled with transferring files on or off an iPad at one time or another. When it comes to moving photos and video wirelessly, you can't beat PhotoSync. PhotoSync makes it simple to transfer your photos and videos to and from computers and other iOS devices. Open PhotoSync, select any amount of photos and videos in your iPad Photo Library along with a destination device (that also needs to have PhotoSync) or a cloud storage service (see Figure 23-6). No cables, no emails, no file size limits, and no fuss. Find out more in Chapter 19.

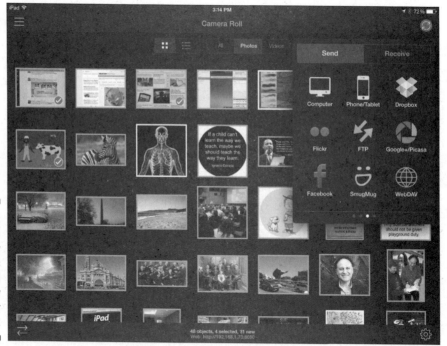

Figure 23-6: PhotoSync wirelessly transfers photos and video to any device or computer.

Newseum

We live in a connected world, and it's important to bring a global perspective to our news and classroom discussions. Newseum is an app and website that offers you the front pages of hundreds of newspapers across the world. With a simple tap, you can browse the newspapers in places as far away as Delhi,

Stockholm, or Sydney. It can be fascinating to get a local perspective on news that's important to people in different cities and to compare and contrast their take on global events.

Skim through a list of newspapers (see Figure 23-7) or browse the world map and find a newspaper by location. Tap any newspaper to open the front page. Add the interesting ones to your list of favorites or share them via email, Twitter, and Facebook. If you want more information, you can use the link to the newspaper's website.

So grab your Sangria or Turkish coffee and open Newseum. It will take reading the daily newspaper to a whole new dimension.

Figure 23-7:
Open front
pages of
newspapers
around
the world
with the
Newseum
app.

Splashtop 2 Remote Desktop

You're out there in the digital wilderness and realize that the file you really need is still on your computer desktop. The meeting starts in five minutes, and you could lose your job if this presentation doesn't go well. Okay, so I have a tendency toward the overdramatic, but there are lots of times you need your iPad to connect to your desktop to find files, use applications, or even just show something. Splashtop 2 Remote to the rescue. Install the Splashtop utility app (see Figure 23-8) on your iPad and download the Splashtop Streamer on your desktop, and then you can access all your content from any device — anywhere, at any time. View and edit your files remotely, use software, watch movies, show a presentation, play music, and more. If your iPad doesn't play that Flash video you really needed to watch or show the class, use Splashtop to connect to your computer and show it that way!

Figure 23-8:
Splashtop 2 Remote connects and controls your computer from your iPad.

TED

The motto of the TED not-for-profit organization is "Ideas worth spreading," and it's certainly true. The acronym TED comes from Technology, Education, and Design, although the organization has now spread beyond those themes. Although I categorize the TED app under the banner of professional development, TED talks inform, amuse, and inspire you no matter your particular field of interest. TED offers international conferences several times a year where innovators (see Figure 23-9) present unique and thought-provoking presentations. TED talks are captured on video and shared across the world via the Internet. Download the TED app to access the wide variety of incredibly fascinating and stimulating talks available on video. The latest version of the TED app also includes a section called Surprise Me. You select a mood such as courageous or funny, tell it how much time you have available, and it suggests a list of talks for you.

Figure 23-9:
Use the Surprise Me feature in TED to find talks that fit a specific mood and length.

iTunes U

iTunes U gives you access to complete courses from leading universities and other schools — plus the world's largest digital catalog of free education content. Download the iTunes U app and open the Catalog to subscribe to a course or just download content as needed. Courses come complete with the latest lessons and updates from instructors and often include assignments to complete.

Whether you're a college student interested in political science, a high-school student taking algebra, or an adult interested in learning how to program apps for the iPad, iTunes U (see Figure 23-10) is a valuable tool to help you learn any time, anywhere. Choose from hundreds of thousands of free lectures, videos, books, and other resources on a wide variety of subjects.

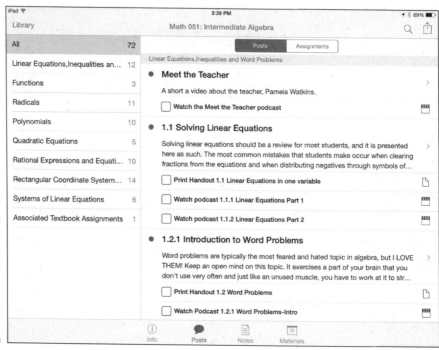

Figure 23-10: Subscribe to iTunes U courses from leading educational institutions.

Chapter 24

Ten Keys to a Successful iPad Implementation

*I*t seems that every school is considering purchasing iPads these days, and Apple has reported that iPad sales to schools are currently outselling MacBook sales by a very large margin. However, the rush to purchase iPads often precedes the careful planning and preparation that's so crucial to their success as educational tools. Technology alone is never the answer. Instead, iPad use needs to be integrated within a holistic approach to 21st-century education that encompasses a thorough and ongoing review of the skills and competencies required in our rapidly changing society and the educational processes that best help students acquire them.

Well-planned technology deployments can be tremendously successful and transformative for schools and students. In this chapter, I list ten vital components of a successful iPad implementation.

Determining Your Technical Readiness

There isn't any point in purchasing iPads if you don't have the technical infrastructure to manage and deploy them. Consider the following questions before going down that road:

✔ Do you have adequate incoming Internet bandwidth to connect all the devices and use them at the same time? Remember that you may also need significant bandwidth for uploading as students start to create and share large media files.

✔ You may have a great Internet connection, but is your internal wireless infrastructure robust enough to manage and distribute a strong, reliable wireless signal all around campus?

✔ Do your classrooms have safe, secure locations to store iPads?

Understanding and Communicating Why You Want iPads

This is the elephant in the room — the most critical question that is rarely discussed and evaluated from an educational perspective. It's imperative that the entire organization be on the same page. That requires a clearly communicated explanation of how iPad use complements your educational mission, which then needs to be clearly communicated to all the various constituent groups, including teachers, students, parents, directors, and administrators.

Targeting 21st-Century Learning Objectives

There's a natural inclination to stay in your comfort zone. Many teachers, especially older ones, prefer to stick to the methods they have always used in the classroom. An iPad program should take full advantage of the educational potential of the technology and be designed to address 21st-century learning objectives. That means integrating multimedia, communication, collaboration, project-based learning, and more. What point is there in purchasing expensive technology and then using it to reinforce outdated pedagogical practices such as frontal lecturing, content delivery, and drill and practice?

Developing Simple iPad Management Strategies

Research and document your plans for the following:

- ✔ Which responsibilities and processes are in place for buying and deploying apps? How will you decide what apps to buy, and who will be responsible for the purchasing?

- ✔ How will you manage user permissions? What restrictions will you enforce? Will you have one common student profile or vary them by class or group?

- ✔ What are your processes for device updates and data backup?

- ✔ Would you consider allowing your older students to manage their own iPads? Have you considered the risks versus benefits of such a policy?

- ✔ Where and how will students store and submit work? Will you use cloud services such as Google Apps? Will you create and/or use a WebDAV server? How will students submit digital work to teachers?

- ✔ How will you deal with instances of damage and theft? Will you buy insurance? Under what circumstances, if any, will students be held accountable? Has this been clearly communicated to parents through a Responsible Use policy?

- ✔ How do you plan to create and use email accounts? Will students be given email, and if so, at what age? If not, will the iPads have generic email accounts to enable outgoing email of content from students to teachers?

Understanding That iPads Aren't Laptops

Many laptop programs use network servers and domain logins that also set permissions. Laptops are controlled, and administrators can often view screen activity. It's important to remember that iPads are not laptops. There's no login, and the ability to secure and control them is minimal. If you're using iPads, utilize their unique assets. Look for ways to take advantage of their mobility, built-in camera, microphone, video, and so on. If monitoring and controlling activities are important criteria to you, it may be advisable to consider staying with laptops.

Overcoming "There's an App for That" Syndrome

You hear it all the time: "There's an app for that." One of the biggest mistakes teachers make is to constantly search for apps that directly address specific curriculum content — everything from 20th-century American history to the geography of California. Many great apps exist, but the real benefit comes from viewing iPads as tools that can be mastered and used creatively as part of the learning process. Encourage students to create mock interviews with famous historic figures, explain scientific phenomena with stop-motion animation, create podcasts for the school community, practice and record speech in a foreign language, create a screencast to explain a principle in algebra, and more. Given the opportunity, students naturally gravitate toward creative and innovative iPad use if they're given the right tools and opportunities.

Share and Share Alike Doesn't Always Work

You learned the value of sharing all the way back in preschool. Although it may be an important life guideline, you'll want to take a different perspective on sharing when it comes to using iPads in school. iPads are designed to be personal devices; you need to protect your user login and all your personal data and files. Sharing them may create privacy and security issues. I generally push for 1:1 deployment of iPads from 4th grade upward. If that causes financial concerns, you need to discuss those concerns and either scale down your deployment or consider an alternative approach, such as allowing children to bring their own devices to school — which comes with its own set of problems, especially for families that cannot afford them. Sharing iPads at upper grade levels, however, is not the solution.

Building an Ongoing Training and Support Structure

Deploying iPads is (I hope) a major step toward addressing the learning needs of 21st-century students. It also involves a major change in school culture. We're all naturally resistant to change. Organizational change requires adequate training and support. It's also important to stress that "training" doesn't mean that one day at the start of the year when you bring someone into school for a half-day workshop. Schedule time for ongoing training sessions throughout the year. Develop teacher support groups within your school and with other schools, where teachers can exchange experiences, share their successes, and learn from each other.

Connecting

The web has many helpful resources. You can easily connect and benefit from the knowledge and experience of other teachers. Join Twitter (www. twitter.com) or sites such as the iPads in Education network (http:// iPadEducators.ning.com).

Enabling the Unpredictable

You've given them wings; now let them fly. Technology is most effective when used as a tool for student empowerment. Don't expect to control every aspect of students' learning. And you don't always need to be the expert. Technology is their canvas. Give them the freedom to paint their own masterpieces.

Just in case you have any doubt regarding my stance on the issue, I want to stress that I don't believe that all education should revolve around technology use. This book is all about appropriate technology integration. Sometimes that means not forcing the issue. There's no doubting the importance of using crayons and paints. Getting your hands dirty planting in a garden is an extremely valuable educational experience, and how can you ever replace the experience of having a teacher or parent read to a child? It's crucial to use technology wisely and creatively. Sometimes that also means knowing when to put it away.

Appendix

Modeling the iPad Classroom

• •

Education is not the filling of a pail but the lighting of a fire.

— *William Butler Yeats*

*T*eachers around the world are starting to recognize the potential of technology to innovate and reform our educational systems. This appendix is for those teachers. It isn't easy when you have to deal with ever-increasing class sizes and work within the constraints of compulsory testing procedures. Slowly but surely, however, teachers are recognizing the transformative potential of technology to empower students and change the ways in which they learn. It's the recognition that education in the 21st century is about developing lifelong learning habits.

Chapter 11 takes a close look at a series of sample math and science lessons. This appendix presents a small additional sampling from teachers across all disciplines who are striving to use technology in unique and innovative ways. I'm extremely grateful for their participation in the book and for the work they do with children every day.

Creating a Band for Students with Disabilities

Submitted by	Mairi Adkin, Ashcraig Secondary School, Glasgow, Scotland
Grade level	S1-S6 Music
Description	Students with disabilities used iPads to play music and participate in performances.
Objectives	Provide and expand musical experiences for students with physical disabilities. Develop ability to work independently and collaboratively.
Apps/tools	Apps such as Yamaha NoteStar, GarageBand, Beamz, Piano Free, Musicnotes, Home Concert Xtreme, and Trackpad Magic

Ashcraig Secondary School caters to pupils with support needs arising from a physical disability, visual impairment, or chronic medical condition. The school has created a band to open up opportunities for students to play instruments and participate in collaborative musical performances. The students have disabilities that would normally make playing an acoustic instrument extremely daunting or even impossible. Using tablet technology and various apps, the pupils have been able to create and present performances in both familiar and unfamiliar contexts.

The project began when two students performed for the school using the smart keyboard tools in the GarageBand app. It demonstrated the potential of using iPads in music and generated increased interest in the concept of a band. Students are now progressively learning how to work collaboratively as members of a school band and are also able to practice and learn independently. If pupils don't have access to a tablet at home, CDs of tracks are burned, and screen shots of chord and note sequences are provided.

Creating a Picasso with Stop-Motion

Submitted by	Tami Rondeau, Southeast Polk Community School, Iowa
Grade level	2nd to 4th grade Art
Description	Students learned about Pablo Picasso, created a cut-paper collage of a head inspired by Picasso, and created a stop-motion movie using their paper collage pieces.
Objectives	Learn about the life and style of a famous artist. Use shape, color, and pattern to design creative collages. Learn how to use movies for expressive communication.
Apps/tools	StoMo and iMotion Pro apps
Materials needed	Colored construction paper, scissors, glue

Students read a book on Pablo Picasso and discussed some of his works and his style, particularly his Cubist portraits. The project was to create a cut-paper collage of a head inspired by the art of Picasso and then create a stop-motion movie highlighting how their collage pieces were assembled to form art in the style of Picasso.

Students drew and then cut out shapes for a head on different-colored construction paper. They used smaller pieces of paper to create eyes, nose, lips, ears, hair, and other elements, which encouraged the students to think about what colors and shapes worked with their collages.

Students were taught how to use a stop-motion app. They used a large piece of white paper as the background for their photo "set." Students went through the process of adding a piece to the collage, taking a photo, and then repeating the process. (See Figure A-1.) The teacher and students discussed how this changed the presentation of their artwork. They were still thinking about shape and color but also had to consider the dynamics of change and motion. They needed to take a minimum of 50 images.

When done, movies were exported and combined into a class collection in iMovie.

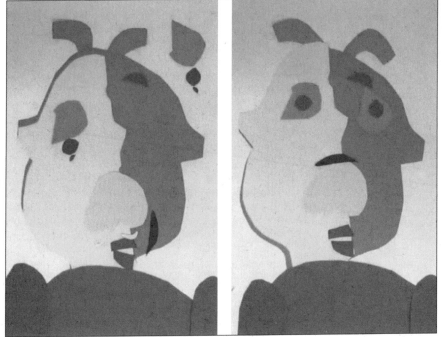

Figure A-1: Students create and animate photo collages of a head in the Cubist style of Picasso.

Image courtesy Tami Rondeau

Creating a Virtual Museum

Submitted by	Julie Hersch and Danit Benito, Temple Israel of Hollywood, Los Angeles, CA
Grade level	4th grade Social Studies

(continued)

(continued)

Description	Students created plaster masks and documented the process on video. The masks were displayed in a museum, and augmented reality was used to play videos when devices were pointed at them.
Objectives	Research and learn about different aspects of Brazilian culture.
Apps/tools	iMovie, SonicPics, and Aurasma apps
Materials needed	Plaster of Paris, Vaseline, bandages

Students were grouped in pairs to study different aspects of the culture of Brazil such as legends, sports, and foods.

In the first stage of the project, students scripted and created short narrated movies about the theme they researched.

Students then designed and created plaster Mardi Gras masks that represented the theme of their movies. Masks featured designs and images of things such as legendary figures, animals, and food. Masks were created by taking a plaster cast of each student's face. As one student in each pair was being fitted with plaster for the mask, the second student was documenting the process on video. Photos and video were also taken as students designed and decorated their masks.

Students integrated the images and video of the mask-making process with the narrated video they had previously created about their theme to create one comprehensive video that would inform museum visitors about their research topic and the process that went into creating their themed mask.

Each video was associated with a trigger image of the appropriate mask using the Aurasma app. This meant that anyone using the Aurasma app could point their device at any one of the masks and it would automatically morph into the video associated with it. Visitors were invited to the museum and loaned an iPad while they walked around.

Storytelling with Stop-Motion Animation

Submitted by	Rosamar Garcia, teacher consultant, Richmond, British Columbia, Canada
Grade level	4th to 12th grade
Description	Students created a story that was presented visually through the medium of stop-motion animation.

Objectives	Generate and communicate ideas, learn the fundamentals of storytelling, and develop a personal voice.
Apps/tools	NFB Stop Mo Studio
Materials needed	Generic storyboard templates, story-map template, chart paper, class-generated brainstorm chart on what makes a good story, Plasticine or clay, figurines for creating characters, cardboard, paint, felts, pastel crayons, colored papers, critic's evaluation form

The teacher started by brainstorming with the class on the topic "What makes a good story?" Students identified stories that have interesting problems; characters the audience can care about; and a plot (beginning, middle, end) where a problem is presented, action developed, and issues resolved. The teacher asked the students to provide examples of these elements from classic or familiar stories.

After the students were divided into pairs or small groups to create a story map, they drew out the scenes to film using a storyboard template. When the storyboard was complete, the students used the art supplies (paint, pastels, felts, cardboard, Plasticine, clay, paper, and so on) to create the characters and the scenery.

Before filming began, the teacher explained the concept of stop-motion animation, in which objects are moved in small increments between shots, and the shots are shown in fast sequence to create an animated movie.

Watch *La boîte*, an animated film by Co Hoedeman, at `www.nfb.ca/film/ boite`. Have students look at the film with a filmmaker's eye to collect ideas about creating special effects, camera angles, close-ups, and pans. Discuss how they might create one or two of these special effects in their own animations.

Before filming, the students assumed roles: iPad camera operator, someone to move the characters between the still shots, others to add scenery changes as necessary, and so on. The students rotated roles so everyone had an opportunity to perform the various jobs.

When the films were completed, students celebrated with a film festival, (complete with popcorn). As they watched the films, students filled out a critic's evaluation form to critique the animations. Critics were asked to note what he or she considered the best thing about the film; his or her favorite part; and a specific element that the film's creators did an especially good job on.

Crafting Enhanced Book Reports

Submitted by	Lisa Johnson, TechChef4u LLC, Austin TX
Grade level	Kindergarten through 2nd grade
Description	Students created book reports by illustrating major scenes that were photographed and enhanced with audio recordings.
Objectives	Articulate understanding of a book's setting, major events, and key figures using a variety of media formats.
Apps/tools	Camera app (or drawing app such as Doodle Buddy), ThingLink app, Tellagami app, Croak.it!, and Canva web service

Book reports are a common activity in school. The teacher sought to utilize different media tools and apps that offer students the opportunity to articulate their understanding of setting, major events, and key figures using art and audio recordings. These augmented book reports allowed all learners to share and showcase evidence of learning using a variety of tools.

Students illustrated major events in the book and took a photo of each hand-drawn illustration. Some drawings were also created in the Doodle Buddy app. The Tellagami app was used to create animated movies using talking avatars. They recorded a Tellagami movie for each section (for example, beginning, middle, end, and favorite part) of the book report. Students personalized their Tellagami by using the hand-drawn images saved to their photo roll as the background of their Tellagami recording and then had the Tellagami avatar repeat what the students wanted them to say. Additional audio snippets were recorded using the Croak.it! app. All recordings were saved on the web, and the link was copied and saved for later reference.

Students used multiple applications (PicCollage, ScrapPad, Scrap It) to create a digital collage of their artwork, which was saved to the photo roll as a single image. The final product was assembled with the ThingLink app. ThingLink allows users to designate hot spots in an image that, when tapped or clicked, display additional information, media, or links to resources on the Internet. Students used their collage photo as the background in ThingLink and designated portions as interactive hot spots. Each hot spot linked to one of their recordings or Tellegami movies. The final student ThingLinks (see Figure A-2) were embedded in a class website or student blog.

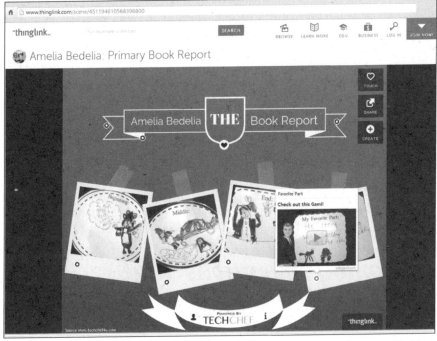

Image courtesy Lisa Johnson

Figure A-2:
Students created interactive ThingLink book reports that played media created in other apps.

Screencasting to Develop Speaking Fluency

Submitted by	Vicki Curtis, associate professor of ESL, Ohlone College, Fremont, California
Grade level	Community-college ESL
Description	ESL students used a screencasting app to record and critique their pronunciation and speaking fluency.
Objectives	Annotate and record correct thought groups to practice speaking fluency.
Apps/tools	Camera, ScreenChomp, Educreations, Facebook

Thought groups are methods native speakers use to combine groups of words without pausing when speaking. Recognizing and using appropriate thought groups helps students improve their fluency when speaking. Common types of thought groups include clauses, phrases, and transitional words and expressions. In this exercise, students used iPads to develop pronunciation skills by using a screencasting app to have them practice thought groups.

Students started by capturing a screen shot of sentences or paragraphs from their e-textbooks. They then imported the image into a screencasting app (see Chapter 17), recording themselves as they used the annotation tool to draw a line above the thought words with their finger while speaking them. They were directed not to lift their finger from the screen until the thought group ended, at which point they could pause. This requirement provided tactile reinforcement of speech timing.

The screencasting app exported their recording as a movie. Students shared the movies with each other and provided feedback. Finally, the video was shared in the class Facebook group for further comment and suggestions.

Designing Inventions That Solve World Problems

Submitted by	Theresa McGee, Community Consolidated School District #181, Hinsdale, Illinois
Grade level	4th grade
Description	Students developed an invention that addresses a problem in our society. The students presented their invention visually and verbally using different iPad apps. The final product was assembled into a podcast that was shared online.
Objectives	Exercise critical thinking and develop mechanical design skills.
Apps/tools	GarageBand, SketchBook Express Pro or Brushes, and iMovie apps

This multimedia learning experience engaged students in all aspects of design thinking through the STEAM (Science, Technology, Engineering, Arts and Mathematics) education model. The process began by exploring innovative designs of contemporary artists and seeing how those ideas could be applied to solve current social problems. Students then developed and designed an invention (see Figure A-3) that they thought would make the world a better place. Visual representations were created using layering features found in iPad apps such as Brushes and SketchBook Pro. Descriptions of the invention's mechanical components, purpose, and marketing concept were recorded using GarageBand. Images and audio recordings were combined in iMovie to create video that was shared as an enhanced podcast. You can find the complete lesson by searching for "Inventing a Better World: Design Thinking Through STEAM Education" in the iBooks Store.

Figure A-3: Students made and narrated movies about inventions they created to solve societal problems.

Image courtesy Theresa McGee

Writing Creatively about Scientific Observations

Submitted by	Dr. Joseph Johnson and Dr. Randy Yerrick, State University of New York at Buffalo
Grade level	2nd through 6th grades
Description	Students predict, sketch, and describe what an object will look like when magnified. Alternatively, they view a magnified image and try to rationalize their hypothesis of the object being magnified.

(continued)

(continued)

Objectives	Explore creative writing through the medium of science content, integrating literary devices such as imagery and metaphor to describe highly magnified images. Practice both creative and scientific writing, comparing the two forms. Experience the processes of hypothesizing and making evidence-based decisions.
Apps/tools	ProScope Micro Mobile digital microscope

What scientists do is sometimes very different from the requirements in other professions. Obtaining a deeper understanding of these differences can be a window to better understanding the nature of science. This understanding can best be developed through actual participation in activities that allow for direct comparisons to be made.

This activity employs the ProScope Micro Mobile device (shown in Figure A-4 and online at `https://www.bodelin.com/proscope/proscope-micro-mobile`), a high-resolution, digital microscope that uses the built-in camera app on iOS devices. This device can share magnified images to nearby iPads via a Wi-Fi signal, allowing the teacher and students to capture images. This cross-curricular activity utilizes the magnified images generated by the microscope.

The images provided by the ProScope can be truly stunning, but they may not bear much resemblance to the original object being magnified. The lesson begins with the teacher presenting an object to the class. He or she asks the students to predict what the object will look like when magnified. Students record their predictions through drawings, providing their explanations as to why it will look that way. Upon viewing the magnified object on their iPads, students can discuss what they saw, how it differed from their predictions, and why. Next, the teacher displays images of magnified objects. The students are able to see and capture the magnified images while the original object remains hidden from their view.

Students hypothesize as to what object they are viewing, providing their rationale for their hypothesis. They can practice their observational skills as they review their captured images and try to figure out what exactly they are seeing. Students are asked to practice creative writing, describing the images they see in such a way that they capture the feeling of the image using imagery and metaphor to describe the image. Next, they write descriptively, providing detailed description of exactly what they see in their image. After the object(s) that were presented are revealed, students can again discuss their predictions. They can also make comparisons between their two pieces of writing; specifically, they can discuss the strengths and purpose of each style.

Figure A-4: Students hypothesize and write about the identity of objects displayed as magnified images.

Image courtesy Dr. Randy Yerrick

Understanding Culture through Stories

Submitted by	Linda Buturian, senior teaching specialist, College of Education and Human Development, University of Minnesota
Grade level	3rd to 5th grades
Description	Students were asked to interview a family member and create a narrated slide show about their family traditions or events.
Objectives	Understand culture and tradition. Foster pride in one's own culture and respect for others' cultures. Develop storytelling.
Apps/tools	Storyrobe, StoryKit, and iMovie apps

Digital stories are academically rich. Students go through processes similar to the development of a formal paper: brainstorming, incorporating research, narrowing focus, creating an outline (or storyboard), peer review, revision, and sharing the final project. In creating a digital story, students build knowledge about their topic and skills in media production, research, and communication. They make connections between their course work and the world around them.

Students were asked to create digital stories that were two to six minutes long — a short video that combines image, audio, and text to convey a narrative or concept. The story assignment required students to create digital stories capturing a conversation with a family member or friend about a tradition or event related to a specific culture. Students integrated the digital story into a presentation they gave to their classmates — a presentation that included a culturally relevant artifact or object.

Designing the Next Space Vehicle

Submitted by	Leah LaCrosse, science teacher, Huron City School, Ohio
Grade level	5th grade Science
Description	Students were required to research a planet and then design, construct, and present an exploration vehicle that was built for the conditions of that planet.
Objectives	Learn about a planet in our solar system by paying attention to specific planet characteristics, such as size, composition, orbiting moons, rotation speed, and presence of rings. Learn about NASA's previous exploratory vehicles, including rovers, satellites, probes, and bases. Design, build, and make a visual presentation for the next NASA exploratory vehicle for the students' planet.
Apps/tools	NASA website, BrainPOP, Solar System, Planets, Dropbox, Drawing Pad, iMovie, Keynote, and Strip Designer apps
Materials needed	Numerous LEGO bricks, random motors, wires and wire strippers, light bulbs and holders, random wheels, various recycled bottles, boxes, egg cartons, and electrical tape.

The students were given the challenge to design and present NASA's next exploration vehicle. The time frame was one week, and students were required to use iPads, building tools, teamwork, and presentation techniques.

The Design to Explore lesson had three overall stages:

- ✔ **Research:** The students used a variety of iPad apps and recommended websites to research the planet for which they would be designing a vehicle. Although students had previous knowledge of the planets, they needed to review specific planet characteristics such as size, composition, orbiting moons, rotation speed, and the presence of rings. These characteristics would help them design the vehicle (rover, satellite, probe, or base). In addition, to get ideas of exploratory vehicles, they researched NASA's previous vehicles.

- ✔ **Design/build:** After the preliminary research, students worked in groups to design their vehicle using the LEGO bricks and recycled materials. The groups designed a mission patch incorporating their vehicles, initials, and planet. For this, they used the Drawing Pad app.

- ✔ **Present.** In creating their presentations, students chose whether to use Keynote, iMovie, or Strip Designer apps. The presentations included information about the planet, the LEGO vehicle, and the mission patch; students were encouraged to add pictures or videos of their vehicles. Students presented their projects to the class as though they were NASA officials, deciding whether to adopt their ideas.

This LEGO project extended into a Skype call with astrophysicist Dr. Neil deGrasse Tyson. During that call, the class sent samples of students' work and discussed their ideas for exploration.

Index

• J •

• K •

• ***S*** •

• *W* •

• *Z* •

About the Author

Sam Gliksman has been a leading voice in the education community, specializing in technology applications for more than two decades. He has been involved with educational and commercial enterprises, having founded and managed a leading software company for many years. He currently works as an educational technology consultant, speaker, and author. As a consultant, he works with schools, school districts and even foreign governments, most recently having been invited to meet and personally consult with the prime minister of Greece.

Sam is recognized as a prominent expert on technology and educational reform and has been very active in promoting the use of mobile technology in education. Sam founded and writes for the popular "iPads in Education" website (`http://ipadeducators.ning.com`) that has an active membership of many thousands of educators worldwide. A dynamic and inspirational speaker, he lectures at national and international conferences as well as giving insightful educational workshops about the use of technology and its potential for reforming education.

Sam can be contacted for workshops and speaking opportunities at his personal website — `www.EducationalMosaic.com`.

Dedication

So much of whatever I have accomplished would never have been possible without the help and support of my wife and soul mate, Debbie. This book is dedicated to her and my three wonderful children who I adore — Lianna, Yoni, and Daniel. I'm so very proud of all of you.

Author's Acknowledgments

Special thanks to everyone at Wiley: Kyle for asking me to write the book and keeping me (almost) on schedule; Charlotte, Kathy, and Cassandra for being amazingly patient and supportive editors; and all the other proof-readers and technical editors that contributed to the final copy. Thanks also to everyone else at Wiley who I may not know by name but who helped get this book published.

Thanks to all the wonderful educators that submitted their creative projects for using iPads in class.

Thanks to Deb for proofreading my writing, correcting my ramblings, and helping to identify my "Australianisms." A huge thanks to our dear friend Nurit for dropping everything to come help on the very last, crazy night.

Finally, thanks to the very special family with which I have been blessed, both in the United States and in Australia. This book could never have been written without your love, encouragement and constant support.

Publisher's Acknowledgments

Acquisitions Editor: Kyle Looper

Project Editor: Charlotte Kughen

Copy Editor: Kathy Simpson

Technical Editor: Cassandra Parets

Editorial Assistant: Claire Johnson

Sr. Editorial Assistant: Cherie Case

Project Coordinator: Erin Zeltner

Cover Image: ©iStock.com/damircudic